Dragon® Professional Individual

FOR DUMMIES®
A Wiley Brand

5th Edition

by Stephanie Diamond

FOR DUMMIES®
A Wiley Brand

Dragon® Professional Individual For Dummies®, 5th Edition

Published by: **John Wiley & Sons, Inc.,** 111 River Street, Hoboken, NJ 07030-5774, www.wiley.com

Copyright © 2016 by John Wiley & Sons, Inc., Hoboken, New Jersey

Media and software compilation copyright © 2016 by John Wiley & Sons, Inc. All rights reserved.

Published simultaneously in Canada

For general information on our other products and services, please contact our Customer Care Department within the U.S. at 877-762-2974, outside the U.S. at 317-572-3993, or fax 317-572-4002. For technical support, please visit www.wiley.com/techsupport.

Wiley publishes in a variety of print and electronic formats and by print-on-demand. Some material included with standard print versions of this book may not be included in e-books or in print-on-demand. If this book refers to media such as a CD or DVD that is not included in the version you purchased, you may download this material at http://booksupport.wiley.com. For more information about Wiley products, visit www.wiley.com.

Library of Congress Control Number: 2015956888

ISBN: 978-1-119-17103-4

ISBN 978-1-119-17107-2 (ebk); ISBN 978-1-119-17106-5 (ebk)

Manufactured in the United States of America

10 9 8 7 6 5 4 3 2 1

Contents at a Glance

Table of Contents

Introduction

• •

*F*inally! Someone has freed you from that medieval torture rack, the keyboard, and its contemporary accessory, the mouse. You've been muttering epithets at your computer. Now you can actually speak to it. Although it still won't take your epithets to heart, it will now at least write them down for your future convenience.

For those who can't type or spell (or at least, not well), and for those whose bodies have been punished by keyboarding, Dragon Professional Individual spells relief (and other words, too). Dragon Professional Individual gives your lips their job back: being your principal data output device. In fact, with Dragon Professional Individual, you may be able to type faster with your lips than with your fingers. At the same time, you can eliminate spelling errors (and spell checking) from your life. Yes, it's true!

Dragon Professional Individual can do great things soon after you open the box, but too often, its talents lie hidden. Recognizing speech is one of those human talents that is still very complex to a computer. Recognizing human speech is as much a miracle for a computer as computing the precise value of *pi* is for a human. (Computing the highly abstract value of pie, oddly enough, is much easier for a human.)

Dragon Professional Individual borders on being miraculous, but to get really practical results, you have to meet this miracle halfway. Perhaps you have been wondering what all the excitement is about, either because you are thinking of getting Dragon Professional Individual or because, so far, Dragon Professional Individual hasn't excited you. *Dragon Professional Individual For Dummies* is here to help.

About This Book

This book reveals the stuff you need to know to turn Dragon Professional Individual from a technical miracle into a working tool on your Windows computer. I also cover how to use Dragon Professional Individual on your smartphone and tablet. Following are a dozen things this book can help you do:

- ✔ Discover what Dragon Professional Individual can and can't do.
- ✔ Help Dragon Professional Individual to recognize your voice.

- ✔ Run Dragon Professional Individual in the best way for your application.
- ✔ Use voice commands to get the formatting you want.
- ✔ Correct Dragon Professional Individual when it makes a mistake.
- ✔ Add to or customize Dragon Professional Individual's vocabulary.
- ✔ Speak better for better recognition.
- ✔ Control your desktop by voice.
- ✔ Transcribe speech from a portable recorder.
- ✔ Use Playback and text-to-speech tools to help proofread.
- ✔ Choose hardware for better performance.
- ✔ Create your own dictation shortcuts and custom commands.

Conventions Used in This Book

Ever try to describe something basically simple and discover that the description made it ridiculously complex instead? Well, it's that way with describing Dragon Professional Individual commands, so I try to simplify the job by using some typographic conventions. You won't really need to think about the typography much (let alone go to any conventions about it), but in case you're wondering about it, here's what it means:

- ✔ I put Dragon Professional Individual commands (the ones you speak, not the menu choices) in bold and initial capitals, enclosed in quotation marks, such as "**Scratch That.**"

- ✔ When part of a Dragon Professional Individual command varies according to what you are trying to do, I indicate the variable part in angle brackets (*<and>*), as in: "**Format That *<font>*.**" The term *<font>* here represents one of the many fonts allowed by that command, like Arial.

- ✔ When part of a Dragon Professional Individual command is text from an example I discuss, I put that part in italics. For example, "**Select *we put that part*"** is a command telling Dragon Professional Individual to select the text "we put that part."

- ✔ Where I want you to pause slightly in a command, I put a comma where the pause should be. For instance, if I tell you to say, "**Caps On, *The Sands of Barcelona,* Caps Off,**" I want you to pause briefly where those commas appear.

Foolish Assumptions

I think you are a person of elevated literary taste and acute discernment, who aspires to converse with computers. Beyond that, I assume certain things about you, my esteemed reader.

I assume you are a new user of Dragon Professional Individual. I also assume you are passably familiar with Microsoft Windows.

I figure you are picking up this book for any of the following reasons:

- ✔ You have installed Dragon Professional Individual and are baffled by it.
- ✔ You are impressed by Dragon Professional Individual but wonder if you are getting the full benefit of it.
- ✔ You'd like Dragon Professional Individual to work more accurately.
- ✔ You can't get all the Dragon Professional Individual features to work.
- ✔ Dragon Professional Individual works, but not consistently.
- ✔ You don't have Dragon Professional Individual, and are wondering if you would like it.

Icons Used in This Book

Like a Dairy Queen ice-cream Blizzard, *For Dummies* books are packed full of cool, crunchy tidbits. Accordingly, you'll find the text studded with attractive two-color icons, pointing out tips, warnings, reminders, and the like. (Yes, of course, black and white are colors!) Here are the icons you'll find:

Tips are insights and shortcuts that make your life easier, your wit sharper, and your hair more silky and manageable.

You don't have to read paragraphs marked with Technical Stuff, but you'll be a finer, more moral person if you do.

I used to know what this icon was for, but I forget. Oh! It notes a topic that I mention and that you should remember.

This icon marks things that are likely to blow up in your face or at least may cause problems if you don't heed the warning.

Beyond the Book

I've provided additional information about Dragon Professional Individual online to help you on your way:

- ✔ **Cheat Sheet:** Check out `www.dummies.com/cheatsheet/dragon professionalindividual` to learn how to start dictation, use punctuation, correct dictation, get help, and use Dragon with other applications.

- ✔ **Online articles:** On several of the pages that open each of this book's Part pages, you'll find links to what the folks at *For Dummies* call Web Extras, which expand on some concept I've discussed in that particular section. You can find them at `www.dummies.com/extras/dragon professionalindividual`.

Where to Go from Here

The next step depends on what you need right now. If you're stuck on a particular aspect of Dragon Professional Individual right now, look it up in the index and turn straight to that topic. If you are a newbie, why not just turn this page?

Let's get started!

Part I
Getting Started with Dragon Professional Individual

In this part . . .

✔ Before you get started with Dragon Professional Individual, you'll discover what the speech recognition software can and can't do and how it gets to know your way of speaking.

✔ The first steps in using this software are to install it, create a User Profile, and train it to understand your voice.

✔ The fun begins when you launch Dragon Professional Individual and learn your way around the interface. I guide you through the process so that you can get up and running quickly.

Chapter 1

Knowing What to Expect

*V*oice recognition is used in places like cars, hospitals, and legal offices. Yet, some people are still skeptical about software that enables you to dictate to your computer and get a transcription of what you said. People think it's very cool, but they secretly wonder if it really works.

It works. (And it *is* really cool.) Right out of the box, today's Dragon Professional Individual reports up to 99 percent accuracy. I bet that's a score you'd like for your own personal output. Well then, read this book and dive right in. You'll be rewarded with higher productivity and hands-free computing.

Sections of this book were written by dictating them into Dragon Professional Individual. It was a lot of fun, and I predict that you will also find Dragon Professional Individual to be useful and fun — if you approach it with the appropriate expectations.

Clarifying What Dragon Professional Individual Can Do for You

Something about dictating to a computer awakens all kinds of unrealistic expectations in people. If you expect it to serve you breakfast in bed, you're out of luck. I didn't write this book by saying, "Computer, write a book about Dragon Professional Individual." I had to dictate it word for word, just as I would have had to type it word for word if I didn't have Dragon Professional Individual.

So what are realistic expectations? Think of Dragon Professional Individual the way that you think about your keyboard and mouse. It's an input device for your computer, not a brain transplant. It doesn't add any new capabilities to your computer beyond deciphering your spoken words into text or ordinary PC commands. If you say, **"Go make me a sandwich,"** Dragon Professional Individual will dutifully type "go make me a sandwich" into whatever word-processing application happens to be open.

Just because your computer can understand what you say, don't expect it to understand what you mean. It's still just a computer, you know.

Here are five specific things you *can* expect to do with Dragon Professional Individual, and where to look for more details about how to do them:

- **Browse the web.** If you use Internet Explorer (IE) (or Chrome or Firefox) and Dragon Professional Individual together, you can cruise around the web without ever touching your keyboard or mouse. Pick a website from your Favorites menu, follow a link from one web page to another, or dictate a URL (web address) into the Address box, leaving your hands in your lap the whole time. See Chapter 13 for details.

- **Control your applications.** If you see the name on a menu, you can say click and the name and watch it happen — not just in Dragon Professional Individual but in your other applications as well. If your email program has a Check Mail command on its menu, then you can check your email by saying a few words. Anything that your spreadsheet has on a menu becomes a voice command you can use. Ditto for hotkeys: If pressing some combination of keys causes an application to do something you want, just tell Dragon Professional Individual to press those keys. See Part II.

- **Control your desktop.** Applications will start running just because you tell them to. Use your voice to open and close windows, switch from one open window to another, and drag and drop stuff from here to there. See Chapter 15.

- **Dictate into a digital recorder and let Dragon Professional Individual transcribe it later.** You need Dragon Professional Individual and a digital (or very good analog) recorder. See Chapter 11.

- **Write documents.** Dragon Professional Individual is darn good at helping you write documents. You talk, and it types. If you don't like what you said (or what Dragon Professional Individual typed), tell Dragon Professional Individual to go back and change it. You can give vocal instructions to make elements bold, italic, large, small, or set in a particular font. Chapters 3, 4, 5, and 6 explain what you need to know to write documents in the Dragon Professional Individual DragonPad itself. If you want to dictate into Microsoft Word or Corel WordPerfect, see Chapter 9. For all other applications, see Chapter 8.

Now, I happen to think that's plenty to get excited about. I can make my own sandwiches, thank you.

Figuring Out What Dragon Professional Individual Can't Do

Even with Dragon Professional Individual, your computer's capability to understand English is more limited than what you can reasonably expect from a human. People use a very wide sense of context to figure out what other people are saying. We know, for instance, what the teen behind the counter at Burger King means when he asks, "Wonfryzat?" (That's fast-food-employed teenspeak for "Do you want fries with that?") We'd be completely confused if that same teenager walked up to us at a public library and asked, "Wonfryzat?"

Dragon Professional Individual figures things out from context, too, but only from the *verbal* context (and a fairly small verbal context at that). It knows that "two apples" and "too far" make more sense than "too apples" and "two far." But two- to three-word context seems to be about the extent of the software's powers. (I can't say exactly how far it looks for context, because Nuance, the manufacturer, is understandably pretty hush-hush about the inner workings of Dragon Professional Individual.) It doesn't understand the content of your document, so it can't know that words like "Labradoodles" and "Morkies" are going to show up just because you're talking about dogs.

However, Dragon does use context in its analysis. Dragon Professional Individual has collected millions of hours of dictation from customers and uses this data to better understand the language. A word receives a frequency score that shows how often the word appears and how often the word appears before or after other words. This data is then used to determine the best choice; for example, when you mention "too" or "two."

Try to speak in slightly longer utterences. The more you say in one breath, the more data Dragon has. But be careful: Try to say too much at one time, and you will likely trail off or start to mumble as you lose concentration.

Consequently, you can't expect Dragon Professional Individual to understand every form of speech that humans understand. In order to work well, it needs advantages like these:

> ✔ **Familiarity:** Each person who dictates to Dragon Professional Individual can train it so that Dragon Professional Individual builds an individualized user model.

Even though you no longer have to train Dragon, it still creates a speaker-dependent profile. After the audio setup is complete, Dragon Professional Individual is already making it unique to you. That's why you must always use your own profile.

✔ **Identification:** Each time you start dictating, you need to identify yourself so that Dragon Professional Individual can load the right user model.

✔ **One user at a time:** Dragon Professional Individual loads only one user model at a time, so it can't transcribe a meeting during which several people talk, even if it has user models for all of them.

✔ **Constant volume:** You can't plunk a microphone down in the middle of the room and then pace around while you dictate.

> • *Use a good, Nuance-approved microphone.* You can find a list at `http://support.nuance.com/compatibility`. Position the microphone the same way every time or sit in front of your computer. Try to stay at the same distance from your PC's internal array microphone.

> • *Don't mumble or let your voice trail off.* Dragon does a pretty good job with accents, as long as you're consistent.

✔ **Reasonable background noise:** Humans may be able to understand you when your favorite drummer is blasting away on your speakers or the blow dryer is on. They may be reading your lips at least part of the time, and they can guess that you're probably saying, "Turn that thing down!" Dragon Professional Individual lacks in the lip-reading department, as well as in the capability to make obvious situational deductions.

✔ **Reasonable enunciation:** You don't have to start practicing "Moses supposes his toeses are roses," but you do need to realize that Dragon Professional Individual can't transcribe sounds that you don't make. See Chapter 16 for an in-depth discussion of this issue.

✔ **Standard turn-of-the-millennium English prose:** If you want to be the next James Joyce, stick to typing. You can have some fun by trying to transcribe Shakespeare or things written in other languages (I had fun in Chapter 25), but it isn't going to work very well (unless you do some really extensive training). On the other hand, Dragon Professional Individual is just the thing for writing books, blog posts, and reports.

Letting someone else use your profile will negatively affect your accuracy.

Selecting the Right Dragon Product

Dragon doesn't have a single product; it's a family of products. And like most families, some members are richer than others. Depending on the features you want, you can pay a hefty price for software. You get what you pay for.

In spite of its members' socioeconomic differences, this family gets along pretty well. All the products are based on the same underlying voice recognition system, so they create the same kinds of user files. This fact has two consequences for you as a user:

- ✔ All the products are about equally accurate at transcribing your speech. However, the Legal version has specific legal terms included, and the language models are more tuned to expect legal phrases. The same idea holds true for the Medical version.

- ✔ Upgrading to a better version is easy.

  You can start out with the inexpensive Dragon NaturallySpeaking Home edition, test whether you like this whole idea of dictation, and then move up to a full-featured version without having to go through training all over again.

Which edition is best for you depends on why you're interested in Dragon in the first place. Are you a poor typist who wants to be able to create documents more quickly? A good typist who is starting to worry about carpal tunnel syndrome? A person who can't use a mouse or keyboard at all? A busy executive who wants to dictate into a recorder rather than sit in front of a monitor? Is price an important factor to you? Do you need Dragon to recognize a large, specialized vocabulary? Do you want to create macros that enable you to dictate directly into your company's special forms?

The more features you want, the more you should expect to pay.

Expanding the use of speech recognition

Speech recognition software is entrenched in many private sector industries. Dragon serves several industries, including the following:

- ✔ **Financial:** Dragon helps financial people manage their paperwork and meet compliance requirements.

- ✔ **Legal and medical:** Transcription and documentation play a major role in keeping things moving in the legal and medical fields. Dragon significantly cuts the time needed to produce various documents.

✔ **Insurance:** This one is self-explanatory. Anything that cuts down on paperwork in the insurance industry is clearly a public service.

The public sector uses Dragon as follows:

✔ **Education:** It is well documented that Dragon can help level the playing field for students who face learning challenges. Teachers can provide better learning experiences to all their students.

✔ **Accessibility:** Dragon makes a major contribution to people who are challenged by the use of a keyboard or mouse. The software provides access to the web and opens up the world to people who might otherwise be denied digital access.

✔ **Public safety:** Dragon's capability to save time on paperwork frees up law enforcement professionals to do the work that keeps us safe.

The latest generation of the Dragon family

The current generation of Dragon products was released in the second half of 2015. In addition to the usual bug fixes and incremental improvements that you expect in a new version of an application, Nuance is splitting its next version of Dragon into Dragon Professional Individual and Dragon Professional Group.

Dragon Professional Individual and Professional Group still have the same great features, including the following:

✔ **Up to 99 percent accuracy:** Every facet of Dragon Professional Individual works faster by cutting down on the time required for the program to recognize dictation and produce output.

✔ **Fast response time:** Response to commands is fast and makes dictating less about stopping and starting. You can pay attention to longer phrases with pauses in between.

✔ **Shortcuts for common commands:** Nuance has anticipated many of the common commands that you want to use and has created shortcuts for them.

✔ **No training to set up:** You don't have to spend time reading documents. Nuance has made this version a five-minute task.

✔ **The well-designed DragonBar:** Using the DragonBar is easier than ever before. It's streamlined and can be collapsed or opened at the click of a mouse. No extended menu needed, either.

Here are some of the new features in Dragon Professional Individual:

- **Advanced custom commands:** You can create and import powerful commands to automate tasks and can also easily insert variable fields in auto-text commands.

- **The ability to transcribe someone else's voice from an audio file:** Another exciting new feature is the ability to transcribe another voice without requiring the speaker to be personally present to train a profile.

- **Improved Help to get a new user up to speed and running quickly:** In-context Help with "What can I say?" that gives you top commands to say depending on which application you are in, enhanced Tutorial, and enhanced online Help support.

The new Dragon Professional Group product is aimed at productivity for the enterprise:

- Enabling and managing multiple desktops with Dragon in an enterprise using administrative tools as well as the option to connect with the Nuance User Management Center, for centralized administration

- Volume licensing with maintenance and support options

Nuance is also introducing Dragon Anywhere. This is a new application available for iOS and Android devices. You can multiply your productivity by dictating to your mobile devices, and the following features are available:

- **Edit and format right on your mobile device:** Enjoy the ability to work right on your device to get your document in shape.

- **No limit on speaking length:** You can talk as long as you want to get the job done to your satisfaction.

Here are the some of the other Dragon NaturallySpeaking products with a few comments about their features:

- **Dragon Home:** This entry-level edition is perfect for people who hate to type. Since the other editions have more powerful features better suited for work, it is recommended for use at home. It is as accurate as the more expensive editions, enables control of the Windows desktop, includes a Dictation Box for dictating into other applications, and enables you to browse the web by voice. The Home version includes Full Text Control for a number of applications and some Natural Language Commands for Word, WordPerfect, and OpenOffice Writer. It doesn't support Full Text Control in Excel or playback of your own voice for corrections. The Home edition is perfect if you're planning to dictate only the first draft of documents, which you then polish using a mouse and keyboard. This version probably isn't the best choice for people with physical disabilities.

- ✔ **DragonPremium:** Premium includes all the Home edition's features, plus a few extras. It's also recommended for home use. It enables you to select a piece of your document and play back your own dictation, a great feature when you're trying to correct a mistake that either you or Dragon made 20 minutes ago. It also opens the possibility of dictating into a recorder (including a smartphone) and letting Dragon transcribe it later. See Chapter 11.

- ✔ **Dragon Legal and Dragon Medical Practice Edition:** At heart, these two editions begin with the Professional edition, but Nuance has done some of the work that I describe about the office geek in the preceding bullet.

  - *Medical edition:* Comes out of the box knowing the names of obscure diseases, body parts, and pharmaceuticals. The Medical versions can be seen as their own family of products. There are versions for different types of healthcare providers and organizations. It is important to know that the Medical versions of Dragon are the only versions that will allow you to dictate into an electronic medical report (EMR or EHR) application.

  - *Legal edition:* Knows *amicus curiae, habeas corpus,* and a bunch of other Latin legal terminology that would make the Professional edition throw up its proverbial hands.

Nuance may be changing the name of Dragon Legal 13 and Dragon Premium 13 in the upcoming future. At the time of this writing, it remains the same.

- ✔ **Dragon for the Mac:** I cover the Dragon Windows products in this book, but Nuance also has a collection of products for the Mac, including Dragon for Mac and Dragon Dictate Medical for Mac. If you know some Mac users, tell them to check these out. (For use with mobile devices, including the iPhone, iPod, or iPad, see Chapter 14.)

In addition to these off-the-shelf products, you can also have Dragon Professional Group installed on your office network. This corporate option goes beyond the scope of what I cover in this book. If you're interested in this option, contact Nuance directly. Training programs for your staff are also available.

Understanding Speech Recognition in Dragon

Nuance has eliminated the training during set-up. But if you really want to make Dragon Professional Individual blazing fast, you should train it to understand you and the special words and phrases you use. So why does Dragon

Professional Individual need to be customized before it understands your speech? The simple answer is that speech recognition is probably one of the hardest things your computer does. Humans may not think speech recognition is hard, but that's because they are good at it. LeBron James probably has trouble understanding why the rest of us think it's so hard to dunk a basketball.

This section explains why deciphering speech is hard for computers and how training Dragon Professional Individual can overcome these difficulties. I hope that understanding these issues will give you confidence that the extra effort is worth it.

Dragon Professional Individual comes out of the box not knowing anything about you. It has to work as well for a baritone with a Scottish accent as for a mezzo-soprano with a slight lisp. It needs time to figure out how you talk.

Training continues for as long as you keep using Dragon Professional Individual. It makes mistakes, you correct them, and it learns. That's the process. It gets better and better the more frequently you use it.

The exact error rate depends on many factors: how fast your computer is, how much memory it has, how good your microphone is, how quiet the environment is, how well you speak, what sound card your computer has, and so on.

Dragon Professional Individual is up to 99 percent accurate out of the box and it gets better as long as you keep correcting it. Don't be lazy.

What's so hard about recognizing speech, anyway?

If three-year-olds can recognize and understand speech (other than the phrase "go to bed"), why is it so hard for computers? Aren't computers supposed to be smart?

Well, yes and no. Computers are very smart when it comes to brain-straining activities like playing chess and filling out tax returns, so you may think they'd be whizzes at "simple" activities like recognizing faces or understanding speech. But after about 50 years of trying to make computers do these simple things, programmers have come to the conclusion that a skill isn't simple just because humans master it easily. In fact, our brains and eyes and ears are chock-full of sophisticated sensing and processing equipment that still runs rings around anything we can design in silicon and metal.

We humans think it's simple to understand speech because all the really hard work is done before we become conscious of it. To us, it seems as if English words just pop into our heads as soon as people open their mouths. The unconscious (or preconscious) nature of the process makes it doubly hard for computer programmers to mimic. If we don't know exactly what we're doing or how we do it, how can we tell computers how to do it?

To get an idea of why computers have such trouble with speech, think about something that they're very good at recognizing and understanding: touch-tone phone numbers. Those blips and bloops on the phone lines are much more meaningful to computers than they are to people. Several important features make the phone tones an easy language for computers, as I discuss in the following list. English, on the other hand, is completely different:

- ✔ **The touch-tone "vocabulary" has only 12 "words" in it.** After you know the tones for the ten digits plus * and #, you're in. English, on the other hand, has hundreds of thousands of words.

- ✔ **None of the words sound the same.** On the touch-tone phone, the "1" tone is distinctly different from the "7" tone. But English has homonyms, such as *new* and *gnu,* and near homonyms, like *merrier* and *marry her.* Sometimes entire sentences sound alike: "The sons raise meat" and "The sun's rays meet," for example.

- ✔ **All "speakers" of the language say the words the same way.** Push the 5 button on any phone, and you get exactly the same tone. But an elderly man and a 10-year-old girl use very different tones when they speak; and people from Great Britain, Canada, and the United States pronounce the same English words in very different ways.

- ✔ **Context is meaningless.** To the phone, a 1 is a 1 is a 1. How you interpret the tone doesn't depend on the preceding number or the next number. But in written English, context is everything. It makes sense to "go to New York." But it makes no sense to "go two New York" or "go too New York."

What's a computer to do?

In order to work effectively for you, a speech-recognition program like Dragon Professional Individual needs to combine four vastly different areas of knowledge. It needs to know a lot about speaking in general, about the spoken English language in general, about the way your voice sounds, and about your word-choice habits.

How Dragon Professional Individual knows about speech and English in general

Dragon Professional Individual gets its general knowledge from the folks at Nuance, some of whom have spent most of their adult lives analyzing how

English is spoken. Dragon Professional Individual has been programmed to know in general what human voices sound like, how to model the characteristics of a given voice, the basic sounds that make up the English language, and the range of ways that different voices make those sounds. It has also been given a basic English vocabulary and some overall statistics about which words are likely to follow which other words. (For example, the word *medical* is more likely to be followed by *miracle* than by *marigold.*)

How Dragon Professional Individual learns about your voice

Dragon Professional Individual learns about your voice by listening to you. Dragon Professional Individual goes on learning about your voice every time you use it. When you correct a word or phrase that Dragon Professional Individual has guessed wrong, Dragon Professional Individual adjusts its settings to make the mistake less likely in the future.

Dragon learns even when you make keyboard edits or delete everything and start over, taking the net result of your dictation or typed text and using it to help improve its accuracy.

Dragon Professional Individual learns in two ways:

- ✔ **The Language Model:** When you make edits with your keyboard, Dragon will update your Language Model and better understand which words you use and when. However, Dragon Professional Individual will never add a word to your vocabulary unless you add it manually in the Vocabulary Editor or use the **"Spell That"** option to make your correction.

- ✔ **The Acoustic Model:** Dragon becomes more accurate by updating your Acoustic Model, which is how you sound and pronounce words. When you make corrections with your voice, Dragon updates both your Language Model and your Acoustic Model because it now has both the text and the audio associated with that text.

Although you can correct with your keyboard, Dragon becomes smarter when you correct with your voice. Either way, though, Dragon gets better!

How Dragon Professional Individual learns your word-choice habits

Dragon Professional Individual learns how you choose words if you choose to have emails or documents analyzed. It may seem as if Dragon Professional Individual is just learning how you say some unusual words. But, in fact, running this tool is worthwhile even if no new words are found, because Dragon Professional Individual analyzes how frequently you use common words and which words are likely to be used in combination.

Dragon Professional Individual comes out of the box knowing general facts about the frequency of English words, but having Dragon learn from emails or documents helps sharpen those models for your particular vocabulary.

For example, if you want to use Dragon Professional Individual to write a report, let it study your previous reports. Dragon Professional Individual will learn that the names of your colleagues appear much more frequently than they do in general English text. It is then much less likely to misinterpret your boss Johan's name as *John* or *yawn*.

Onward to Customizing!

By enabling you to install Dragon Professional Individual, your computer has taken on one of the hardest tasks a PC ever faces. It needs your help. If you use it with patience and persistence, and if you gently but firmly correct your Dragon Professional Individual assistant whenever it makes a mistake, you'll be rewarded with a computer that takes your verbal orders and transcribes your dictation without complaint (and even without a coffee break, unless you need one).

But I read in a magazine . . .

Quite a few magazine and newspaper articles have been written about voice recognition in general, and Dragon Professional Individual in particular. Almost all of them contain an example that's something like this: A guy says into a microphone, **"Send email to Bob about Friday's meeting. Period. Bob, comma, glad you're going to be there. Period."**

As if by magic, an email application opens, a message window appears, Bob's email address is pulled out of an address book somewhere, "Friday's meeting" is entered on the subject line, and the following text is entered into the message body: **"Bob, glad you're going to be there."**

The example is completely legitimate, as you can see in Chapter 12. But you need to keep something in mind: If you say, **"Do the numbers on February's revenue receipts,"** your spreadsheet just sits there.

Like any good magician's trick, more appears to be happening than actually happens. The computer has not suddenly been granted intelligence that rivals that of a human. The Nuance programmers have created a handful of scripts for doing everyday tasks, like generating email messages and entering new events into a calendar program. They've made the commands sound like the instructions you would give a personal assistant, and they've set things up so that a lot of similar-sounding commands produce the same result. But if you say, **"Zip a message off to Bob,"** nothing happens.

Impressive? Yes. Magic? Not quite. It's still just a computer.

Chapter 2

Installing Dragon and Starting Basic Training

In This Chapter

▶ Installing Dragon Professional Individual on your computer

▶ Creating a user profile

▶ Assisting Dragon in recognizing your voice

*B*y now, you have decided that Dragon Professional Individual is best for you, you've concluded that your hardware configuration is appropriate, and you may be sitting in front of your computer ready to get started. It's exciting to anticipate using a tool that can make you more productive every day!

But before you can start saving all that time, you need to install the program and create a user profile. Installing Dragon Professional Individual is easy. In most cases, you just put the DVD into your DVD-ROM drive and follow the directions on the screen. Setting up your profile is really quick, too. You will be asked some questions about your speaking style, but the good news is that they're all questions you know the answers to.

There is no training process to complete to get started. You can go back and read aloud some well-known material chosen for you to improve performance. The program will work on its own to improve accuracy, and you can help it along. I cover that in later chapters. In the late 1990s, training Dragon was a long, boring process. But fear not! Those days are over. By the end of this chapter, you will be ready to start dictating your project plan for that next great start up!

Installing Dragon Professional Individual on Your Computer

Whether you're installing Dragon Professional Individual for the first time or installing over a previous version, the process is easy. If you have user profiles from Dragon NaturallySpeaking versions 12 or 13, the Upgrade Wizard finds those user profiles and sets them up in version 14. Otherwise, you're guided through the creation of a new user profile. Follow these steps:

1. **Find the envelope that contains the installation DVD.**

   The DVD in the white envelope has a label with a serial number on it. The serial number enables you to activate the program, so keep it handy. You'll see duplicates of the number in a peel-off label format for your convenience.

2. **Paste the duplicate serial numbers in places that you can easily access.**

   For safekeeping, peel two of them off (leaving one on the envelope) and put them on your software receipt, in the front of this book, or in a file folder where you'll be able to find them again.

3. **Plug in a microphone.**

   Microphones other than those with a USB plug into your computer's sound card. If you have a desktop computer, turn the computer so that you can see the back where all the cables are. Your computer likely has color-coded jacks for the microphone and the headset along with small icons showing a mic and a headset. The headset has two color-coded plugs that correspond to the ones on the headset. Insert the plugs into the jacks as shown in the photo they supply.

   If you don't want to plug in an external mic, you also have the option to use the internal microphone.

4. **Put the installation DVD into your DVD drive.**

   The Windows AutoRun feature starts running the installation program automatically.

   If you wait 30 seconds or so and nothing happens, don't worry. Nothing is wrong. Do this instead: Double-click the Computer icon on the Windows desktop. When the Computer window opens, find the icon corresponding to your DVD-ROM drive, and double-click it. Find the `setup.exe` file in the DVD-ROM window and double-click it. Now you are exactly where you would be if it had started automatically. It will take a minute to prepare the files.

   You may see a screen asking you to reboot before installing. Make your choice. If you have already restarted more than once, click Yes to proceed.

5. **A welcome screen appears, as shown in Figure 2-1.**

   You are asked to wait as the setup process begins.

Figure 2-1:
InstallShield
Wizard
welcome
screen.

6. **After the InstallShield Wizard prepares the setup process, click the Next button.**

   You are presented with an End User License Agreement, as shown in Figure 2-2.

7. **If you agree to the terms of the license agreement, select the I Accept radio button and then click Next.**

   The Customer Information window appears, as shown in Figure 2-3.

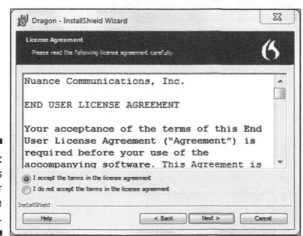

Figure 2-2:
Nuance's
End User
License
Agreement.

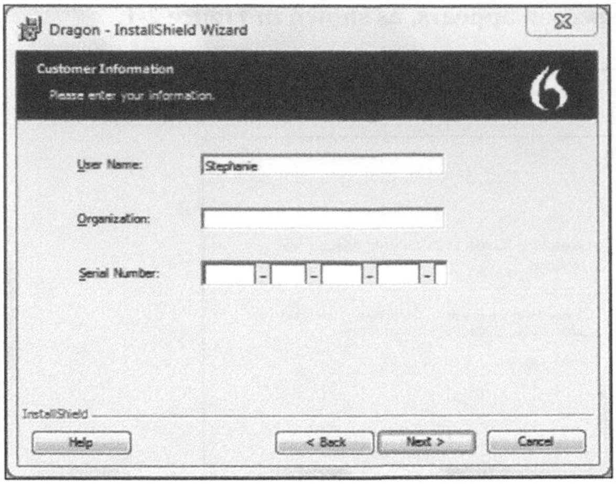

Figure 2-3:
Customer
Information
window.

8. **Type your username and serial number where prompted and then click Next.**

    You are presented with a Region Selection screen. Dragon uses this to determine the right vocabulary for your dictation.

    The serial number will never have any letter *O*s in it. If you see something that looks like an *O*, it's always a zero.

9. **Choose your region, as shown in Figure 2-4, and click Next.**

    You see the installation window as shown in Figure 2-5.

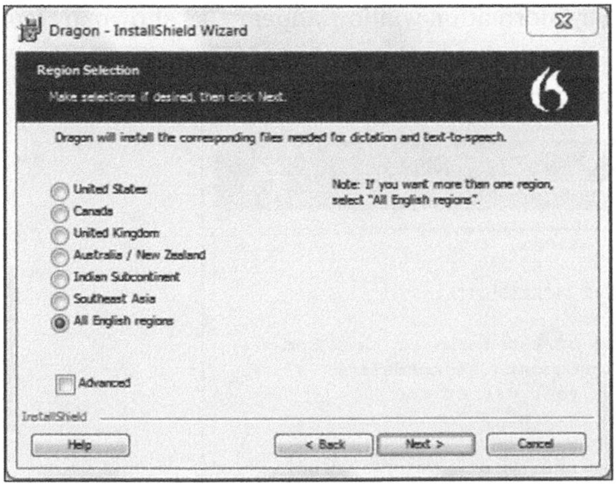

Figure 2-4:
Choose your
region.

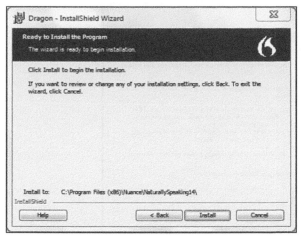

Figure 2-5:
Installation.

10. Click install.

Files begin to install as shown in Figure 2-6. Installation may take a few minutes.

After the files install, the InstallShield Wizard is finished. See Figure 2-7.

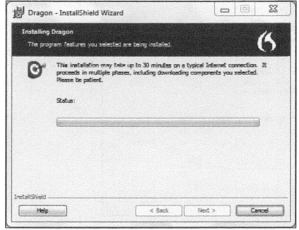

Figure 2-6:
Files are
being
installed.

11. (Optional) Deselect the Check for Updates check box if want to look for program updates later.

I recommend that you leave the check box selected so that you start your training with the most up-to-date files.

Figure 2-7:
InstallShield
Wizard has
completed
its magic.

12. Click Finish.

A screen appears, and you're asked to choose a way to register the software, as shown in Figure 2-8.

Figure 2-8:
Choices for
product
registration.

13. Select one of the two radio buttons to register.

You can choose Register Online or Remind Me in 7 Days. Make your choice based on your needs.

14. Click OK.

You might be asked to reboot your computer to make the necessary changes, as shown in Figure 2-9.

15. **If you're asked to restart your system, click Yes.**

    Congratulations! You've successfully installed Dragon Professional Individual.

Figure 2-9: Go ahead and reboot your computer if Dragon asks.

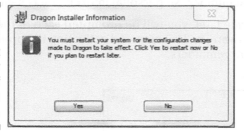

Creating a User Profile

If you wonder how Dragon Professional Individual maintains up to 99 percent accuracy rate, the secret is in the user profile. The profile learns your unique speech patterns and word choices. But, as with any good assistant, you need to provide Dragon Professional Individual with clear, accurate instructions for it to follow.

When Dragon is installed, you will see the Dragon icon on the desktop.

1. **Double-click the icon on the desktop (or on the Start screen in Windows 8) or choose Start ➪ All Programs ➪ Dragon Professional Individual from the Windows Start menu.**

    The Dragon Professional Individual opening screen appears, as shown in Figure 2-10.

Figure 2-10: The Dragon Professional Individual opening screen.

The first time after you install the program, you will be asked to activate your software, as shown in Figure 2-11. You can activate it immediately (Activate Product) or within five more uses (Trial Mode). Activation is required to use the program after the fifth use. If you click Activate Product, you must be connected to the web in order to verify that you are using a valid serial number. No personal information is sent.

If you choose to activate later, you will be prompted each of the next five times you use the software, so I recommend activating the product and avoiding the persistent reminders.

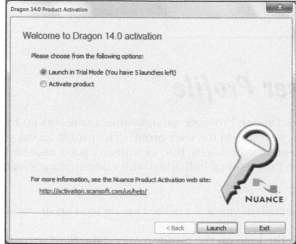

Figure 2-11:
Choose
when to
activate the
software.

Dragon 14.0 Product Activation

Welcome to Dragon 14.0 activation

Please choose from the following options:

- Launch in Trial Mode (You have 5 launches left)
- Activate product

For more information, see the Nuance Product Activation web site:
http://activation.scansoft.com/us/help/

NUANCE

< Back   Launch   Exit

2. **Select the Activate Product option.**

   Your serial number will be displayed.

3. **Click Next.**

   A 'Successful Activation' screen is displayed.

4. **Click Launch.**

   You see another welcome screen. You're another step closer to greater productivity and hands-free dictation!

If you're a new user who doesn't have a user profile from a previous version of NaturallySpeaking you will be prompted to create a profile name. This name will appear on future lists and menus so that you can tell Dragon Professional Individual which user you are.

Pick a name that you will recognize as your own. Be aware that your username is case sensitive when you make a choice. If you type your name as **Tom** with a capital *T,* you won't be able to use *tom* later.

Next, you'll need to step through some profile options. You are asked to:

1. **Choose your speech options, as shown in Figure 2-12.**

    • *Select your region:* It's important for Dragon Professional Individual to prepare files that are specific to your region of the world. Choose your region from the drop-down list.

    • *Select your accent:* I'm sure we all agree that it's the other person who has an accent, but there really are identifiable accents depending on where in the world you first learned to speak. Choose an accent from the drop-down list.

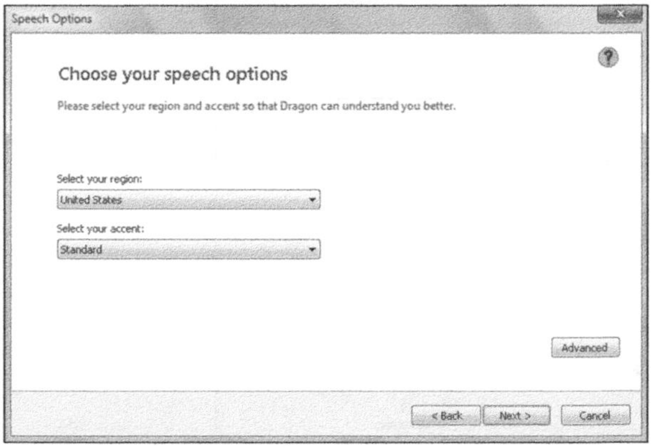

Figure 2-12:
Speech
options help
Dragon
better
understand
what you
are saying.

2. **Click Next.**

    If the program can locate your microphone, it will show up in the first audio device box, as shown in Figure 2-13. If you want to choose a different audio device, double-click it in the second box.

3. **Click Next.**

    You will be shown how to position your microphone correctly. (See Figure 2-14.) This instructional screen requires no information from you. It gives you advice on how to position your microphone and shows two graphics illustrating the approved techniques.

    The main idea is that the microphone needs to be near your mouth, but not in front of it. (In front *seems* natural, but you get interference from your breathing on the microphone.) It should be far enough to the side that you don't bump it with your mouth when you talk. You may need to twist the arm a bit to get the microphone positioned just right.

    Put the microphone a distance of two fingers from your mouth; that's the perfect amount of space. Also, make sure the word *talk* under the boom cushion is pointing toward your mouth; otherwise, you will not be heard.

Figure 2-13:
Choose an
audio
device.

Figure 2-14:
Position
your micro-
phone
according to
the provided
advice.

You only have to set up your user profile one time. However, there are other user profile options, including adding a dictation source to an existing profile. I tackle those options in Chapter 19.

4. Click Next.

Now you need to read a bit of text to make sure your microphone is configured correctly. See Figure 2-15.

5. When you are ready, click Start.

Begin reading until you get an audio signal that the recording process is complete. A Complete button will also appear indicating you are finished if you have the speakers muted on your system.

6. Click Next.

You see a screen that lets you know that the program is customizing itself for you.

When the customization finishes, a screen comes up asking you to choose whether you want to help Nuance improve the software, as shown in Figure 2-16. Make your choice.

Figure 2-15:
Helping
Dragon
adapt to
your voice
and ensure
your mic
works.

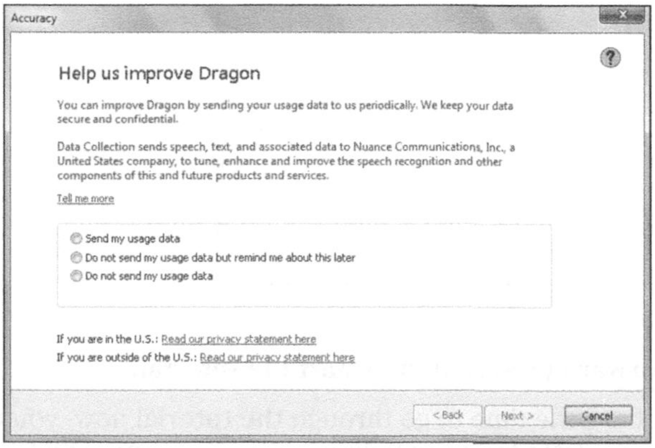

Figure 2-16:
Choices for
improving
current and
future
software
versions.

7. **Click Next.**

   A screen pops up to introduce the new mobile application Dragon Anywhere, as shown in Figure 2-17.

8. **Click the Learn More button if you want (I discuss Dragon Anywhere in Chapter 14) or click Next.**

   The software is ready to use, as shown in Figure 2-18.

9. **Click Finish.**

   A screen pops up and you see the Interactive Tutorial, as shown in Figure 2-19. If you have the time, I recommend that you step through the tutorial.

Figure 2-17:
Dragon
Anywhere

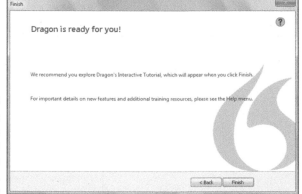

Figure 2-18:
The
software is
ready to
use.

10. **Click the Forward (>>) button to start the tutorial.**

    If you don't have the time to go through the tutorial now, you can always access it later from the Help menu in the upper-right corner of the DragonBar. When you're learning, it's great to use as many different modes as possible: watching, hearing, and, in the case of this book, doing it step by step.

11. **If you choose not to go through the Interactive Tutorial at this time, click the X in the upper-right corner.**

    If you need help of any kind, access the Help icon on the DragonBar.

    There's also a Dragon on the web link in the Help icon. This takes you to the information and support site for Dragon Professional Individual. For more information about the help available to you, see Chapter 21.

    A reminder screen pops up as shown in Figure 2-20. It reminds you to say, "What can I say?" if you need help.

12. **Click "Got It," and you're done.**

You've completed your set up. I'm sure you're already starting to feel confident that you and your new Dragon Professional Individual assistant will be great friends. If you're ready, head to Chapter 3 and start mastering the controls.

Figure 2-19: Interactive Tutorial teaches you efficient dictation skills.

Figure 2-20: "What can I say?" reminder screen.

Chapter 3

Launching and Controlling Dragon

*O*kay, you're at the point where you are deciding whether to skip this chapter and jump into dictating or to read this chapter and feel more prepared. Why not take the time to learn how to take control?

In this chapter, I show you the different ways to launch and control Dragon Individual Professional. I also tell you what tools you can use to get better performance and behavior, and where to find those tools. I refer you to other chapters in this book for the details. If Dragon Professional Individual is already up and running and you simply can't wait any longer, go and dictate! (See Chapter 4.)

Launching Dragon Professional Individual

To get started with Dragon Professional Individual, launch the product in one of the following ways:

▶ Double-click the Dragon icon on your desktop.

▶ On the Windows taskbar, choose Start ➪ Programs ➪ Dragon.

✔ You can also use the system tray (set by the Tray Icon Only option). Right-click the microphone icon and you'll see all the same menu options you have in the DragonBar. (More on the DragonBar later in this chapter.)

On the Windows 8 Start screen, you may see many Dragon-related icons; make sure to pick Dragon Professional Individual.

By choosing one of these options, you launch the Dragon Professional Individual DragonBar. You can dictate documents and control how Dragon Professional Individual works. You can customize this to suit your preferences.

Choosing or Switching User Profiles

When you launch Dragon Professional Individual, it may ask you to choose a *user.* If it doesn't ask, don't worry. You probably have only one user: you.

Remember that when you first set up Dragon Professional Individual, you created and named a User Profile and then showed Dragon Professional Individual how that user (you) sounded. Now, when you launch Dragon Professional Individual, you must choose that user so that Dragon Professional Individual can recognize you.

After launching, Dragon Professional Individual displays the Open User dialog box. Click the User Profile name you created when you set up Dragon Professional Individual, and then click the Open button. You're ready to roll.

Each person must have his or her own User Profile. If you need to add a user, go to the DragonBar and choose Profile ➪ New User Profile. This launches the same New User Wizard you used to set up Dragon Professional Individual for yourself. See Chapter 2 for details on that wizard. For more about multiple users and their vocabularies, see Chapter 19.

You can switch users without restarting Dragon Professional Individual. Follow these steps:

1. **From the DragonBar, choose Profile ➪ Open User Profile.**

   Dragon Professional Individual may ask whether you want to save your speech files. Unless for some reason you don't want to save any corrections you have made to Dragon Professional Individual's behavior, choose Yes. Dragon Professional Individual then displays the Open User dialog box.

2. **Click the username from the User list and then click the Open button.**

Meeting the Face of Your Dragon Professional Individual Assistant

As anyone who has ever used software knows, its value is most often determined by the design of the user interface. If it's hard to find menus, options, and features, most people give up before they ever find out if the product actually works. If you want simple, think Google Search Box. It doesn't get any easier than that!

Happily, the folks who develop the Dragon software have given a lot of careful attention to its user interface over the years. With Dragon Professional Individual, they've hit it out of the park. When you first launch Professional Individual, you see the Dragon Professional Individual DragonBar, as shown in Figure 3-1.

Figure 3-1:
The new
Dragon
Professional
Individual
DragonBar.

What can you do with the Dragon Professional Individual DragonBar? You can use the menu bar to access various tools for customizing and improving the performance of your Dragon Professional Individual assistant and you can click the microphone icon here to turn your microphone on and off. I consider it the base of operations.

The Dragon Help Center is a nice, controlled environment where you can find all the major commands used with Dragon Professional Individual. You don't have to wonder about commands. With your microphone on, all you have to do is say, **"What can I say?"** A menu opens that asks you to choose the type of commands you want to see. The function is context sensitive, so it displays commands about the application you are working on at the time.

For instance, if you're in Microsoft Word, asking "What can I say?" shows you the commands you need to use for Word. This makes learning application-specific commands much easier. See Chapters 20 and 21 for more about the Dragon Help Center. To access the Help Center directly from the DragonBar, click Help ⇨ Help Topics, and the Help Center opens.

A closer look at the DragonBar

The DragonBar in Dragon Professional Individual is docked at the top of the screen. If you prefer, you can change the placement by dragging the cross-hatched rectangle (called the Grabber bar) on the left, as shown in Figure 3-2.

Figure 3-2:
Options for docking the DragonBar.

Docking menu

The DragonBar button has links to the following:

- **New DragonBar:** This is the default view that you see when it opens.

- **Classic DragonBar:** This link lets you go back to the DragonBar design used in version 12 and previous versions. Although you may be tempted to do this if you are a long-time user of Dragon, I recommend trying the new one. When you get used to the new design, you will find you are more productive. Also, at some point, you will no longer have the option to switch, so best to start using it now.

- **Tray Icon Only:** This minimizes the DragonBar and places a microphone icon in your system tray. Right-click the icon to see all the menu options that were available to you when the DragonBar was visible.

- **Auto-collapse:** If you prefer to have the DragonBar showing all options at all times, you can select not to auto-collapse the bar by clicking the Auto-Collapse link. You can also collapse the DragonBar by clicking the –/+ sign on the left.

- **Exit Dragon:** This is how you exit Dragon. When exiting, you may be asked to run maintenance on your profile. I recommended that you do this whenever possible to make your profile more accurate. Just make sure you have some time because the program will take slightly longer to close.

To set the option to have QuickStart launch when Windows starts up, go to Tools ➪ Options ➪ Miscellaneous and select the check box for Launch Dragon in QuickStart mode when Windows starts.

If you want to reference the Classic DragonBar from previous versions, it is shown in Figure 3-3. Even though the new DragonBar looks different, all the menu items you know and love are there.

Here are the items on the new Dragon Professional Individual toolbar, shown in Figure 3-4:

Figure 3-3:
The Classic
DragonBar.

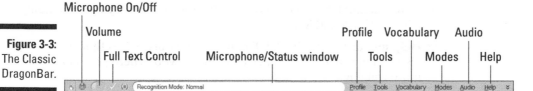

Figure 3-4:
Details of
the new
DragonBar.

✔ **The Microphone On/Off button:** This is the most critical item, for obvious reasons. If your microphone is off, you'll be doing nothing more than talking to yourself. Your assistant will be waiting to hear from you. The microphone icon is color-coded and tells you the status of your microphone. Red is off, green is on, and blue is asleep.

✔ **Volume display:** The volume display is located within the microphone area. It displays increasingly large circles alongside the icon when the volume is up and smaller ones when it's down. Adjust your voice accordingly.

✔ **Full Text Control indicator:** If you see a small green circle at the end of the DragonBar, you know that all the Full Text Control functions of the application you are in are available and working.

✔ **Profile menu:** This is where you manage all the functions related to User Profiles, such as adding new users and backing up a User Profile.

- ✔ **Tools menu:** The Tools menu has several important items, including the DragonPad (discussed later in this chapter) and the administrative settings.

- ✔ **Vocabulary menu:** This menu contains the all-important Vocabulary Editor and is the place where you go when you want to have your Dragon Professional Individual assistant learn more from your documents and emails.

- ✔ **Audio menu:** Here you will be able to launch accuracy training along with Playback and Read.

- ✔ **Help menu:** This is chock-full of helpful resources and tips. It also includes a link to Nuance.com on the web, where you'll find more training.

- ✔ **Mode menu:** This is found at the end of the DragonBar where you see Now Listening for . . . . You use several modes when dictating, including Dictation mode and Command mode. When you want to move from one to another, you make the switch by using the drop-down menu.

- ✔ **Start Playback and Stop Playback:** To make this function work, select the text you want to play back by highlighting it or saying, "**Select <xyz>**." Choose Audio ➪ Read That, and the text will be read.

Choosing options

Now that you're in charge, you can order Dragon Professional Individual to work your way. It's time to choose some options! From the DragonBar, choose Tools ➪ Options to open the Options dialog box. There are seven different category options. Take time to check them out and configure your assistant exactly the way you want it to behave.

Five options you may want to try right off the bat are as follows:

- ✔ **Trade-off speed for accuracy:** Miscellaneous tab

- ✔ **Automatically back up User Profile every fifth time:** Data tab

- ✔ **Change microphone on/off, correction hotkeys:** Hot Keys tab

- ✔ **Double-click to correct in Dragon Professional Individual window:** Correction tab

- ✔ **Automatic playback on correction:** Correction tab

Each tab has a Restore Defaults button. Hurray! Click it if you feel you changed something in error and want to put things back the way they were when you first launched Dragon Professional Individual.

Following is a brief explanation about what's in each tab:

- **Correction:** This tab is useful to explore if you want to have things like Spell commands bring up a Spelling Window. Take your time and go back to these options after you have worked in your documents for a while. As you might guess, corrections are a fact of life. At least they can be dealt with your way.

- **Commands:** In this section, you have a slider you can configure for the amount of time you want a pause before you dictate a command. It's set on the shorter end. Try this first before you extend it to see what's comfortable. Remember that you'll be dictating both speech and commands, and you want Dragon to understand how you like to do this.

- **View:** In this tab, you can set your placement of the DragonBar in addition to the way shown in Figure 3-2. Additionally, you can set the Results Box that was displayed in previous versions of Dragon Professional Individual.

- **Playback/Text-to-speech:** Text-to-speech is a fun and functional feature of Dragon Professional Individual. It uses a computer-synthesized voice to read text aloud. This will be the voice of your assistant, so choose accordingly. (In the English version, you can choose American English Samantha or British English Serena.) It can sound a bit comical until you get used to it. Adjust the up-arrow and down-arrow keys for volume and speed.

- **Miscellaneous:** This tab includes lots of useful stuff. Most important is the Speed versus Accuracy slider. Move this to the right for fewer recognition errors, or to the left for a quicker, if less accurate, job. The choice is yours.

- **Data:** Here you can change the amount of disk space reserved for playback. The default is 100MB. I don't recommend using less than that, but if you need the space you can set it to use less. If you need more space for playback, you can set it to use more. If you are using Dragon Professional, choose Never for the Save Recorded Dictation with Document option so your files don't become large and unwieldy.

- **Hotkeys:** You're either a devoted hotkey user or you aren't. There's no middle ground. If you like hotkeys, here's where you change them. Why change? You may have trouble pressing the key. Or you may need to use the key for something else (like using the numeric keypad + and – [minus] keys for calculations).

  All the buttons on the Hot Keys tab work the same way: Click the Edit button, and a Set Hot Key dialog box pops up. When it does, don't try to type the names of the keys; just press them. For instance, press the Ctrl key, and {Ctrl} appears. Click OK when you're done.

On the Hot Keys tab, you see the following options you may want to set:

- *Microphone On/Off:* If you choose a regular keyboard key (like a letter), you must use Ctrl or Alt with it. Otherwise, function keys, arrow keys, and other non-typewriter keys are all fair game either by themselves or in combination with Ctrl or Alt.

- *Correction:* This key pops up the Correction dialog box to correct the last phrase you spoke or the highlighted text. The rules are the same as for Microphone On/Off.

- *Force Command Recognition:* Hold this key down to try to make Dragon Professional Individual interpret what you say as a command, not text. It can be only Ctrl, Alt, Shift, or some combination of them.

- *Force Dictation Recognition:* This does the opposite of Force Command Recognition (makes what you say come out as text). Rules for keys are the same as Force Command Recognition.

Before Dragon Professional Individual, previous versions of NaturallySpeaking had a Results Box that showed what Dragon thought you said as you dictated. In versions 12 and higher, this has been streamlined to a results display. As you dictate, you will notice a little Dragon icon displayed near your text. When you pause dictation, the words show up in your document. Nuance made this change after discovering that users were distracted by following the Results Box.

I think this is a great improvement and I recommend you do not switch back to the Results Box option if you are new to Dragon Professional Individual. If, however, you are used to seeing the Results Box and want to display it, do the following:

1. **Go to Tools ➪ Options ➪ View tab.**

   Look at the section toward the bottom called Results Box.

2. **Click the drop-down arrow under Auto-hide Delay and select Never Hide or some amount of time it will display.**

   You can also choose whether you want it to stay in one place by selecting the anchor check box or whether you want to show preliminary results.

"Okay, so I have familiarized myself with the controls. Now how do I dictate?" you may be asking. Easy: Plug in your microphone, put it on, click the Microphone On/Off button (also duplicated on the Windows taskbar's system tray), and talk! But wait. . . .

Why Use the Dragon Professional Individual DragonPad?

Before you start dictating by employing one of the myriad applications you can use with Dragon, I want to introduce you to the DragonPad. To open it, go to the DragonBar and choose Tools ⇨ DragonPad.

DragonPad is a simple word processor into which you can dictate or type a document. You then can print the document, copy it to another program window, or save the document as a file that other programs can read.

Dragon Professional Individual works with really robust word processors like Word and WordPerfect, so you may be wondering why I mention this simple Dragon Professional Individual function.

Here are some of the reasons you may want or need to dictate into the Dragon Professional Individual window:

- ✔ You don't have Microsoft Word or Corel WordPerfect (or your version of those programs doesn't work with Dragon Professional Individual).

- ✔ You just need the basic word-processing functions and you're in a hurry.

- ✔ Your PC is tight on memory. The Dragon Professional Individual window uses less memory than some other applications.

- ✔ You see that the circle on the DragonBar is not green, which indicates that you need to open a Dictation Box.

- ✔ Your alternative is to use some application in which Dragon Professional Individual offers only basic dictation and not other features.

Using the word-processor features of the Dragon Professional Individual DragonPad

The Dragon Professional Individual window's menu and toolbar may seem familiar to you. They are, with the addition of speech features, the same as the menu and toolbar in WordPad (the small-scale word processor that comes with Windows).

If you're already familiar with WordPad or similar word processors, you can skip this section and move right on to Chapter 4.

Choosing from the menu bar and toolbar

Even if you have never used DragonPad, if you have used any word processor, you'll find all the choices on the DragonPad menus and toolbars so familiar (except for the speech-related choices) that you'll hardly need this section. But just in case you aren't familiar, following are the details, as shown in Figure 3-5.

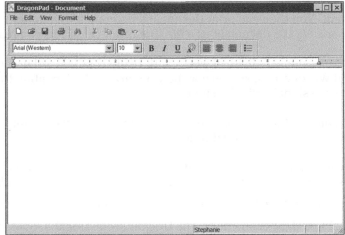

Figure 3-5:
The DragonPad interface.

Use the DragonPad menu bar and toolbar buttons as you would in any Windows program. As with most Windows toolbars, pause your mouse cursor over a button to see the button's name or function.

Because you're running Dragon Professional Individual, you can also choose items on the menu bar by using voice commands (as you can in nearly any other application, too). To choose from the menu bar, follow these steps:

1. Use the verbal command, "Click *<menu text>*."

By *<menu text>*, I mean anything listed on the menu bar, such as File, Edit, or Format.

2. Choose an item from the menu that appears by saying its name.

If you want consistency in your commands, you can instead say **"Click"** and then its name. For instance, you can say, **"Click File"** and then say, **"Save."**

In Dragon Professional Individual, you can have more control over when you need to say **"Click."** To change your options, go to Tools ⇨ Options ⇨ Commands. In the check boxes Require Click to Select Menus and Require Click to Select Buttons and Other Controls, make your choices. If you're just getting started and you aren't sure how you want to use these controls, leave them selected. You can always return later.

Editing: Cut, paste, and the usual suspects

The Edit menu of Dragon Professional Individual holds no surprises for anyone who has used a word processor in Windows. It has the usual suspects: Copy, Cut, and Paste using the Windows Clipboard, plus Undo, Select All, Find, and Replace.

If you add the Format bar to the Dragon Professional Individual window, you can alternatively use the familiar Cut, Copy, and Paste buttons on that bar. The button with the binoculars icon is a shortcut to the Find dialog box.

Choosing Edit ⇨ Select All (hotkey: Ctrl+A) is useful when you want to copy all the text in the window in preparation for pasting it into a different program. See Chapter 5 if you want details about copying text from Dragon Professional Individual by using voice commands.

Formatting: Fonts, indentations, alignments, bullets, and tabs

The Format menu is where all the formatting stuff hangs out. Like the Edit menu, the Format menu is straightforward if you have used a word processor before. Here are the menu choices that change the format:

- ✔ **Font:** Choose Format ⇨ Font to get a Font dialog box to make your typeface, style, size, and color choices. Or add the Format bar to your screen by choosing View ⇨ Format Bar and choose your font on that toolbar. You can set font styles of bold, italic, or underline in alternative ways, just as in many other programs. Click the B, I, or U button on the Format bar; or press Ctrl+B, Ctrl+I, or Ctrl+U, respectively. You can choose font color from the Font dialog box or by clicking the Color button (the palette icon) on the Format bar.

- ✔ **Indents and alignments:** Choose Format ⇨ Paragraph to get a Paragraph dialog box. Type in an indentation for the left edge, right edge, or just the first line of the paragraph. (For hanging indents, set a left indent, like 0.5 inch, and then an equal but negative indent, like –0.5, for first line.)

> Click Alignment to choose from Left, Center, and Right alignment. Or if the Format bar is on your screen, click the Align Left, Center, or Align Right button.

> ✔ **Tabs:** To set tab stops (where the cursor stops when you press the Tab key), choose Format ➪ Tabs. In the Tabs dialog box that appears, type a position (for example, 0.8 inch) in the Tab Stop Position box, and then click the Set button. Continue until you have set all your tabs, and then click OK. Click Clear All to restore tabs to the normal half-inch defaults.

> ✔ **Bullets:** Dragon Professional Individual offers only one style of bullets. To turn bullets on, choose Format ➪ Bullet Style (or click the Bullets button on the Format bar). Repeat that choice to turn bulleting off.

You can also set tab stops on the Ruler. (To put the Ruler bar on your screen, choose View ➪ Ruler Bar.) Just click wherever you want a tab stop. A tiny L-shaped mark appears; you can drag it to any position you like. To remove it, drag it up or down off the ruler.

Saving and opening documents

You save a Dragon Professional Individual document the old-school way: with a menu choice or toolbar button. As in any other application, you can use a voice command to make the menu choice, such as saying, **"Click File,"** and then saying, **"Save"** or just saying, **"Press Control S."**

The New, Save, Save As, and Open commands in the Dragon Professional Individual File menu work as they do in nearly every other Windows application. So do the New, Open, and Save buttons on the toolbar (the first three). In case you forget (or nobody ever told you), here's what they do:

✔ To start a new, blank document, choose File ➪ New (or click the New button).

✔ To open an existing document file, choose File ➪ Open (or click the Open button).

✔ To save the document as a file, choose File ➪ Save (or click the Save button).

✔ To save a new copy of the current document under a new name or in a new location, choose File ➪ Save As.

Dragon Professional Individual enables you to save your work in one of the following ways (file types), so you can pass your work along to others or save it for a fun day of editing later on:

- ✔ **Plain text (**.txt**) files:** Text files do not preserve formatting, only the text plus line or paragraph breaks and tabs. (Tab stop *positions* are not saved, however.) Most everything can open a .txt file.

- ✔ **Rich Text Format (**.rtf**) files:** Rich Text Format files are filled with all the formatting you can do in Dragon Professional Individual. Nearly all major word processors can open these files, so your formatting survives the translation if you use .rtf.

When you choose File ➪ Save the first time (or anytime you choose File ➪ Save As), you have to choose which file type to use. A Dragon Professional Individual dialog box appears, warning you that saving a text file will lose formatting. It presents you with two buttons to choose between: Rich Text Document or Text Document. (If you press the Enter key at this point, Dragon Professional Individual will choose RTF.)

Choose Rich Text Format if you want to import your document into a word processor or some other application that enables character formatting (such as bold) and paragraph formatting (such as center-aligned). Choose Text if the application (such as a simple email program) does not support formatting. When you click the button for your choice, Dragon Professional Individual presents the typical Save As dialog box you will recognize from other Windows applications. Type a name for the file and choose a folder.

To open an RTF file in your word processor or other application, the usual menu choice is File ➪ Open. In the Open dialog box that appears, click the box labeled Files of Type (or something like that) and look for Rich Text Format (RTF).

If you want to verbally edit documents, you need to load them into the Dragon Professional Individual window. In addition to being able to open the RTF and TXT files it writes, Dragon Professional Individual can read some Microsoft Word (.doc) files. Using your word processor, check the dialog box that appears when you use the File ➪ Save As command. Click the Save As Type box there and choose a Word version (.doc or .docx), Text (.txt), or Rich Text (.rtf).

You don't have to rely on DragonPad to edit your text. If your first choice is to edit in your favorite word processor or other supported application, choose that.

Customizing the window

In case you are wondering, you can change the appearance through the View menu in DragonPad. By "appearance," I mean stuff like toolbars, text wrapping in the window, and units of measure on the ruler (metric, English, or typesetting).

To view all the toolbars in the DragonPad, click View to get a list of available toolbars. Click next to a toolbar in that list to put a check mark beside it to turn on whatever toolbar you check. Click again to clear any check mark. The default is set with all boxes selected.

To control how text wraps (continues onto the next line) on your screen, how your mouse selects text, or what units of measure you use, choose View ⇨ Settings. The Settings dialog box springs into action, where you can customize any of the following:

✔ **Measurement units:** Dragon Professional Individual normally uses inches for measurement units (used on the ruler and in paragraph formatting). To change measurement units, click the Options tab of the Settings dialog box. You can then choose Inches, Centimeters, Points, or Picas.

✔ **Selecting words:** When you select with your mouse, Dragon Professional Individual (like many Windows programs) normally selects entire words when you stretch the selection highlight to more than one word. If, instead, you want to be able to set the end point of your selections in midword, click the Options tab, then click to clear the check box labeled Automatic Word Selection.

✔ **Text wrapping:** To control how text wraps on your screen, click Rich Text. (Click Text, instead, if you intend to save your file as plain text.) Then click either Wrap to Window (to fill your window with text) or Wrap to Ruler (to force lines to break at the right margin on the ruler). No Wrap makes your text hard to read. Choose Wrap to Ruler if you intend to print from the Dragon Professional Individual window and want to see exactly how your printed lines of text will break while you type.

None of the wrap settings affect how lines of text break when you print, copy, or save a document as a file. The DragonPad always prints according to the page margins you set up, regardless of wrap settings. It never puts line breaks in text that is saved as a file or copied to another program's window. It always leaves the line breaks to that other program, and so avoids any ragged-right margin problems.

Tools and When to Use Them

I know you're saying, "Let's dictate, already!" (See Chapter 4.) But Dragon Professional Individual will never get any better at its job if you don't use the tools found in the DragonBar menus. They help you get the most accuracy from your Dragon Professional Individual assistant. I give you the details of these tools throughout the book, but here's the big picture.

Following are some of the tools that you most likely need:

- **Correction menu box:** Use this to educate Dragon Professional Individual whenever it makes a recognition error. You may have to use it several times for the same error, but Dragon Professional Individual will make the error less often. The Correction dialog box also appears in response to the **"Correct That"** voice command, the – (minus) key on the numeric keypad, and the Correct That icon on the toolbar. (See Chapters 4 and 5 for details.) You can also say, **"Correct *<xyz>*, "** where "xyz" refers to the words you want to select for correction.

- **Microphone check:** Run the microphone check by choosing Audio ➪ Check Microphone if Dragon Professional Individual seems to be making more errors than it did previously. It adjusts the volume of the microphone input and ensures the correct microphone input is selected. (See Chapter 2.)

- **Vocabulary Editor:** Use this tool to add specific words to your vocabulary or to train Dragon Professional Individual in your pronunciation. It's also useful for creating shortcuts in which a single spoken phrase like **"My Address"** causes Dragon Professional Individual to type some complex text. (See Chapter 17.) Use the Vocabulary Editor if you want more advanced functions, to edit or manage existing words in the Vocabulary.

- **Add New Word or Phrase:** Go to this menu item under Vocabulary to quickly add a specific word.

- **Add New Auto-Text:** Go to this menu under Tools to quickly add these shortcuts in which a single spoken phrase like **"My Address"** causes Dragon Professional Individual to type some complex text.

- **Vocabulary Editor:** Use this if you want more advanced functions, to edit or manage existing words in the Vocabulary.

- **Manage Custom Commands:** Use to edit or manage existing auto-texts or command shortcuts (although it works with the Vocabulary Editor, its probably not the more intuitive way to do that).

- **Audio training:** Use audio tools to tell Dragon Professional Individual how you pronounce a particular word or command. (See Chapter 17.)

Table 3-1 lists the Dragon tools or technologies to use in specific circumstances and where to read the full details about them.

If you are running Dragon Professional Individual but can't see its window, click the Dragon Professional Individual microphone button on your Windows taskbar. Then you can access the tools from the Dragon Professional Individual system tray icon menu.

Table 3-1	When to Use Tools, and Where They Are		
What You Need to Do	*What Dragon Technology to Use*	*Menu/Toolbar Choice*	*Where to Read More*
Correct a Dragon Professional Individual error	Correction dialog box	Correction button on the DragonBar or − (minus) on the keypad	Chapters 4, 5
Adjust for changes in microphone	Microphone check	Audio ➪ Check Microphone	Chapter 18
Improve recognition of individual words	Audio Tool	Audio ➪ Improve Recognition of Word or Phrase	Chapter 18
Add a specific word to your vocabulary	Vocabulary Tool	Vocabulary ➪ Add New Word or Phrase	Chapter 17
Add words in this document to vocabulary	Vocabulary Tool	Vocabulary ➪ Learn from Specific Documents	Chapter 17
Delete, train, or edit word properties in your vocabulary	Vocabulary Editor	Vocabulary ➪ Open Vocabulary Editor	Chapter 17
Create a shortcut phrase for long text	Vocabulary Editor	Vocabulary ➪ Open Vocabulary Editor	Chapter 17
Add a new user	Profile Tool	Profile ➪ New User Profile	Chapters 2, 20
Switch to a different user	Profile Tool	Profile ➪ Open User Profile	Chapter 19
Transcribe recorded speech	Transcription Tool	Tools ➪ Transcribe Recording	Chapter 11
Create custom commands	Commands Editor	Tools ➪ Add New Command	Chapter 20
Modify commands	Commands Editor	Tools ➪ Command Browser	Chapter 20

Make sure to look at the Recognition modes that are available in Dragon Professional Individual. To access them, go to the DragonBar and choose the mode you want at the end of the bar from the drop-down menu. Then select the one you need. The five available modes are as follows:

- ✔ **Dictation & Commands mode:** This is the default mode. In this mode, the program can discern the difference between commands, words, and numbers.

- ✔ **Dictation mode:** In this mode, most of what you say is interpreted as dictation, except for a few standard commands like **"New line."**

- ✔ **Command mode:** Not surprisingly, this mode will only recognize commands. Use this one if you only want to move around in a document.

- ✔ **Numbers mode:** Can you guess this mode's function? Yep, this one only recognizes numbers. This may be helpful when you are doing your monthly tally of something.

- ✔ **Spell mode:** In this mode, you can only spell things out. This can be useful for creating things like a household inventory of serial numbers.

Part II
Creating Documents and Spreadsheets

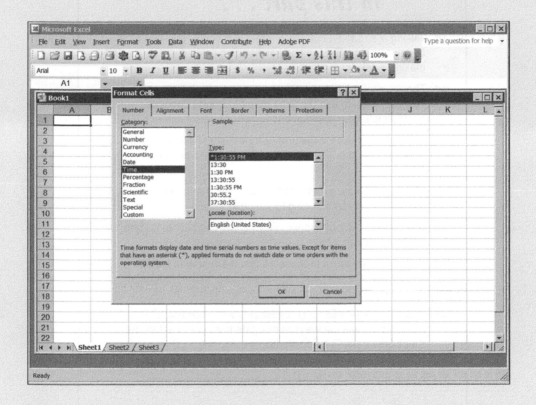

 Want to practice so that your dictation will be flawless? I show you how, using punctuation and formatting. It's easy once you get the hang of it. Go to www.dummies.com/extras/dragonprofessionalindividual.

In this part . . .

- Talking is so simple that you'll forget that you're creating emails and documents. Get the hang of dictating using punctuation and making quick corrections.

- The DragonPad makes editing and correcting your text easy. You'll see how to use the DragonPad to create flawless content to insert into your applications.

- Are you a stickler for the proper formatting? I show you how to get exactly the format you want in your text-editing applications.

- Most people hate proofreading. You'll find out how to catch mistakes easily by listening to your text.

- If you have a favorite application, I show you how to dictate into it so you don't have to devise new ways to work.

- Everyone uses word processors. You learn how to make short work of emails and reports by using natural language commands to format and edit.

- Want to navigate Excel spreadsheets with your voice? I highlight the easiest ways to navigate the cells in either the Quick Edit or the Full Edit mode.

- What could be better than dictating and letting someone else do the transcribing? You find out how to make this happen.

Chapter 4

Simply Dictating

· ·

In This Chapter

▶ Dictating text and commands

▶ Controlling the microphone

▶ Reviewing tips for dictation

▶ Punctuating and capitalizing

▶ Entering spaces and tabs

▶ Entering different numbers and dates

▶ Making quick corrections

▶ Tackling common dictation problems

· ·

*I*t seems to me that dictating should be a far easier way to communicate than by tapping your fingers across a keyboard. And the basics of dictating are, in fact, pretty easy. You just need to know a few tricks that I tell you about in this chapter.

The "basics" of Dragon Professional Individual are its keyboard-like capabilities to turn voice into text. Dragon Professional Individual can do lots of other things (edit, format, make tables, launch programs, and more) too, but those tasks are covered in later chapters. The keyboard-like features are the ones you find in all versions of Dragon.

This basic keyboard capability works not only in Dragon Professional Individual DragonPad but also in any (well, nearly any) Windows application. See Part III for using Dragon Professional Individual with Internet applications.

Chapter 5 goes into detail about correcting errors, moving your cursor around verbally, and other fine points of editing using Dragon Professional Individual. Chapter 5 also discusses some of the more advanced editing features Dragon Professional Individual offers in certain applications. For now, I focus on basic dictation in Dragon Professional Individual.

Dictating 101: How to Dictate

After you have installed Dragon Professional Individual on a computer with all the necessary system requirements (see Chapter 2), you're on the road to a beautiful friendship with your assistant. Open the program into which you'd like to dictate and take the following steps:

1. **Launch Dragon Professional Individual. Choose Start ⇨ Programs ⇨ Dragon.**

   You can use Dragon Professional Individual with a large number of applications. If you intend to use Dragon Professional Individual with another application, launch that application at this point, too.

2. **Put on your headset, and make sure the microphone is positioned as it was during initial training.**

   The microphone should be positioned about a half-inch away from one corner of your mouth, off to the side. It should never be directly in front of your mouth.

3. **Turn the microphone on.**

   The microphone icon on the DragonBar needs to be green in order for you to dictate. If the icon is red, click it or press the + key on your keyboard's numeric keypad to turn it green, as shown in Figure 4-1.

Figure 4-1:
Click the microphone icon in the DragonBar to turn the microphone on.

The microphone icon in the toolbar of the Dragon Professional Individual DragonBar works exactly the same way as the icon in the system tray. Make sure one of these is open and ready for you to dictate.

4. **Click where you want the text to go if the cursor isn't already there.**

   Or select (highlight) the text that you want to replace with dictated text.

5. **Speak carefully, just as you did when you read the text aloud to Dragon Professional Individual during the initial setup. Don't rush, and don't speak the words with . . . spaces . . . between . . . them.**

   As you speak, Dragon Professional Individual shows you what it thinks you said.

6. **Speak your punctuation, such as** "Period" **or** "Comma," **as you go, and if you want a word capitalized, say the word** "Cap" **beforehand.**

   However, you don't need to say **"Cap"** if it is the first word of the sentence.

   See the later section, "Punctuating and Capitalizing," for details.

If Dragon Professional Individual makes errors (remember, it's only up to 99 percent accurate), correct them rather than edit them. For basic instructions, see "Making Quick Corrections," later in this chapter. See Chapter 5 for additional details on correcting and for instructions for editing by voice.

Figure 4-2 is an example of how dictation works in Dragon Professional Individual. These paragraphs show the basic keyboard-style input I discuss in this chapter.

Figure 4-2:
The callouts in this example show what to say to get punctuation, capitalization, and numbers.

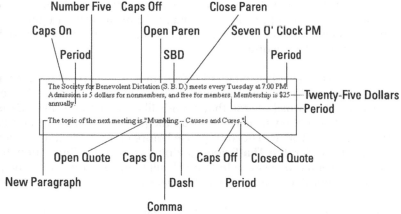

Speak continuously. Don't pause between your words (until you come to the end of a phrase)! Dragon Professional Individual is designed to recognize continuous speech. If you deliberately put pauses between your words, Dragon Professional Individual will make more errors, not fewer. (Pausing between phrases is okay, however.)

Use your keyboard and your mouse just as you would normally — to type, make menu selections, or use command keys (like Ctrl+Z). Or you can use Dragon Professional Individual to perform keyboard and menu commands. See Chapter 15 for details.

Distinguishing between Text and Commands

Dragon Professional Individual lets you mix dictation (words that are converted into text) and commands (instructions to the computer). You don't have to press or click anything to tell Dragon Professional Individual, "Here comes a command; don't write this." You just say the command.

Sometimes, however, you may not get what you expect. For instance, **"Cap"** is a command to capitalize the upcoming word. You may, however, dictate a sentence like, "We want to cap expenditures for this year" and see it come out like this: "We want to Expenditures for this year."

Use pauses to control the interpretation. Most commands involve two or more words. Dragon Professional Individual must hear them together, as a phrase, to interpret them as a command. To make sure Dragon Professional Individual interprets a phrase as text instead of a command, pause between two or more of the words.

To have Dragon Professional Individual interpret "cap" as text, for instance, pause between "cap" and the word it operates on, like "expenditure." For a two- or three-word phrase that sounds like a command (like **"Caps On"**), pause between the words to break up the phrase ("They put their caps . . . on their heads.") You also need to pause before commands that affect what you just said, as **"Scratch That"** does, undoing your preceding action. If you don't pause, Dragon Professional Individual will lump "scratch" with the preceding word and consider it all as text. Fortunately, such a pause is natural.

Most people aren't that careful. They speak the phrase and then say, "Oh, rats" (silently, to themselves, or else Dragon Professional Individual will dutifully type *that* out). Instead of "Oh, rats," when you see the error, say, **"Scratch That"** to remove the blooper. Then repeat the phrase with the pauses adjusted. Don't worry; this isn't as complicated as it sounds. It becomes quite natural.

You can adjust the amount of time that Dragon Professional Individual considers is a sufficient pause. (See Chapter 3.)

Pausing doesn't help with punctuation and numbers that you want spelled out. For instance, you can't dictate, **"He typed a comma and continued."** You get the comma symbol, not the word. For those problems, use the Vocabulary Editor (described in Chapter 17) to add the written word *comma* with a new spoken form (for example, "word comma"). Then you can say, **"He typed a word comma and continued."**

Although using pauses is the most reliable way to distinguish between text and command, Dragon Professional Individual offers an alternative solution. This alternative doesn't work for so-called "dictation commands" that have to do with capitalization, tabs, and line or paragraph breaks, but it does work for many other commands, such as formatting commands. To force your utterance to be taken as text, hold down the Shift key while you speak. To force it to be taken as a command, hold down the Ctrl key.

Controlling Your (Cough! Sneeze!) Microphone

Some people switch the microphone off and on to avoid inserting the garbage text that comes from coughing, sneezing, or answering the phone. Dragon Professional Individual gives you several ways to control the microphone:

- ✔ Press the + key on the numeric keypad to switch the microphone between "on" and "off." I find this switch to be the most convenient one.

- ✔ Click the microphone icon that appears either on the DragonBar or in the system tray of your Windows taskbar.

- ✔ Say, **"Go to Sleep"** or **"Stop Listening"** to disable the microphone. The microphone icon turns blue and a moon symbol appears next to the microphone icon. To wake up the microphone again, say, **"Wake Up"** or **"Listen To Me."** (Or click the sleeping microphone icon, or press the + key on the numeric keypad twice.) This sleeping and waking stuff is not the same as "off" and "on." What's the difference? When the microphone is asleep, it's still listening for the command, **"Wake Up."** If you turn the microphone off, it isn't listening at all.

There is no **"Microphone On"** command that corresponds to the **"Microphone Off"** command. You have to say **"Wake Up"** or **"Listen To Me."** If the microphone is off, you must manually turn it on because it is not listening for anything.

You can change the microphone hotkey (normally the + key on the numeric keypad) by choosing Tools ➪ Options and clicking the Hot Keys tab in the Options dialog box that appears. Then click the Microphone On/Off button in the dialog box; a tiny Set Hot Key dialog box appears. Now press the key or key combination you would prefer for the hotkey, and then click OK.

Tips for Talking

Dictating text, especially if you're used to typing on a keyboard, can seem a little clumsy at first. You need to do things a bit differently than when you type. Following are eight tips to make your dictating easier:

- ✔ **Try not to watch the screen as you talk.** The two activities are somehow not very compatible. I find I lose my train of thought if I look at what's being typed. Instead, look out the window or gaze off into the distance to compose and speak. Nuance removed the Results Box because people found it distracting.

- ✔ **Dictate in phrases.** You don't have to dictate the entire sentence, with all its punctuation, all at once (although using longer phrases improves accuracy). For instance, as I dictated the preceding sentence, I paused after "the entire sentence" and paced a while in thought. I also paused before and after the commas.

- ✔ **Punctuate and capitalize as you speak.** Although you can certainly go back and punctuate and capitalize text after you dictate, punctuating as you speak is often easier, after you become used to it.

- ✔ **Proofread what you have dictated.** Dragon Professional Individual will make some mistakes, particularly when you first get started. Sometimes those mistakes are both potentially embarrassing and so plausible-sounding that they are hard to detect! Dragon Professional Individual provides two tools that address this problem:

  - • *Playback:* Directly accessible from the DragonBar Audio menu, this feature plays back a recording of your voice (not available in the Home edition).

  - • *Read That:* This feature actually synthesizes a voice from your text.

  See Chapter 7 for more information on these proofreading features.

- ✔ **Avoid the temptation to use unusual or classic texts, such as the Gettysburg Address, when trying out Dragon Professional Individual.** Instead, use normal, day-to-day language. See Chapter 25 of this book if you want to play around with Dragon Professional Individual. If you really intend to dictate poetry or something other than contemporary English regularly, use multiple users (see Chapter 19). Out of the box, Dragon Professional Individual is designed for conventional and contemporary English; using it otherwise can cause errors.

✔ **Expect dictating to be a bit awkward at first.** If, like me, you are used to typing, you may find that composing your thoughts verbally is disconcerting at first.

✔ **Compromise between using your voice and the keyboard if you can.** Keep your hands on the mouse and keyboard for cursor and menu control, and then use Dragon Professional Individual as a fast way to type and format text. For example, you might highlight some text with your mouse and then say, **"Cap That"** or move your cursor somewhere and dictate.

✔ **To get used to Dragon Professional Individual gradually, try typing normally using the keyboard; then, every so often, dictate a bit of text that you find awkward to type.**

If you're stumped about what command to say, you can always ask Dragon, **"What can I say?"** and you'll see the appropriate commands.

Punctuating and Capitalizing

Dictating isn't quite like speaking. Unlike human listeners, Dragon Professional Individual can't interpret the inflections and pauses in your voice as punctuation. When you dictate, you have to make an effort to help Dragon Professional Individual out, although Dragon Professional Individual does do some punctuating and capitalizing automatically. Here's how to work with Dragon Professional Individual to get your words correctly capitalized and your apostrophizing properly punctuated.

Punctuating your remarks

Speaking punctuation marks as you dictate is annoying but necessary if you want to avoid the tedious process of going back and inserting punctuation. Tables 4-1, 4-2, and 4-3 show you what words to say to insert punctuation marks as you speak.

Table 4-1	Single Punctuation Marks
Punctuation Mark	*Spoken Form*
.	**"Period"** (or **"Dot,"** or **"Point"**)
!	**"Exclamation Mark"** (or **"Exclamation Point"**)
?	**"Question Mark"**
,	**"Comma"**
'	**"Apostrophe"**
's	**"Apostrophe Ess"**
&	**"Ampersand"**
:	**"Colon"**
;	**"Semicolon"**
'	**"Open Single Quote"**
'	**"Close Single Quote"**
. . .	**"Ellipsis"**
$	**"Dollar Sign"**
-	**"Hyphen"**
--	**"Dash"**

Table 4-2	Paired Punctuation Marks
Punctuation Mark	*Spoken Form*
"	**"Open Quote"**
"	**"Close Quote"**
(	**"Open"** (or **"Left"**) **"Parenthesis"** (or **"Paren"**)
)	**"Close"** (or **"Right"**) **"Parenthesis"** (or **"Paren"**)
[	**"Open Bracket"**
]	**"Close Bracket"**

Here are some tips for dictating punctuation:

✔ Dragon Professional Individual puts no space before an apostrophe, so you can easily make a noun possessive (such as in "Tom's bicycle") by speaking the word (**"Tom"**) and then saying, **"Apostrophe Ess."** Dragon Professional Individual may supply an apostrophe automatically if, from the context, it thinks you are describing a possessive noun or contraction, but it can't always do that accurately. It's more reliable, if more awkward, to speak the word and then add, **"Apostrophe Ess."**

Table 4-3	Math and Computer Symbols
Punctuation Mark	**Spoken Form**
{	**"Open Brace"**
}	**"Close Brace"**
/	**"Slash"**
\	**"Backslash"**
@	**"At Sign"**
~	**"Tilde"**
_	**"Underscore"**
*	**"Asterisk"**
>	**"Greater Than Sign"** (or **"Open Angle Bracket"**)
<	**"Less Than Sign"** (or **"Close Angle Bracket"**)
|	**"Vertical Bar"**
#	**"Pound Sign"** (or **"Number Sign"**)
-	**"Minus Sign"**
+	**"Plus Sign"**
.	**"Point"**
%	**"Percent Sign"**
`	**"Backquote"**
,	**"Numeric Comma"**
^	**"Caret"**

✔ Dragon Professional Individual uses a double dash character when you say the word **"Dash."** If you would rather use a different character, you can paste that character into your vocabulary list using Dragon's Vocabulary Editor (described in Chapter 17), and create your own spoken command for that character, such as, **"Em Dash."**

✔ You can hyphenate any multi-word utterance (such as the phrase, "all-encompassing") by saying, **"Hyphenate That"** immediately after speaking the phrase.

✔ If you meant to use a punctuation word as text, such as the word *period,* and Dragon Professional Individual used that word as punctuation instead, say, **"Correct That"** and choose the interpretation you prefer. See "Making Quick Corrections" later in this chapter for instructions.

Discovering Natural Punctuation

If you'd like to wade slowly into the process of speaking punctuation, you'll be happy to know that Dragon Professional Individual provides a function called Natural Punctuation, which automatically adds periods and commas where Dragon thinks they should go. If you start a new line or a new paragraph or come to what Dragon Professional Individual thinks is the end of a sentence based on your pause, it will add a period. Choose DragonBar ➪ Tools ➪ Auto-Formatting Options and select the check box that says Automatically Add Commas and Periods to turn that feature on.

This doesn't prevent you from saying **"period"** or **"comma,"** but if you forget or are new to the process, you have a backup. Remember that it won't add any punctuation other than periods and commas. You still need to say them. (See preceding tables for punctuation you can use.)

Capitalizing on your text

Dragon Professional Individual does some capitalization for you, as you dictate. For example, it generally capitalizes the first letter of a sentence. (Its cue to capitalize is that you have started a new paragraph or punctuated the end of a sentence.) It also capitalizes words that it thinks are proper nouns or that it has been taught to capitalize in its vocabulary training or editing. In general, as long as you don't do any manual typing between finishing one sentence and starting the next, Dragon Professional Individual automatically takes care of the initial capitalization.

When Dragon Professional Individual doesn't capitalize for you, you have several ways to capitalize words yourself. The two best and easiest ways to capitalize are either *before* you speak a word or phrase or *immediately afterward.*

You can also select any text with your mouse or by voice and then apply capitalization and other formatting. See Chapter 5 for more about that technique.

Here are the basics of capitalizing the initial letters of words:

- ✔ To capitalize the first letter of any word, before speaking it say, **"Cap"** followed immediately by your word. Don't pause between **"Cap"** and whatever the word is, or Dragon Professional Individual will type *cap* instead of doing it!

- ✔ After you say some words and Dragon Professional Individual types them in your program window, say, **"Cap That"** or **"All Cap That."** **"Cap"** means the initial letters are capitalized. **"All Cap"** means all the letters of a word are capitalized.

✔ If you are about to speak a series of words that must be capitalized, say, **"Caps On."** Speak those words (pausing for as long as you like anywhere in this process), and then say, **"Caps Off."** To capitalize *all* the letters in a series of words (LIKE THIS) use the phrases **"*All* Caps On"** and **"*All* Caps Off"** instead.

Table 4-4 lists all the various ways to capitalize.

Table 4-4		Capital Ideas
To Do This	*Example*	*Say This*
Capitalize the first letter of a word.	Like This	**"Cap <*word*>,"** or "<*phrase*> **Cap That,"** or **"Caps On <*one or more phrases*> Caps Off"**
Capitalize all letters in a word.	LIKE THIS	Use any of the same three preceding approaches for first-letter capitals, but say, **"All Caps"** in place of **"Caps."**
Use all lowercase letters in a word.	like this	Use any of the same three approaches, but say, **"No Caps"** in place of **"Caps."**
Capitalize something already dictated.	Like This	**"Capitalize <*xyz*>"**

"Caps On" and **"Cap That"** don't really mean, "Capitalize the first letter of *every* word." A more accurate interpretation would be, "Capitalize the first letter of every *important* word." Dragon Professional Individual tends to omit initial capitals for prepositions, articles, and all those other little words whose correct names I (and probably you) forget. Even though Dragon Professional Individual is probably being editorially correct according to the *Chicago Manual of Style* or other such authority, such selective capitalization may not be what you have in mind. If you want Dragon Professional Individual to capitalize absolutely all the words, you have to say the command **"Caps"** before each word.

Taking Up Space

Understanding a letter or other document depends not only on the words but on the spaces between the words as well. Getting your document spaced out is relatively easy. Dragon Professional Individual automatically does some word, sentence, and paragraph spacing. You can control that spacing, or add space of your own.

Controlling paragraph spacing

Dragon Professional Individual has two commands that you can say to create the space that divides paragraphs: **"New Paragraph"** and **"New Line."** What's the difference?

- ✔ **"New Paragraph"** puts a blank line between paragraphs. It is like pressing the Enter key twice: It inserts two paragraph marks (invisible) into your text. It also makes sure that the first word of the next sentence is capitalized.

- ✔ **"New Line"** does not put a blank line between paragraphs. It is like pressing the Enter key once. The next line isn't capitalized unless you ended the last line with a period, question mark, or exclamation point.

One quick way to set a word to always be capitalized is to select a word or symbol in the vocabulary, go to its properties, and make the change there.

Dragon's way of doing the **"New Paragraph"** command might cause a problem for you if you are going to use any kind of paragraph formatting (such as bullets or, in Word, paragraph spacing). It's better to use the **"New Line"** command instead. Otherwise, in many instances, you double the effect of the paragraph formatting: You get two bullets or twice the spacing you intended, for example.

When you are creating bullets and want the first word of each to be capped, remember to say, **"Cap"** after saying, **"New line"** each time if you are not using periods at the end of your bullets.

If you want to type the words *new paragraph* instead of creating a new paragraph, put a pause between the two words: **"New"** [pause] **"paragraph."**

Controlling spaces and tabs

Dragon Professional Individual does a pretty good job of automatic spacing. It usually deals with spaces around punctuation in the way that you want it to. Occasionally, however, you will want to add a few spaces or a Tab character in your text.

Automatic spaces

Dragon Professional Individual automatically puts spaces between your words. It looks at your punctuation to figure out the rest of the spacing. If, for some reason, you don't want spaces between your words, speak the command **"No-Space On,"** speak your words, and then say, **"No-Space Off."** Or if you anticipate that Dragon Professional Individual is about to precede your next word with a space that you don't want, say, **"No-Space"** and then your next word, with no pauses between.

Dragon Professional Individual does different amounts of spacing after other punctuation marks. It is done in a way that usually works. For instance, Dragon Professional Individual puts one space after a comma, unless that comma is part of a number, such as 12,000 (whether spoken as **"Twelve thousand"** or **"Twelve comma zero zero zero"**). Dragon Professional Individual also offers a so-called "numeric comma" that's never followed by a space. You can find these choices by going to Tools ⇨ Auto-Formatting Options.

Adding spaces and tabs

The quickest way to add a space is to say the word **"Spacebar."** For a tab character, say, **"Tab Key."** Just as Dragon Professional Individual does for **"Comma"** or **"Period,"** it accepts these words or phrases as a character that it should type.

Another way to do the same thing is to say, **"Press Spacebar"** or **"Press Tab."** In fact, you can tell Dragon Professional Individual to press any key on the keyboard by saying the word **"Press"** and then the name of the key. So, to press the spacebar, you can say, **"Press Spacebar."** Or to press the F1 key, you say, **"Press F1."**

When should you use **"Press Spacebar"** or **"Press Tab"**? If you sometimes write about the keyboard, you may end up training Dragon Professional Individual to type out the word *spacebar* or *tab* when you speak it, instead of inserting a space character. Sometimes, you may need to use the word *tab* in other contexts. (For example, **"Run me a tab."**) In that event, the **"Press"** command will be the more reliable way to get a space or tab character.

Entering Different Numbers and Dates

When people speak about numbers and dates, they use so many different forms that it's remarkable that a software program can actually figure them out. Yet, Dragon Professional Individual can do it. You can say, **"Eight o'clock AM"** and Dragon Professional Individual types 8:00 AM. Or you can say, **"Forty-five dollars"** and Dragon Professional Individual types $45.

Most of the time, Dragon Professional Individual types numbers and dates just the way you want it to, without doing anything special. The most common correction that you'll have to do is tell Dragon Professional

Individual to use numerals rather than words for digits zero through nine. To do so, say, **"Numeral"** before speaking the digit. Table 4-5 lists some of the ways you can say numbers and dates.

If a number, date, or time doesn't come out in the form that you want, you may be able to choose the form you want by saying, **"Correct That"** and then choosing from the list in the Correct That dialog box. For instance, when speaking the words **"Seven o'clock,"** Dragon Professional Individual initially typed *seven o'clock*. But, by saying, **"Correct That"** and choosing 7:00 from the pop-up menu choices displayed as shown in Figure 4-3, Dragon Professional Individual learned that I wanted the numerical form. See Chapter 5 for more about the **"Correct That"** command.

Table 4-5	Numbers and Dates
To Get	*Say*
.5	**"Point"** (or **"Period"** or **"Dot"**) **"Five"**
0.45	**"Zero point four five"** or **"oh point four five"**
One	**"One"**
1	**"Numeral one"**
42	**"Forty two"** or **"Four two"**
192	**"One ninety two," "One nine two,"** or **"one hundred (and) ninety-two"**
4627	**"Four thousand six hundred (and) twenty seven," "forty-six hundred twenty-seven,"** or **"four six two seven"**
4,627	**"Four comma six hundred (and) twenty seven"** or **"four comma six two seven"**
$152.07	**"One hundred fifty-two dollars and seven cents"** or **"dollar sign one five two point zero seven"**
Aug. 28, 1945	**"August twenty-eight comma nineteen forty-five"**
May 11, 2010	**"May eleven comma two thousand (and) ten"**
2:12 p.m.	**"Two twelve pee em"**
7:00 a.m.	**"Seven o'clock ay em"**
V	**"Roman numeral five"**
XLV	**"Roman numeral forty five"**
842-8996	**"Eight four two hyphen eight nine nine six"**

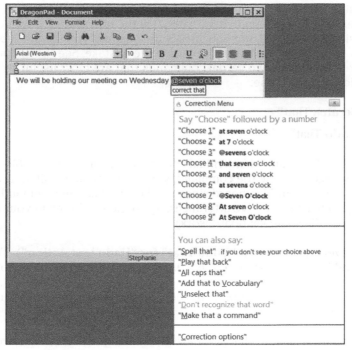

Figure 4-3:
The choices
displayed to
correct a
number
format.

Making Quick Corrections

Although making corrections technically falls into the editing category, and editing is discussed in Chapter 5, you usually want to make a few corrections the instant you see an error. Errors fall into two categories:

- Errors that you make — which I call "bloopers"
- Errors that Dragon Professional Individual makes in interpreting your speech

You deal with those errors in two different ways: *scratching* and *correcting*. Read on!

Scratching your bloopers

Making a verbal "blooper" is easy to do with speech input. You call across the office to someone or mutter something sarcastic, and Dragon

Professional Individual dutifully types it. If you make a mistake verbally, however, you can also undo it verbally. (On the other hand, if Dragon Professional Individual, not you, makes the mistake, you should "correct" Dragon Professional Individual, not undo the mistake. See the upcoming section for details.) The two verbal commands that are most useful for undoing your bloopers are these:

- ✔ **"Scratch That"**
- ✔ **"Undo That"**

The Dragon Professional Individual command for undoing your bloopers is **"Scratch That."** To use the command, you must not have edited anything with your mouse and keyboard since you last spoke. The command will undo up to ten consecutive utterances, up to the last break in your dictation (where you did some keyboard work).

Alternatively, you can say, **"Undo That"** (or **"Undo Last Action"**). That verbal command is the equivalent to the **"Undo"** command, so it works not only on dictated text, but also on anything that you could normally undo. For example, if you had just applied bullet-style formatting, you could undo that formatting.

Of course, nothing says that you have to use Dragon Professional Individual to undo your bloopers. You can use your keyboard or mouse (press Ctrl+Z, for example, press the Backspace key, or select the text and press the Delete key) just as you would if you had typed the mistake.

If physically pressing the Backspace or Delete key isn't an option for you, here are two verbal commands you can use for the same purpose:

- ✔ **"Backspace"** (or **"Press Backspace"**)
- ✔ **"Delete"** (or **"Press Delete"**)

You can backspace or delete several characters by saying, **"Backspace 7"** to backspace seven characters, for example, or **"Delete 8 characters"** to delete eight characters to the right of the typing cursor. The **"Backspace"** command can be more reliable. (Because the word *delete* is more commonly written out in text than the word *backspace,* Dragon Professional Individual sometimes errs on the side of writing out *delete* rather than doing the **"Delete"** command.)

Resuming dictation with an earlier word

Tripping over your tongue is easy when dictating. Also, composing sentences on the fly isn't easy, and sometimes you want to change your mind about the phrase you just used.

You can solve both problems (misspeaking and changing your mind) with the **"Resume With <*word*>"** command. For **<*word*>**, substitute the word you want Dragon Professional Individual to back up to. That word must be within the last 100 characters you have dictated, and you must have dictated continuously (typed or edited nothing by hand) since that word.

For instance, following is dictation where someone makes an error in the first line, gives a correction using **"Resume With,"** and completes the phrase correctly:

> Speaking the original error: **"I keep on getting my tang tungled up."**

> (Brief pause, as the user realizes the error)

> Backing up: **"Resume With *my*."**

> Correcting from that point: **"tongue tangled up"**

The resulting text is *Getting my tongue tangled up.*

This command is particularly useful when you dictate into a portable recorder. See Chapter 11 for more about using commands when you dictate into a recorder.

Correcting a Dragon Professional Individual error

If Dragon Professional Individual has misinterpreted something that you said, you can fix that mistake and help train your Dragon Professional Individual assistant. To accomplish this, you have to correct the error rather than just typing in the correct text, scratching the error, or undoing it. What's the difference?

In Dragon terms, correcting something means to tell Dragon Professional Individual what you actually said rather than merely editing the text in the document. When you correct an error, you not only fix the resulting text, but you also educate your Dragon Professional Individual assistant to understand your individual speech habits. Correction is one of the main ways in which Dragon Professional Individual gets better over time. Don't shortchange your assistant by not correcting it.

I describe all the different ways of correcting Dragon Professional Individual in Chapter 5, but here are two easily remembered ways using the command **"Correct That"**:

- ✔ If Dragon Professional Individual just made the error, say, **"Correct That"** or **"Spell That."** Either the Correction menu box or the Spelling Window appears. (You can also spell from the Corrections menu box.)

- ✔ If Dragon Professional Individual made the error a while back, select the erroneous text and say, **"Correct That"** to get the Correction dialog box.

Another quick way to make the correction would be to say, **"Correct <*xyz*>"** (where <*xyz*> is the word that Dragon didn't recognize).

This second way of correction works only in the Dragon Professional Individual window and in what are called "Full Text Control" applications. In other applications, you select the text, and then you must speak replacement text. If the new text is also erroneous, say, **"Correct That."** See Chapter 8 for more tips on using Dragon Professional Individual with other applications.

When the Correction dialog box appears, it lists numbered alternatives. Verbally choose one of the alternatives by saying, **"Choose <*number*>."** For instance, say, **"Choose five."** This approach is my favorite. If none of the alternatives are correct, you may verbally spell out the replacement text.

Another way to handle it if none of the options are correct is to redictate what you meant to say. If you get that wrong, say **"Spell That"** and you can spell it out. When you use the Spelling Window, the word is added to the vocabulary for future use.

With regard to corrections, remember that editing with the keyboard helps improve Dragon but editing with voice improves it even more.

Tackling Common Dictation Problems

Following are some common problems users experience with dictation. You can fix many of them by using the Correction menu box, described earlier in this chapter, or by word or vocabulary training (see Part IV for the details of vocabulary and word training):

✔ **Sound-alike words:** When two words normally sound exactly alike, even human speakers make mistakes. The way that humans distinguish one word from the other is by the context. That's how Dragon Professional Individual works, too. If it didn't work that way, you couldn't say a sentence like "It was too far for two people to go to purchase two tickets" and have any hope that Dragon Professional Individual would get it correct. Vocabulary training and using the Correction menu box will alleviate this problem to some degree.

✔ **Commands as text:** Sometimes, if you say, **"Go To End of Line,"** Dragon Professional Individual will type those words instead of performing the command. One solution that may work is to pause very slightly before speaking each word. Another solution is word training, as described in Part IV. A quick fix is to hold down the Ctrl key while speaking a command, which forces Dragon Professional Individual to interpret your utterance as a command.

✔ **Text as commands:** Sometimes you want to actually type something like "go to end of line," but Dragon Professional Individual instead interprets your utterance as a command. Avoid pausing before and after that phrase, if you can. A quick fix is to hold down the Shift key while dictating, which forces Dragon Professional Individual to interpret speech as text.

✔ **Extra words:** If Dragon Professional Individual gives you small, extra words in your text, it may be interpreting microphone noises as words. Make sure the microphone isn't in front of your mouth, or else it will pick up tiny puffs of breath and interpret them as words. (Also, if applicable, make sure the microphone cover isn't brushing against your beard or moustache, if you have one.) This is a good time to rerun the microphone check in the Audio section of the DragonBar. You may simply be in a new environment that is causing this with new background noises or you may have changed the volume before you started dictating.

✔ **Acronyms and other non-words:** Contemporary English uses a lot of acronyms, abbreviations, initials, and other unconventional words. You can add these terms to Dragon Professional Individual by using the Vocabulary Editor, described in Chapter 17, or by using the "Add new word or phrase" menu selection under Vocabulary. You can also add them by speaking them and then correcting the Dragon Professional Individual interpretation with the Spelling Window. The Dragon Professional Individual vocabulary already includes many common abbreviations. If Dragon Professional Individual thinks it hears initials, and those initials aren't otherwise in its vocabulary, it capitalizes them and puts a period after each letter.

- ✔ **Email addresses:** If you use a particular email or web address a lot, you can add it to your vocabulary like other "non-words," as the preceding bullet describes. Otherwise, you can say an email address, such as "person@company.com," much the way you would in conversation. To make sure everything is lowercase, say, **"No Caps On,"** then the email address, and then **"No Caps Off."** For the address itself (person@company.com, for instance), say, **"person at company dot com."** If you are getting spaces within the name in the email address, you can also bring up the Spelling Window and add it there.

- ✔ **Web addresses:** Use the **"No Caps On"** and **"No Caps Off"** commands as suggested in the preceding bullet to prevent capitalization. Speak a web address in the form, **"www dot *<company>* dot com."** For a full address (such as http://www.company.com) say, **"http www dot *<company>* dot com,"** saying nothing about the colon or slashes. Dragon Professional Individual adds the colon and slashes and recognizes the terms *com, gov, mil, net, org,* and *sys* just as you would normally say them. If you prefer, you can verbally spell out the letters in those terms.

Chapter 5

Selecting, Editing, and Correcting in DragonPad

In This Chapter

▶ Using voice commands to move the cursor

▶ Selecting text

▶ Inserting and deleting text

▶ Undoing actions after you change your mind

▶ Correcting Dragon Professional Individual mistakes and training it to do better

*I*n my most optimistic moments, I like to imagine that I will write a document (like this chapter) by starting at the beginning and continuing flawlessly to the end. I've heard of such miracles, but unfortunately have never experienced one myself. Whether you write your documents by hand, use a keyboard to enter them into a computer, or dictate them to an assistant, from time to time you're probably going to want to insert new text into the middle of the document, delete some text, rearrange a few paragraphs, and rewrite a sentence here and there.

If you prefer, you can continue using the mouse and keyboard to do this editing, just as if you had never heard of Dragon Professional Individual. In fact, dictating your first drafts and editing by keyboard isn't a bad way to get your feet wet with Dragon Professional Individual. And you can add the editing voice commands to your repertoire as you get more experienced.

Or you can plunge right in and do all your editing by voice, just as if you were dictating your changes to a real person instead of your virtual Dragon Professional Individual assistant. But, unlike a real person, your assistant works nights and holidays without complaining and never rolls its eyes when you rewrite a sentence for the tenth time. (Yeah, I've done that too.)

In addition to making changes that are a normal part of your creative process, you also want to correct the errors that get into your documents whenever your Dragon Professional Individual assistant thinks that you said something different from what you actually said. Occasional mistakes of this sort (known as *recognition errors*) are inevitable, just as occasional typographical errors always manage to sneak into typed documents. The Dragon Professional Individual mistakes tend to be funnier than typos, because they are correct English words that sometimes give your sentences entirely new and unintended meanings (for example, "Quoth the raven, 'Never bore.'").

Although you can just write (or dictate) over these mistakes, Dragon Professional Individual has a special correction procedure that teaches it not to make similar mistakes in the future. Just as you teach your children to perfect their language skills by correcting their errors, you teach your Dragon Professional Individual assistant to understand you better by using the correction procedure.

Moving Around in a Document

When you're in a cab, you can tell the driver where to go in three ways (excluding the ever-popular "Follow that car"):

- ✔ You can give directions, as in "Turn left and go three blocks."
- ✔ You can specify a location without saying what's there, as in "Go to 49th and Madison."
- ✔ You can name a destination without saying where it is and count on the driver to find it, as in "Take me to the airport."

The same basic ideas work when you tell Dragon Professional Individual where to move the cursor in its document window. You have two options:

- ✔ You can give a directional command, like **"Move Up Five Lines."**
- ✔ You can say some text and count on Dragon Professional Individual to find it by saying, **"Insert After wish you were here."**

These commands are summarized in Table 5-1, as well as in the Help Center. To display helpful commands to use, say, **"What Can I Say"** and the suggestions will pop up. The following sections of this chapter provide more detailed instructions for using these commands and their various synonyms.

You don't have to use the voice commands if you'd rather not. The mouse and the arrow keys on the keyboard can also move the cursor. It's your choice.

Table 5-1	Commands for Moving Around in a Document		
First Word	*Second Word*	*Third Word*	*Fourth Word*
"Go To"	"Top," "Bottom"		
"Go To"	"Top," "Bottom"	"of"	"Selection," "Line,"
"Move"	"Up," "Down," "Left," "Right"	"<1–20>"	"Words"
"Move"	"Back," "Forward"	"<1–20>"	"Words"
"Insert"	"Before," "After"	"xyz"	

Giving the cursor directions and distances

You can use the **"Move"** command to move the cursor in different directions: forward or backward a certain number of characters, words, lines, or paragraphs. The short form of the **"Move"** command uses just three words (as in **"Move Down Three"**).

The short, three-word version of the **"Move"** command imitates the cursor keys on the keyboard. The three words are **"Move,"** a direction (**"Up, "Down," "Left,"** or **"Right"**), and finally a number from **"1"** to **"20."** You don't specify any units. So, for example:

- ✔ **"Move Down 12"** gives you the same result as if you press the down-arrow key 12 times. In other words, the cursor goes down 12 lines.

- ✔ **"Move Right 2"** moves the cursor two characters to the right, the same result you get from pressing the right-arrow key twice.

When you want to move a certain number of words, just add **"Words"** to the command. Use the four-word **"Move"** command. First you say **"Move"**; then say a direction (**"Back"** or **"Forward"**); then say a number (**"1" – "20"**); and finally, say a unit (**"Words"**). For example, **"Move Back Six Words."**

You can also use the units **"Characters"** or **"Lines"** instead of **"Words."** When the units are **"Words"** or **"Characters,"** you can use **"Left"** or **"Right"** instead of **"Back"** or **"Forward."** When the units are **"Lines,"** you can use **"Up"** or **"Down"** instead of **"Back"** or **"Forward."** For example, **"Move Left Three Characters"** means the same as **"Move Back Three Characters"** or **"Move Left Three."**

Finally, the word "a" can be used as a synonym for the number 1. **"Move Back a Word"** is the same as **"Move Back One Word."**

If you just want to scroll the text up or down, and you don't care about moving the cursor, say **"Press Page Up"** or **"Press Page Down."** The **"Start Scrolling Down"** and **"Start Scrolling Up"** commands work in word processors now, too.

Going to the head of the line

Like telling your cab driver to go to the end of a street, you can tell Dragon Professional Individual to go the beginning or end of various chunks of a document: the beginning or end of the document, current line, or whatever block of text is selected. (The current line is the line where the cursor is now.)

The simplest destination commands are

- ✔ **"Go To Bottom,"** which moves the cursor to the end of the document
- ✔ **"Go To Top,"** which moves the cursor to the beginning of the document
- ✔ **"Go To Top** (or **Bottom**) **of Line** (or **Selection**)"

Dragon Professional Individual understands a number of synonyms for these commands. In particular, you can use **"Move To"** instead of **"Go To"** as long as you specify the chunk of text you're moving within. Begin with **"Move To"** and then use **"Start," "Beginning,"** or **"End,"** and then specify, **"Line," "Selection,"** or **"Document."**

Sometimes Dragon Professional Individual understands one form of a command more consistently than another. For example, when I say, **"Go To,"** it's often interpreted as "due to," "do to," or "good." I'm sure I could eventually train Dragon Professional Individual to recognize my slurring pronunciation of **"Go To,"** but I find it easier just to say, **"Move To"** instead.

Don't make the mistake of saying **"Go to"** or **"Move to"** followed by a word instead of a location. The only way you can tell Dragon to move to a word is by using the **"Insert Before XYZ"** (or **"Insert After XYZ"**) command.

Specifying a destination by quoting text

Sometimes you want to put the cursor right smack in the middle of a block of text on your screen, not near the beginning or end of anything. And you'd rather not count lines or words or characters. You'd like to tell Dragon Professional Individual to put the cursor after this phrase or before that one.

You want the **"Insert"** command. Suppose you dictated, **"She sells seashells by the sea shore,"** and you want to put the cursor between "sells" and "seashells." You can say,

✓ **"Insert After *sells*"** or

✓ **"Insert Before *seashells*"**

Each of these commands accomplishes the same result.

If the words "sells" and "seashells" appear in several locations, you will see all the instances numbered. You can choose the one you want.

If text is selected already, you can move the cursor to the beginning or the end of the selected text by using the commands **"Insert Before That"** or **"Insert After That."** These commands are equivalent to **"Go To Beginning of Selection"** and **"Go To End of Selection,"** respectively.

Editing by Voice

Editing a document involves several activities: inserting new text, deleting text, replacing text by dictating over it, and rearranging the document by cutting text from one place and pasting it into another. All these topics are covered in this section. I discuss reformatting text in Chapter 6.

You can use these techniques to fix the Dragon Professional Individual mistakes as well as your own. But in the long run, you'll be happier with your Dragon Professional Individual assistant's performance if you teach it to do better by using the correction commands. See "Fixing Dragon Professional Individual's Mistakes," later in this chapter.

Because Dragon Professional Individual can transcribe only the words in its vocabulary, both your errors and its own are cleverly disguised as actual English words. They're even correctly spelled. In these circumstances, proofreading becomes an art. Be sure to check out the proofreading tricks in Chapter 7.

Selecting text

You can select text in three ways:

✓ Select text near the cursor by using commands like **"Select Next Two Characters."**

✓ Select text by saying it, as in **"Select *we'll always have Paris.*"**

✓ Select a large block of text by saying the beginning and the end, as in **"Select *once upon a time* through *lived happily ever after.*"**

Table 5-2 summarizes these commands.

Table 5-2	Commands for Selecting Text		
First Word	*Second Word*	*Third Word*	*Fourth Word*
"Select"	"Next," "Previous"	"<1–20>"	"Characters," "Words," "Paragraphs"
"Select"	"<text>"		
"Select"	"Again"		
"Select"	"<text>"	"Through"	"<text>"

Selecting text near the cursor

To select text immediately before or after the current location of the cursor, use the **Select** command in a four-word sentence of this form: **"Select,"** followed by a direction (**"Next"** or **"Previous"**), followed by a number (**"<1–20>"**), followed by a unit (**"Characters," "Words,"** or **"Paragraphs"**). For example:

> ✔ **"Select Next Seven Words"**
>
> ✔ **"Select Previous Three Paragraphs"**

If you want to select only one character, word, or paragraph, leave the number out of the sentence, as in **"Select Next Character"** or **"Select Previous Word."**

You can use **"Back"** or **"Last"** as synonyms for **"Previous,"** and **"Forward"** as a synonym for **"Next."**

Selecting text by saying it

If text is visible on your screen, you can select it by saying, **"Select"** and then saying the text you want to select. For example, suppose Shakespeare is editing the file `Hamlet.doc`, and the phrase "To be or not to be" is visible. He can select the phrase by saying, **"Select to be or not to be."**

Sometimes, the phrase you select occurs several times in the current window. Which occurrence is selected? Dragon Professional Individual will display numbers next to the text and you select the one you want.

Selecting more text than you want to say

When you want to select a large block of text, you don't want to have to repeat all of it just to tell Dragon Professional Individual where it is. Dragon Professional Individual provides a special command for this purpose:

"Select . . . Through." Pick a word or two at the beginning of the selection and a word or two at the end, and then tell Dragon Professional Individual to select everything in between by saying, **"Select <*beginning text*> Through <*end text*>."** For example, if your Dragon Professional Individual window contains the Pledge of Allegiance, you can select it all by saying, **"Select I pledge allegiance Through justice for all."**

Deleting text

The simplest way to delete text is to use the **"Scratch That"** command to delete recently dictated text, as I explain in Chapter 4. You can use **"Scratch That"** up to ten consecutive times. Another way to delete recently dictated text is the **"Resume With"** command, also covered in Chapter 4.

To delete text immediately before or after the current location of the cursor (as outlined in Table 5-3), begin with **"Delete"** and then give a direction (**"Next"** or **"Previous"**), a number (**"1" – "20"**), and finally a unit (**"Characters," "Words,"** or **"Paragraphs"**). For example:

✔ **"Delete Next Seven Words"**

✔ **"Delete Previous Three Paragraphs"**

Table 5-3	How to Make a Deleterious Statement		
First Word	*Second Word*	*Third Word*	*Fourth Word*
"Delete"	"That"		
"Delete"	"Next," "Previous"	"Character," "Word," "Paragraph"	
"Delete"	"Next," "Previous"	"*<1–20>*"	"Characters," "Words," "Paragraphs"
"Delete"	"*<xyz>*"		
"Backspace"			
"Backspace"	"*<1–20>*"		

If you want to delete only one character, word, or paragraph, you can leave the number out of the sentence, as in the following:

✔ **"Delete Next Character"**

✔ **"Delete Previous Word"**

You can use **"Back"** or **"Last"** as synonyms for **"Previous,"** and you can use **"Forward"** as a synonym for **"Next."**

Saying **"Backspace"** gives the same result as pressing the Backspace key on the keyboard: The character immediately behind the cursor is deleted. To backspace up to 20 characters, say, **"Backspace,"** followed by a number between 1 and 20. **"Backspace"** is a simpler version of the **"Delete Previous Character"** command. For example, saying, **"Backspace Five"** produces the same results as saying, **"Delete Previous Five Characters."**

You can turn off the **"Delete XYZ"** command by choosing DragonBar ⇨ Tools ⇨ Options ⇨ Commands. You may find yourself accidentally deleting text in a document and not understand why.

Sharp tongues: Cutting and pasting by voice

To cut or copy text from a document, select it (using the techniques from the "Selecting text" section earlier in this chapter) and then say either **"Cut That"** or **"Copy That."** To copy the entire document (which is useful if you like to compose in the Dragon Professional Individual DragonPad or Dictation Box and then paste the results into an application), say, **"Copy All to Clipboard."**

If something is on the clipboard, you can paste it into your document by saying, **"Paste That."** You can also now say, **"Copy XYZ"** or **"Cut XYZ."**

Just undo it

Sometimes the result of editing or dictating something isn't what you pictured. All is not lost; you can still undo it. Just say, **"Undo That"** or **"Undo Last Action."** These two commands are equivalent.

In the Dragon Professional Individual window, **"Undo That"** is like flipping a switch: If you say it twice, you wind up back where you started. In other words, the second **"Undo That"** undoes the first **"Undo That."** When you use Dragon Professional Individual with other applications, what you get varies from one application to another. In some applications, saying, **"Undo That"** twice undoes the application's last two actions.

What **"Undo That"** actually does is type a Ctrl+Z. Different applications handle a Ctrl+Z in different ways, which is why they respond to **"Undo That"** differently.

Fixing Dragon Professional Individual's Mistakes

Even though Dragon Professional Individual is up to 99 percent accurate out of the box, it will occasionally make a hilarious error. That's because Dragon Professional Individual is incapable of a simple typo or misspelling. All its mistakes are still correct English words — just not the words you said or meant to say. But as funny as some mistakes might be, you don't want to create documents that amuse your readers because of unintentional errors. You want those mistakes fixed, preferably in a way that keeps them from happening again the next time you dictate. That's what Dragon Professional Individual's **"Correct That"** and related correction commands are for.

If you don't care about correcting Dragon Professional Individual, and all you want to do is remove an error from the document you're working on, just select the offending text and dictate something else over it. Or, if you catch the error immediately, you can get rid of it by saying **"Scratch That"** or **"Undo That,"** as described in "Editing by Voice," earlier in this chapter.

If you make any corrections during a session, Dragon Professional Individual reminds you to save your speech files before exiting. Be sure to choose Yes. Otherwise, all the lessons Dragon Professional Individual learned from these corrections are lost.

Correcting a Dragon Professional Individual recognition error

Depending on how quickly you catch the error, you can correct it in one of the following two ways:

- ✔ If you catch the error as soon as Dragon Professional Individual makes it, say, **"Correct That"** or **"Spell That."** See "Casting a spell," later in this chapter for more about **"Spell That."**

- ✔ If you don't catch the error immediately, say, **"Correct <*incorrect text*>."** (You can also select the erroneous text verbally or with your voice and then say, **"Correct That."**)

Table 5-4 summarizes these ways of making a correction. If you would rather not use voice commands at all, select the text and then press the – (minus) key on the numeric keypad of your keyboard or click the Correct button on the Dragon Professional Individual DragonBar Extras section. (You can substitute a different key for the – [minus] key; see the discussion of Dragon Professional Individual options in Chapter 3.)

Table 5-4	Making Your Corrections		
First Word	*Second Word*	*Third Word*	*Fourth Word*
"Correct"	"That"		
"Spell"	"That"		
"Correct"	"*<text>*"		
"Correct"	"*<text>*"	"Through"	"*<text>*"

No matter how you do it, the Correction menu box appears, as shown in Figure 5-1.

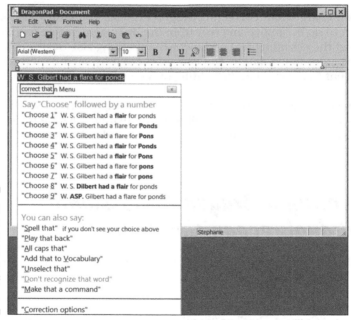

Figure 5-1:
Dragon
Professional
Individual
generates a
list of
alternatives.

The dictation error that Figure 5-1 illustrates occurred when I said, **"W. S. Gilbert had a flair for puns."** What Dragon Professional Individual thought I said was, **"W. S. Gilbert had a flare for ponds."** When I said, **"Correct That,"** the Correction menu box shown in Figure 5-1 appeared.

Dragon Professional Individual chose some alternative interpretations of what I said, listed in the box, up to a maximum of nine. Figure 5-1 shows Dragon Professional Individual got most of the phrase right.

If the correct phrase is listed in the Correction menu box, you need only tell Dragon Professional Individual which number it is. If I had said, **"W. S. Gilbert had a flair for ponds,"** then I could make the correction in Figure 5-1 by saying **"Choose 1."** You can also click the correct version with the mouse. When you indicate your choice, the Correction dialog box closes and the correction is made in the text.

Sometimes, none of the options offered is correct, as is the case in Figure 5-1. In those instances, you should try to redictate over the highlighted text. If Dragon gets it wrong again, say, **"Spell That."** The Spelling Window opens. Start spelling the correct version aloud. (See "Casting a spell," later in this chapter.) With each new letter, more alternatives appear in the box as Dragon Professional Individual continues trying to guess what the correct version is. If the correct version appears, you can stop typing or spelling and choose it by number. The Correction menu box closes and the correction is made in the text.

Here are two additional reminders and tips:

- ✔ Don't attempt to dictate replacement text in the Spelling Window. Dragon Professional Individual tries to interpret your utterances as letters!

- ✔ If you are correcting a large block of text, you can say, **"Correct <*beginning of incorrect text*> Through <*end of incorrect text*>."**

Casting a spell

One way to correct a simple mistake is to select the mistaken word and spell the correct one. You can do this from the Correction menu by saying **"Spell That"** if you don't see the choice you want.

Suppose you dictated **"New York"** and Dragon Professional Individual interpreted it as "Newark." You could correct it as follows:

1. **Find the mistaken word, "Newark," in the active window.**

2. **Say,** "Select Newark."

   If Dragon Professional Individual hears you correctly this time, the mistaken word is selected. If "Newark" occurs several times in the active window, you may need to say, **"Choose 'n'"** to select the occurrence that you want to correct. See "Selecting text by saying it," earlier in this chapter.

3. **Say,** "Spell That" **and the Spelling Window opens. Say,** "Cap N-e-w space bar cap Y-o-r-k." **Or you can use the International Communications Alphabet by saying,** "Spell That cap November Echo Whiskey space bar cap Yankee Oscar Romeo Kilo."

The Spelling Window now has the correctly spelled "New York" selected. You will also see the choices to say **"Play That Back,"** **"Train,"** and **"Tell Me More about This Window"** (for help). These are described in the next section.

4. **Say** "Click OK" **or** "Press Enter." **Or you can click the OK button or press the Enter key.**

Dragon Professional Individual replaces the incorrect "Newark" in the text with the correct "New York." Also, Dragon Professional Individual makes an invisible little note to remind itself not to be so quick to hear "Newark" instead of "New York." (See the later sidebar "Bravo! Charlie Tangos with Juliet in November," for more about the International Communications Alphabet, or ICA.)

But what if you didn't see the choice you wanted? You could choose the Spell That option from the Correction menu and bring up the Spelling Window, shown in Figure 5-2. Follow these steps:

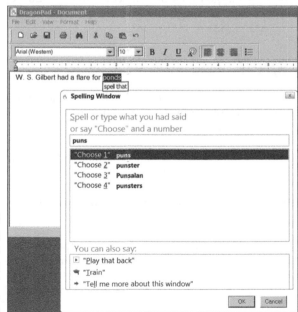

Figure 5-2:
Using the
Spelling
Window for
correction.

1. **Choose "Spell That" from within the Correction menu.**

   The Spelling Window appears with several choices. One of the choices is in the typing window.

2. **Click in the typing window if you want to type your correction, or start spelling it if you want to use a verbal command.**

3. **Say** "Click OK" **or** "Press Enter." **Or you can click the OK button or press the Enter key.**

If you use a lot of proper nouns (names of people, places, and things), learning the ICA might be worthwhile. You can use the ICA to spell a word even during dictation, not just in the Correction menu box.

Recurring errors

The correction process is supposed to prevent the same errors from happening in the future, but sometimes Dragon Professional Individual makes a particular error a couple of times. In these cases, you need something stronger than just correction; you need to train Dragon Professional Individual (otherwise known as boot camp for assistants).

Begin by identifying the error and typing or dictating the correct version into the Correction menu box. Then say, **"Spell That"** and the Spelling Window opens. Instead of clicking the OK button in the Spelling Window, click Train. This opens the Train Words dialog box, where you record the correct word. See Chapter 17 for detailed instructions.

Playing back an error

Dragon Professional Individual includes a Playback feature that you can use to listen to your dictation. In particular, when you are correcting a mistake, you can click the "Play That Back" link in the Correction dialog box to hear what you said. You may discover that you aren't dealing with a recognition error at all and that you didn't say what you think you said. See Chapter 7 for more about the Playback feature.

Bravo! Charlie Tangos with Juliet in November

The problem with dictating letters is that many sound alike. If you've ever had to spell your name to someone over the telephone, you know how easily *d*'s become *t*'s or *m*'s turn into *n*'s.

This is an old problem, so it isn't surprising that someone solved it a long time ago by creating the International Communications Alphabet. In the ICA, the names of the letters all sound different, so you can spell aloud with confidence if you know the ICA vocabulary:

a. alpha

b. bravo

c. charlie

d. delta

e. echo

f. foxtrot

g. golf

h. hotel

i. india

j. juliet

k. kilo

l. lima

m. mike

n. november

o. oscar

p. papa

q. quebec

r. romeo

s. sierra

t. tango

u. uniform

v. victor

w. whiskey

x. xray

y. yankee

z. zulu

Chapter 6

Basic Formatting in Text-Editing Applications

· ·

· ·

*T*ext that is all the same font, size, and style can be pretty boring. Because of advances in web design, everyone's expectations for design are higher. Formatting puts some zing into your content and makes it exciting. Your favorite applications are, most likely, loaded with formatting buttons and icons. You can, of course, continue to use them, but Dragon Professional Individual lets you produce many of the same results with voice commands.

In this chapter, I tell you about voice commands especially for formatting, like **"Bold That."** In the Dragon Professional Individual DragonPad (and specific other applications), you can get the job done quickly with formatting commands.

Knowing the Short Formatting Commands

Dragon Professional Individual provides several different commands for most actions. These commands fall into two basic types. On one hand, you can use short, very specific commands for most actions, such as **"Underline That"** for underlining text or **"Center That"** for centering a paragraph. Table 6-1 shows the short formatting commands.

Table 6-1	The Short Formatting Commands	
To Do This	*Example*	*Say This*
Make selected text bold.	**Like This**	**"Bold That"**
Italicize selected text.	*Like This*	**"Italicize That"**
Underline selected text.	<u>Like This</u>	**"Underline That"**
Make selected text normal.	Like This	**"Restore That"**
Center the current paragraph.	Like This	**"Center That"**
Right-align the current paragraph.	Like This	**"Right-Align That"**
Left-align the current paragraph.	Like This	**"Left-Align That"**

On the other hand, you can use the slightly longer but more general commands **"Format"** and **"Set"** to do almost anything if you know the correct syntax. For example, **"Format That Bold"** and **"Format That Centered"** bolds or centers text, respectively, whereas **"Format That Courier 18"** changes the font to 18-point Courier. Whether you find it easier to remember a lot of short commands or a general family of longer commands that follow predictable patterns is largely a matter of preference.

Left, Right, and Center: Getting into Alignment

To change the alignment of a paragraph, move the cursor into the paragraph and use one of the following commands:

- ✔ **"Center That"**
- ✔ **"Left-Align That"**
- ✔ **"Right-Align That"**

(If you're currently dictating a paragraph, you don't have to move the cursor; it is already in the correct paragraph. Just speak the command.)

To change the alignment of up to 20 consecutive paragraphs, follow these steps:

1. **Move the cursor to the beginning of the first paragraph.**

2. **Say,** "Select Next *<number>* Paragraphs," **where *<number>* is the number of paragraphs you want to realign.**

   For example, say, **"Select Next Two Paragraphs."**

3. Say, "Center That," "Left-Align That," **or** "Right-Align That."

In Figure 6-1, you see what happens when you select two paragraphs and say, **"Right-Align That."**

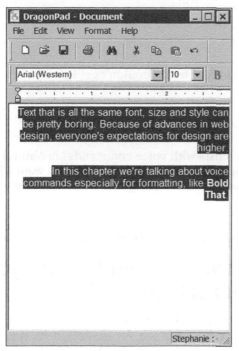

Figure 6-1:
Right-
aligning two
paragraphs.

To change the alignment of the entire document, follow these steps:

1. Say, "Select Document."

2. Say, "Center That," "Left-Align That," **or** "Right-Align That."

You can use the **"Format"** command to substitute for any of the alignment commands:

✓ **"Format That Centered"** gives the same result as **"Center That."**

✓ **"Format That Left Aligned"** gives the same result as **"Left-Align That."**

✓ **"Format That Right Aligned"** gives the same result as **"Right-Align That."**

Using Bullets and Numbered Lists

Clear, concise writing requires more than just simple paragraphs. For example, *For Dummies* books just couldn't exist without

- Bullets
- Numbered lists

Or perhaps I should say that these books couldn't get by without

1. Numbered lists
2. Bullets

How can you create bulleted lists with voice commands? In Natural Language and Full Text Control applications, dictate the text that you want a bullet next to and then say, **"Format That Bullet Style."** To get a second bullet, say, **"New Line."**

Formatting in applications other than Dragon Professional Individual

The Dragon Professional Individual formatting commands in this chapter work only with the Dragon Professional Individual word processor and specific other applications: the Natural Language applications (for example, Word, WordPerfect, and OpenOffice.org) and the Full Text Control applications (for example, DragonPad, WordPad, and Microsoft Outlook).

In general, if you want to create or edit a formatted document in an application that is not compatible, you have two choices:

- Work in the Dragon Professional Individual DragonPad and then paste the result into the other application.

- Work in the application's own window and get all your formatting commands from the menus.

Choosing formatting commands from the menus means you can use voice control for *anything* the application can do, not just formatting. For example, if you want to make some selected text bold in an unsupported application, you couldn't use the Dragon Professional Individual **"Bold That"** command, but you could access the Bold command on the application's own Style menu by saying, **"Click Style, Bold."** Specially supported word processors such as Word and WordPerfect have more formatting features than Dragon Professional Individual gives you direct commands for. In these cases, you can access the word processor's own menus by voice as well as by mouse or keyboard. For example, Dragon Professional Individual provides no **"Footnote That"** command for inserting footnotes into Word documents, but you can use the Footnote command on Word's insert menu by saying, **"Click References"** and then **"Insert Footnote."**

In this chapter, I give commands for dictating in the Dragon Professional Individual window. (The same commands also work in Full Text Control applications, including Natural Language Commands in Word or WordPerfect, for example.) This command doesn't work in all applications. If your document is in an application that doesn't support Full Text Control, make the bulleted list in the DragonPad and then copy and paste it into your document.

The Dragon Professional Individual DragonPad doesn't provide a means for generating numbered lists automatically. You have to construct them yourself. For example, say, **"New Line. One period. Cap *this is the first entry on my numbered list*. Period. New Line. Two period. Cap *this is the second entry*. Period."** The result is

1. This is the first entry on my numbered list.

2. This is the second entry.

Changing Font

Dragon Professional Individual provides commands like **"Bold That"** to change the style of a font. You can use the **"Set"** or **"Format"** commands to change the size or style of a font, to choose a new font family, or to change everything at the same time.

Changing your style: Bold, italic, and underlined text

One way to create bold, italic, or underlined text is to select the text and then say, **"Bold That," "Italicize That,"** or **"Underline That."**

These three commands are equivalent to clicking the corresponding buttons (**B**, *I*, or <u>U</u>) on the toolbar. If you select some underlined text and say, **"Un-Underline That,"** the underlining is removed.

To dictate bold, italic, or underlined text, follow these steps:

1. **Move the cursor to the place in the document where you want the text to be.**

2. **Say,** "Bold That," "Italicize That," **or** "Underline That," **depending on what kind of text you want to produce.**

3. **Dictate your text.**

When text is already bold, italic, underlined, or some combination of all three, you can change it back to plain Roman text by selecting it and saying, **"Restore That."**

The **"Format"** and **"Set"** commands can substitute for any of these commands. For example, the following three commands have the same effect:

- ✔ **"Bold That"**
- ✔ **"Format That Bold"**
- ✔ **"Set Font Bold"**

You can also use **"Format That"** or **"Set Font"** with **"Italics,"** **"Underline,"** or **"Regular."** For example,

- ✔ **"Format That Regular"** is equivalent to **"Restore That."**
- ✔ **"Set Font Bold"** and **"Format That Bold"** are equivalent to **"Bold That."**

You can also use Quick Voice Formatting commands for Bold, Underline, Italicize, Capitalize, Copy, Delete, and Cut by saying, **"Select <*text*>"** or **"Select <*start*> through <*end*>,"** saying the command (for example, **"Bold"**), and then saying the words to which you want to apply the command.

Changing font size

To change the size of a font, you must know the point size that you want. If, for example, you want to change some text to 18 point, you can select it and say

- ✔ **"Set Size 18."**
- ✔ **"Format That Size 18."**

In Figure 6-2, the **"Format That Size 18"** command is given.

Not all point sizes exist for all font families. If you request a nonexistent point size, your command is ignored.

If you want to start dictating in a new font size, move the cursor to the place where you want to begin dictating and give a **"Set Size"** or **"Format That Size"** command. For example,

- ✔ **"Set Size 10."**
- ✔ **"Format That Size 24."**

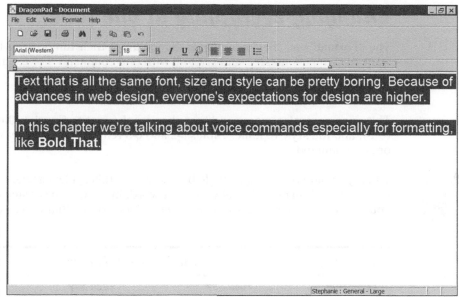

Figure 6-2:
Changing
the font
size to 18.

When you begin to dictate, the text appears in the size type that you requested, if that size exists in the current font family.

Changing font family

Who said you can't choose your family? Dragon Professional Individual recognizes most font families. You can use the **"Set"** or **"Format"** command to change from one of these font families to another. For example,

- ✔ **"Set Font Times."**
- ✔ **"Format That Times."**

Both change the current font to Times New Roman on any text that was selected when you issued this command. If you did not select any text, any new text you dictate at the insertion point will be in Times New Roman font.

If you want to use a font whose name Dragon Professional Individual doesn't recognize, you must choose it from the menu, either by voice or using the mouse. See Chapter 15 for a discussion of controlling the menus by voice.

Changing everything at one time

The **"Format"** and **"Set"** commands demonstrate their full power when you want to change font, size, and style all with one command. For example,

▌✔ **"Format That Courier 14 Italic."**

This is an equivalent command that changes the font to Courier, the font size to 14, and the style to italic. Tables 6-2 and 6-3 tell you how to speak a Format or Set command.

When you put something in angle brackets and italics, like **<style>,** it is a placeholder. You don't literally say that word; instead, you replace it with your own particular choice of word from a list of styles that I give you.

Table 6-2	The Syntax of Format		
Command	*Then Say*	*Then Say*	*Then Say*
"Format That"	"Capitals"		
	"All Caps"		
	"Bold"		
	"Italics"		
	"Underline"		
	"Regular"		
	"Left-Aligned"		
	"Right-Aligned"		
	"Bullet Style"		
	"Size"	"*<4–120>*"	
	"*<font family>*"	"*<4–120>*"	"*<style>*"

"Plain," "Plain Text," and **"Regular"** mean the same thing: not bold and not italic. They do not remove underlining. To undo underlining, see the earlier section, "Changing your style: Bold, italic, and underlined text."

Table 6-3	The Syntax of Set			
Command	*Then Say*	*Then Say*	*Then Say*	*Then Say*
"Set"	"Size"	"*<4–120>*"		
	"Font"	"*<style>*"		

You can change color with the **"Font"** commands in the Dragon Professional Individual DragonPad. Also, you can say, **"points"** as part of the command, too. For example, **"Set size 20 points."**

Understanding Smart Formatting

In version 13 and up, there is a feature that you likely will come across during dictation. It's called the Smart Format Rules box. This box pops up when you change the format of a word that already has a standard format setting.

For example, say you dictate the sentence **"Continue knitting for 25 inches."** The word *inches* would display as "inches," as shown in Figure 6-3.

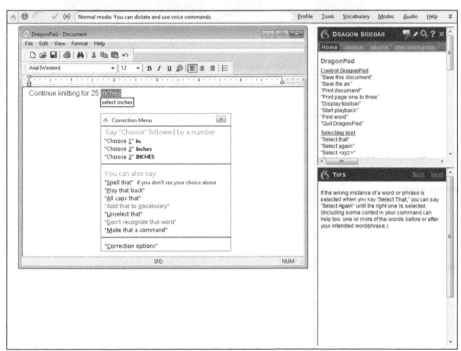

Figure 6-3:
Correction
menu.

If you want to change the format to something nonstandard, like "in." By choosing "2," the Smart Format Rules box pops up, as shown in Figure 6-4, and asks if you want to make this new format the alternate written form. If you want to accept this change, say, **"1."**

You may see this box pop up when you are using either the Correction menu or the Spelling Window. You are not required to select anything when the box comes up. It's up to you whether a format should be changed. You can simply click the *x* in the window, say **"Cancel,"** or just keep dictating and the box will disappear.

If you want to disable this feature, you will find it under the DragonBar in Tools⇨Options. Just deselect the box where it says, Show Smart Format Rules.

As a rule of thumb, it's helpful to understand that smart rules apply to such things as email addresses, phone numbers, dates, or anything that has a format convention.

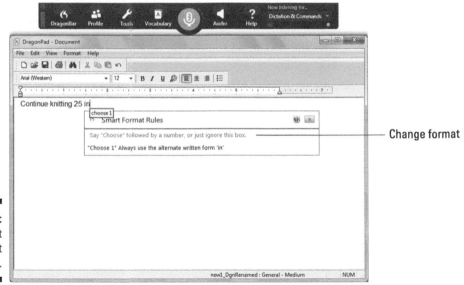

Change format

Figure 6-4:
Smart
Format
Rules box.

Chapter 7

Proofreading and Listening to Your Text

In This Chapter

▶ Using voice commands to play back

▶ Proofreading and correcting with playback

▶ Converting text to speech

*O*n one hand, Dragon Professional Individual never misspells a word. On the other hand, Dragon Professional Individual can make some mistakes by choosing the wrong (if perfectly spelled) word. A person who writes to the bank, "I have trouble paying this year" rather than, "I am double paying this year" is going to have a big problem. No computerized grammar checker or other kind of checker is likely to catch that error. Proofreading is the only answer.

Of course, you don't need to hear your text in order to proofread it, but in Dragon Professional Individual, you can hear your dictation in one of two ways:

✔ **Playback of your voice:** Dragon Professional Individual records your voice as you dictate and can play it back to help you proofread (not available in the Home edition).

✔ **Reading the text:** You can read what Dragon Professional Individual has generated from your dictation — or of any other text that you bring into the Dragon Professional Individual DragonPad or any other supported application. The Dragon Professional Individual text-to-speech feature uses a computer-synthesized voice to convert any text into speech.

Why play your own voice back? For one thing, it tends to make the Dragon Professional Individual errors stand out. If you read what Dragon Professional Individual typed as you listen to your voice, the discrepancy between, say, the written word *double* and the word you spoke, *trouble,* becomes obvious.

Also, playback lets you know what you *actually* said, rather than what you *think* you said. Knowing what you actually said is important when you correct Dragon Professional Individual. If Dragon Professional Individual has typed *fourth-quarter profits are down,* for instance, and you think you said, "in the fourth quarter, profits are down," you should correct Dragon Professional Individual — even if you like its phraseology better! If, on the other hand, you really *did* say, "fourth-quarter profits are down," do *not* correct Dragon Professional Individual. Playing back your voice helps you do a better job of correcting Dragon Professional Individual.

What about text-to-speech read back? Why listen to synthesized speech, instead of your recorded voice, when you proofread? Though not a perfect reader, text-to-speech lets you hear what Dragon Professional Individual actually typed. The Dragon Professional Individual errors (wrong words) are sometimes more obvious when you hear them than when you see them.

Text-to-speech can be useful for other purposes. If you have a visual impairment, for example, you can verbally copy documents or email messages to the Dragon Professional Individual DragonPad and play them.

A quick way to access the commands to **"Read That"** or **"Play That Back"** is by going to the DragonBar, choosing Audio, and selecting the command from the menu items.

Using Voice Commands for Playback

The simplest form of playing back your voice is to speak the command **"Play That"** (or **"Play That Back"**) after you dictate some text. The **"Play That"** command reads back the last thing you said. **"Play That Back"** is just another form of the same command.

A more practical use of the **"Play That"** command is to proofread larger blocks of text than just your most recent utterance. You can select the text you want to proofread and then say, **"Play That."** You can use any means you like to select the text: your mouse, your keyboard, or a Dragon Professional Individual voice command such as **"Select Document,"** **"Select Paragraph,"** or **"Select Line."** (See Chapter 5 for details of various selections.)

Instead of selecting text first and then giving the **"Play"** command, you can specify what chunks of text are to be played back, right in the command. Use any of the following commands; you can say either **"Play"** or **"Play Back,"** as you prefer (I only show the **"Play"** form here):

- ✔ **"Play Line"**
- ✔ **"Play Paragraph"**
- ✔ **"Play Document"**
- ✔ **"Play Window"**
- ✔ **"Play Screen"**
- ✔ **"Play To Here"**
- ✔ **"Play From Here"**

The **"Play To Here"** and **"Play From Here"** commands let you play everything up to the current typing cursor position **("here")** or from that position to the end.

Pressing Ctrl+Shift+S starts the playback from your typing cursor's current position. (It's the same as **"Play From Here."**)

Dragon Professional Individual stores about a half hour of dictated text. (Pauses don't count.) Nothing you dictated before that point can be played back.

If you want to increase the size of the space used for storing dictated text, choose DragonBar ➪ Tools ➪ Options and click the Data tab.

Proofreading and Correcting with Playback

Voice playback is a nice feature for proofreading and editing your documents. Dragon Professional Individual provides convenient buttons on the DragonBar and hotkeys on the keyboard for controlling the Playback feature as you proofread.

Note that playback doesn't work for text entered in the following ways:

- ✔ Text that has been typed in
- ✔ Text that you didn't dictate in the first place
- ✔ Text that you dictated, but later moved

To hear such text, use the Dragon Professional Individual text-to-speech feature instead.

When you are ready to proofread your document and correct Dragon Professional Individual errors, follow these steps:

1. **Select the text you want to proofread.**

   For instance, say, **"Select Document,"** or select text by using your mouse.

   You can select and play in one command by saying a command like **"Play Document"** or **"Play Paragraph"** instead. You can then skip to Step 3.

2. **Say,** "Play That."

   Or press Ctrl+Shift+S or click the Playback link on the toolbar shown in Figure 7-1.

3. **Scan the text with your eyes as your dictation plays back.**

   At this point, poise your finger over the minus (–) key on the numeric keypad. (The numeric keypad is usually on the far right end of your keyboard.) Strike this key quickly when you hear an error! To help you follow the text, a yellow arrow points as it continues reading.

4. **When you come to a Dragon Professional Individual error, press the – (minus) key on the numeric keypad of your keyboard.**

   The playback stops and the Correction menu box pops up, displaying the last four spoken words.

   You must press the minus key within four words or punctuation marks of when you hear the error, or you will overshoot the error.

5. **Choose the correct interpretation from the list in the Correction menu box.**

   (See Chapter 5 if you aren't familiar with the Correction menu box.)

   When you make your choice, the Correction menu box closes and playback continues immediately. Continue correcting errors as in Steps 4 and 5 until you reach the end of the text to be played.

If you press the minus key too late, you'll overshoot the error. That is, the Correction menu box displays a phrase after the one you want. Here are a few solutions for that issue and other related problems:

- ✔ If you realize you have overshot the error, but still haven't pressed the minus key, press the left-arrow key (one of the navigation keys on the keyboard). This backs Dragon Professional Individual up by about eight to ten words. Press the left-arrow key repeatedly until you catch the phrase you want. Alternatively, you can click the Begin Rewind button (with the |< symbol) on the toolbar.

- ✔ If you have already pressed the minus key and the Correction menu box pops up with the wrong phrase in it, you can use the left-arrow key to keep the correction box open. When you get to the error, correct it and start playback again from that point.

- ✔ Keep in mind that when you click the minus key, the Correction menu box displays only the last four words (or punctuation marks). If playback is already more than three words ahead of the error, press the left-arrow key to skip backward.

- ✔ A secret (well, undocumented) alternative to the minus key in the DragonPad is the down-arrow key (among the navigation keys on your keyboard). I find this key more convenient because it's next to the left-arrow key. You can also change the hotkey for corrections to any key you like with the Tools ➪ Options command in Dragon Professional Individual. See Chapter 3 for details.

If you really like using Playback, you can make corrections more efficiently when using the Classic DragonBar, too. From the DragonBar menu, select Classic DragonBar. After the Classic DragonBar loads, select the small arrows on the far right side of the screen to show the Extras bar. There you find a set of buttons for Playback. Here's what they do:

- ✔ **Stop the playback:** Click the Stop button (with the square) in the toolbar or press the Esc key (or Ctrl+1).

- ✔ **Play back at high speed:** Click the Begin Fast Forward button (with the |> symbol).

- ✔ **Skip forward in your text:** Press the right-arrow key until you reach your text.

- ✔ **Skip backward at high speed:** Click the Begin Rewind button.

- ✔ **Skip backward in your text:** Press the left-arrow key until you reach your text.

Playback in the Correction menu box

A good reason for playing back your dictation is so that you can properly correct Dragon Professional Individual. You want to be sure that the text you type in the Correction menu box is what you actually said!

One way to ensure that your correction matches your spoken word is to click the Play That Back selection in the Correction menu box. Dragon Professional Individual then plays your original speech for the phrase being corrected.

If you like this feature, you can tell Dragon Professional Individual to play the recorded speech whenever you use the Correction menu box. Choose Tools ➪ Options from the Dragon Professional Individual menu. In the Options dialog box the Correction tab is open. Select it to place a check mark in the Automatic Playback On Correction check box. Click OK to close the Options dialog box.

Using the Text-to-Speech Feature

The Dragon Professional Individual text-to-speech feature is a great piece of wizardry. Although not perfect, it can help your PC do a reasonable job of turning text into speech. It might even be disconcerting if it sounded like a real person. Are you ready for that?

Text-to-speech isn't limited to proofreading. It's a general-purpose tool for listening to documents. For instance, you could play a document by copying it into the Dragon Professional Individual DragonPad or any text window. A visually impaired person could do the whole job with the verbal copying and window-switching commands described in Chapter 15.

One reason for using text-to-speech is to help proofread your text. But which is better for proofreading — playback of your own voice or reading it with text-to-speech?

Many people find that playing back their own speech is the best way to find errors. With playback, you hear the correct text and spot errors with your eyes. Because you're comparing the original dictation to the resulting text, playing back tends to be a more accurate way of proofreading.

If you're an auditory learner, however — for instance, if you find you pay better attention to the spoken word than to the written word — you might try text-to-speech read back. With the reading back, you hear the text that Dragon Professional Individual wrote and mentally judge whether that was what you intended. You aren't presented with your original dictation, just the

Dragon Professional Individual interpretation. A second advantage of reading it back is that it works even if you edit text manually; playback can't handle manual edits.

To start Read, select some text in the Dragon Professional Individual DragonPad or any text window (using the mouse, the keyboard, or a voice command). Then, choose Audio ⇨ Read That from the DragonBar or speak the verbal command, **"Read That."**

Read verbal commands are the same as Playback verbal commands, except instead of saying, **"Play,"** you say, **"Read."** Here are the Read verbal commands:

✔ **"Read That"** (referring to text you have selected)

✔ **"Read That Back"** (same as **"Read That"**)

✔ **"Read Line"**

✔ **"Read Paragraph"**

✔ **"Read Document"**

✔ **"Read Window"**

✔ **"Read Screen"**

✔ **"Read Up To Here"** (where "here" is wherever your typing cursor is)

✔ **"Read Down From Here"**

You can stop reading back in the Dragon Professional Individual DragonPad or other text window by pressing the Esc key. If you hear a Dragon Professional Individual error during read-back, first stop the read-back, and then select the erroneous text any way you like (with your mouse and keyboard or a verbal command). With text selected, launch the Correction menu box in any of the usual ways, including pressing the minus key on the numeric keypad or saying, **"Correct That."**

If you hear an error that you (not Dragon Professional Individual) made, stop reading back first by pressing the Esc key. Then, select and edit your text any way you like (by speech or by using the keyboard and mouse).

Chapter 8

Dictating into Other Applications

*Y*ou can get quite a bit done just by dictating into the Dragon Professional Individual Dictation Box and then using cut-and-paste techniques to move the text into documents belonging to other applications or by clicking the Transfer button in the Dictation Box. But you haven't seen the full potential of Dragon Professional Individual until you've used it to dictate directly into other applications. At that point, Dragon Professional Individual becomes an essential component of your computer, like the keyboard and the mouse.

In this chapter, I focus on general techniques that you can use with many applications, using the Dictation Box and Full Text Control in the Dragon Professional Individual terminology. I tell you about the interactions you can expect in different sets of applications, plus the details. When you aren't sure why something is working a certain way, you can turn here to at least find out how it should work.

The bottom line in using Dragon Professional Individual with other applications is that basic dictation works pretty much the same, but the capabilities to do other tasks vary. Nuance has a newly redesigned Dictation Box that makes it easy to use.

Finding Levels of Control

In addition to entering text into another application's windows, Dragon Professional Individual voice commands can also control another application's menus. When you combine these techniques with the desktop control commands and dialog box techniques described in Chapter 15, you get a true no-hands computer experience.

One of the most frequently asked questions about Dragon Professional Individual is, "Does it work with *<name of application>*?" The answer is yes. If the application has menus, dialog boxes, or a window into which you can type text, then you can use Dragon Professional Individual with it. The more interesting question isn't *whether* Dragon Professional Individual voice commands work with some application, but *which* commands work with which applications.

Over the years, I've watched Dragon Professional Individual software evolve to the point where it's sometimes hard for me to demonstrate a mistake. The out-of-the-box accuracy is truly stunning. The number of programs and apps available to dictate into has exploded as well. For this reason, I want to present you with a way of thinking about using other applications so that you know what to expect.

Dragon Professional Individual has different levels of control with different programs (on the web, as software, or as a mobile app). Commands that work in some applications don't work in others. You'll save yourself a lot of frustration if you understand the level of control you have in a particular type of application.

Table 8-1 summarizes these basic control levels:

- ✔ **Desktop:** Even if you have no applications other than Dragon Professional Individual open at all, you still have a few dictation powers:

    - Open files and applications on the desktop or the Start menu.

    - Switch from one open window to another.

    - Use the mouse commands.

    See Chapter 15 for details.

- ✔ **Nearly Any Windows Application:** You have all the desktop commands plus

    - Basic menu control

    - Dictation

    - Navigation

- ✔ **The Dictation Box with another application:** You retain all the desktop interactions. You can enter text by dictating. You can use the application's hotkeys and menus. You can move around in a document by using the Move and Go commands. You have a limited amount of selection and correction capabilities.

    See "Creating Documents with the Dictation Box," later in this chapter.

- ✔ **Full Text Control:** You have all the Dictation Box capabilities, plus the capability to create, edit, or format content. In other words, editing and correcting work exactly the way they do in the Dragon Professional Individual DragonPad.

You can check if an application has Full Text Control by looking at the DragonBar and seeing if the circle at the end is green. If it is, you have Full Text Control. For example, if you use OpenOffice.org Writer, version 3.3 or 3.4, you have Full Text Control.

✔ **Natural Language Commands:** These allow you to speak commands in a more natural way. For example, rather than having to say, **"Click File; Click Save As,"** you can simply say, **"Save Document."** You speak as you normally would. You have the full editing, correcting, and formatting control of the Dragon Professional Individual DragonPad, plus a Dragon Professional Individual menu is visible above the other application's menu bar.

Using this menu, you can do virtually anything that you can do with the DragonBar: Create a new user profile, launch Accuracy Tuning, check your microphone, and so on.

This level is available in applications such as Microsoft Word 2010 and 2013, Internet Explorer 9 or higher, and current versions of Mozilla Firefox and Google Chrome.

Table 8-1	Dragon Professional Individual in Different Applications				
Application	*Windows Desktop*	*Nearly Any Windows Application*	*Dragon Professional Individual Dictation Box with Another Application*	*Full Text Control Applications*	*Natural Language Commands*
Launch applications	X	X	X	X	X
Control windows	X	X	X	X	X
Clipboard		X	X	X	X
Basic menu control		X	X	X	X
Dictation		X	X	X	X
Navigation		X	X	X	X
Dragon Professional Individual DragonBar			X	X	X
Menus		X	X	X	X
Full Text Control				X	X

(continued)

Table 8-1 *(continued)*

Application	Windows Desktop	Nearly Any Windows Application	Dragon Professional Individual Dictation Box with Another Application	Full Text Control Applications	Natural Language Commands
Additional formatting				X	X
Additional natural phrases					X

Getting Started

You may already be comfortable dictating into the Dragon Professional Individual DragonPad, and you may have developed confidence that you can create documents there. If so, then you have already mastered the techniques that allow you to dictate to other applications. You just need to know which commands you can use in which situations.

If you aren't already familiar with dictating in the Dragon Professional Individual Dictation Box, the next sections tell you what you need to know.

Dictating your first words

The first step in achieving dictation mastery of other applications is to make the words you say appear in a window controlled by the other application. (You can worry later about whether those words are correct or what you should do if they aren't.)

To get those first words to show up in the correct window, do the following:

1. **Open Dragon Professional Individual and another application.**

   In the figures, I'm dictating into DragonPad, but you can use any application you want. It doesn't matter whether you open Dragon Professional Individual or the other application first.

2. **Click the microphone icon in the DragonBar to turn the microphone on.**

   If the icon is green, the microphone is on; if the icon is red, the microphone is off. Change from one state to the other by clicking the microphone icon. By default, the microphone is off at startup.

3. Activate the window of the other application.

- If the application is already opened but not visible, you can say, **"List open applications."**

  A numbered list of open applications pops up. Choose the application you want.

- If the application has not been opened, say, **"Open <*application name*>."**

  The application should open and the cursor should be blinking in the text-editing window. If not, click in the text-editing window.

In the open text window, I dictated, **"Dear Betty, <New paragraph> We would like to issue congratulations to you and your dog Fluffy, for winning the gold medal at the big event this week. We know that you have worked hard. Period"** The DragonPad window then looked like Figure 8-1.

Figure 8-1: DragonPad takes dictation from Dragon Professional Individual.

If you aren't going to use the Dragon Professional Individual DragonBar for a while, minimize it by clicking the DragonBar menu and choosing Tray Icon Only. A minimized window uses less of your computer's resources for display and leaves more for the really important tasks, like figuring out what you just said. But don't *close* the Dragon Professional Individual DragonBar. If you do, you'll instantly lose your dictating capabilities.

Turning the microphone on and off

One item from the Dragon Professional Individual DragonBar is always available to you when Dragon Professional Individual is running: the microphone. Without it, you're talking to yourself.

The microphone box is green when it's on. Click it to switch between on and off.

You can use the + (plus) key on the numeric keypad (at the far right end of your keyboard) as a microphone on/off button.

Knowing which capabilities you have in any application

No matter what application you find yourself working in, you can do the following (as long as Dragon Professional Individual is running):

✔ **Use the Dictation Box.** When another application is open, you can access it from the DragonBar menu. Choose Tools➪Dictation Box, say, **"Show Dictation Box,"** or press Ctrl+Shift+D.

✔ **Use menus.** See "Ordering from the Menu," later in this chapter.

✔ **Use hotkeys.** In any application that has hotkeys, you can use them with the **"Press"** command followed by the name of the hotkey.

Points to ponder

Dragon Professional Individual uses several windows at once. Normally, you launch an application, you get an application window, and you work in that window. End of story. Not so with Dragon Professional Individual, and for good reason: You want to be able to use voice input in lots of different places, not just in a single window.

The core of Dragon Professional Individual — the basic program that turns your speech into text or actions — actually runs in the background. It is hidden:

✔ This hidden program puts its text into whichever application window you are using at any given moment.

✔ If you give a menu command, such as **"Click File,"** the command goes to that application's window, too.

To be technically precise, Dragon Professional Individual works with whichever application is active at the time. An application is active if its title bar is darkened. Click an application's title bar, or anywhere in its window, to make it active.

✔ **Dictate text.** In most applications, you have the simple capability to dictate a phrase (including capitalization, punctuation, and hyphenation) and see it appear on the screen.

✔ **Undo your last action.** The **"Undo That"** command works in all applications.

✔ **Move the cursor around in a document with the** "Move" **and** "Go" **commands.** The **"Move"** and **"Go"** commands work in any application. See Chapter 5.

✔ **Use the mouse commands.** See the section about mice understanding English in Chapter 15.

✔ **Control windows.** You can open and close windows, start applications, and switch from one window to another. See Chapter 15.

Creating Documents with the Dictation Box

Wondering when to use the Dictation Box? Work at the Dictation Box level when you find you don't have all the voice commands you normally use. For example, when I'm using the Snagit software, I don't have access to all the commands, so I pop open the Dictation Box as shown in Figure 8-2. Use one of the methods described in the preceding section and see what happens.

In the sections that follow, I give you an idea of what kinds of actions you can take with the Dictation Box and tell you how to do them.

Figure 8-2:
Opening the
Dictation
Box in
Dragon
Professional
Individual
while in
another
application.

Using the Dictation Box

When you dictate into an application where only the Dictation Box applies, you don't have access to several capabilities that you would have in a Full Text Control application or a Natural Language application. But, fear not, you can

- ✔ Easily move around in a document.
- ✔ Select and edit text.
- ✔ Delete text.
- ✔ Make corrections.

Doesn't seem like much of a sacrifice, right? The Dictation Box gives you the option to do things in applications that otherwise don't want to play nicely with Dragon Professional Individual.

First, confirm that your application doesn't have Full Text Control (the circle at the end of the DragonBar on the right is gray instead of green). Put your cursor in the desired application and say, **"Show Dictation Box."** The Dictation Box opens.

If you are a long-time user of Dragon, the Dictation Box is set to automatically appear when you start dictating into a window that does not have Full Text Control. This can be turned on and off by choosing DragonBar ➪ Options ➪ Miscellaneous. *Note:* You may not experience this if you upgrade from a previous version because your previous settings are retained.

You can now change font type, size, color, bold, italic, and underline of text within the Dictation Box. You can do this using some of the same commands as you would in Word or by clicking the Settings button in the Dictation Box and choosing Change Font. You can also click the Default Font button to make your font changes to the default the next time the Dictation Box is used.

Moving around in a document

The **"Move"** and **"Go"** commands work the same way in the Dictation Box as they do in the Dragon Professional Individual DragonPad. The **"Insert Before"** and **"Insert After"** commands also work here. See Chapter 5. You can also use the mouse commands to position the cursor.

If you're just reading a document and don't care where the cursor is, use the **"Press Page Up"** and **"Press Page Down"** commands.

If an editing job turns out to require more work than you feel like doing in the Dictation Box application, take it back to the shop. Cut the text out of the application window and paste it into the Dragon Professional Individual DragonPad, where you have more tools to work with. After you get the text the way you want it, cut and paste it back to the original application.

Making corrections

Your ability to make corrections at the Dictation Box level is affected by how recently you spoke it:

- ✔ If you spot a Dragon Professional Individual mistake immediately after it happens, you can say, **"Correct That"** to invoke the Correction menu.

- ✔ To correct a Dragon Professional Individual error that happened a while ago, select the text with your mouse and then dictate new text.

  If the new text is still wrong, say, **"Correct That"** to invoke the Correction menu. You can also say, **"Correct <xyz>"** or **"Select <xyz>"** to highlight and correct the text.

The Correction dialog box itself always works the same way, no matter what application you call it from. See Chapter 5.

Using Full Text Control Applications

In some applications, Dragon Professional Individual gives you the capability to select, correct, or move the cursor to text in a document by saying the text. This capability is called Full Text Control, and the applications in which you have this capability are called Full Text Control applications.

Following are some applications that have the Full Text Control capability:

- ✔ **Notepad**
- ✔ **WordPad**
- ✔ **Microsoft Word**
- ✔ **Outlook:** When you use Word to edit Outlook's email messages, the Word windows also use Full Text Control.
- ✔ **Internet Explorer, Mozilla Firefox, and Google Chrome:** Internet Explorer's Full Text Control capability applies only to web pages that expect your input, such as online forms or web email interfaces.

The cut-and-paste commands like **"Cut That"** or **"Copy That"** work in some, but not all, Full Text Control applications. In the applications where they don't work, you can easily accomplish the same purpose with menu commands. For example, use **"Click Edit, Cut"** instead of **"Cut That."**

The formatting commands described in Chapter 6 all work in WordPad, but not in some of the other Full Text Control applications. (You wouldn't expect them to work in Notepad, for example, because Notepad doesn't allow formatting in any case.)

Dictation only works if Dragon Professional Individual is running. You can minimize the Dragon Professional Individual window while you dictate into another window, but if you close Dragon Professional Individual, you won't be able to dictate.

Ordering from the Menu

The engineers at Nuance can't anticipate every command that any stray application could possibly use, so they've done the next best thing: They made the **"Click"** command turn an application's own menus into voice commands.

Here's how to use it:

1. Say, "Click *<menu name>*" **to expand a menu.**

Any title that appears on an application's menu bar will work: **"Click File," "Click Edit,"** and so on.

What if it doesn't work?

So there you are, dictating into an application. You aren't sure whether the command you want (for example, **"Set Font Arial"**) will work here or not, so you try it once and it doesn't. Does that mean it just doesn't work and you should never try it again? Maybe, maybe not. Here's how to decide:

✔ Maybe Dragon Professional Individual didn't understand you properly. So try the command again, and watch to see what Dragon Professional Individual thinks you said. If "set phone to aerial" appears, then the jury is still out on whether the command works here or not. Keep trying.

✔ On the other hand, if **"Set Font Arial"** shows up as text on your screen, but still nothing happens font-wise, then you can reasonably conclude that the command isn't going to work.

---

2. After the menu expands, say an entry on the menu.

For example, after you say, **"Click Edit,"** you can say, **"Paste"** if Paste appears on the Edit menu. The result is the same as if you had chosen Edit⇨Paste.

Extending Posts to Facebook and Twitter

Generally, you can dictate into an application while running Dragon Professional Individual if you have an open text window. Using Dragon Professional Individual, you can use a special command that calls up a text window and posts directly into Twitter or Facebook. Following are three versions of a voice command you can use:

✔ **"Post That to *<Facebook/Twitter>*":** Notice the use of the word *that.* In this version of the command, *that* refers to text you have already dictated and want to post on Facebook or Twitter. So, when you say this command, the text is in the box when the window opens.

✔ **"Post to *<Facebook/Twitter> <text>*":** In this version of the command, the window opens and the text you uttered in the command is placed in the text window.

✔ **"Post to *<Facebook/Twitter>*":** Using the command this way opens a blank text window for either Facebook or Twitter and then lets you dictate text.

If one of these preceding commands isn't recognized, a blank window opens. You'll have to dictate it again or cut and paste the dictation into the window.

You must give authorization for Dragon Professional Individual to post to your Facebook or Twitter account the first time you use this command (as shown in the following instructions). You are, of course, still subject to all the Twitter or Facebook restrictions on your account as you would normally be.

To use DragonPad to post to Twitter, use the following steps:

1. Open the DragonPad by saying, "Open DragonPad."

The DragonPad opens.

2. Dictate your message.

3. Once you have your message the way you want it, say, "Post that to Twitter."

A text window with the title "Post to Twitter" will open and your message will be in it, as shown in Figure 8-3.

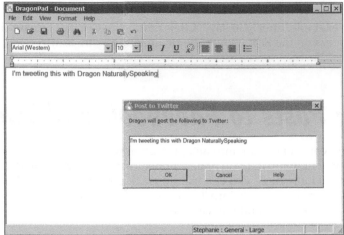

Figure 8-3:
The Post to
Twitter
window.

4. **Say,** "Click OK."

An authorization window as shown in Figure 8-4 appears.

5. **Dictate or type in your email and password.**

6. **Say,** "Click Sign In," **and your message will be posted.**

Figure 8-4:
Giving
Dragon
permission
to post to
your site.

Chapter 9

Dipping into Word Processing

. . . .

In This Chapter

▶ Editing and moving text

▶ Listening to your text

▶ Understanding Natural Language Commands in Word

▶ Formatting and editing with Natural Language

▶ Inserting tables with Natural Language

▶ Working in OpenOffice.org Writer

. . . .

*I*f you have used Dragon Professional Individual for even a short amount of time, you know that there are many different ways of accomplishing the same thing. You can use some applications, such as Microsoft Word, PowerPoint, and Excel, and Corel WordPerfect, with Natural Language Commands.

In this chapter, I look at all the ways you can work in Word or WordPerfect for an easy, uncomplicated experience. I discuss how Natural Language Commands make it even more intuitive. At the time of this writing, Word 2010 (English), Word 2013, Word 2016, and WordPerfect X6 and X7 are supported.

If you work with online applications, look at using OpenOffice.org Writer as your word-processing program.

Saying the Right Thing

If you are new to using Dragon Professional Individual with Word, you want to know the quickest ways to find the right thing to say. Here are some things to do when you're stumped:

> ✔ **Ask for help.** You can always say, **"What can I say?"** and a dialog box will pop up with commands that pertain to the application you are working in. If the application is not supported with specific commands, you'll see global commands that work in most applications.

- **Open the Command Browser.** Go to Tools ➪ Command Browser and use the Keyword Filter to find the right command. (See Chapter 17.)

- **Say, "Give Me Help."** The Dragon Help window opens, and you can say or type a keyword. (When you are done, say, **"Close Help."**) You can also say, **"Search Dragon Help for <xyz>"** or **"Search Nuance Support for <xyz>."**

- **Say what you see.** Natural Language Commands don't cover everything. You still need to use menus for some functions. You can either use your mouse or voice commands for menu choices. For example, say the menu item, like, **"Click View,"** and then choose from the drop-down menu that opens.

- **Mouse over with your cursor.** If you aren't sure what a particular item is called on the Word menu, mouse over it with the cursor and you'll see the name of the choice. Then use that name when calling that menu or button.

In Word (2010, 2013, and 2016), get to the File Menu items by saying, **"Click File Tab."** This then displays such items as New, Open, Save, and so forth.

Creating, opening, and closing documents

To get started with Word, you don't need any special Natural Language Commands. You're already familiar with them. Some of the commands you'll most likely use are

- **"Open Microsoft Word"**
- **"Open New Document"** (You must have Word open already to use this.)
- **"Save Document"**
- **"Close Document"**

Employing the "Playback" and "Read" commands

A familiar set of features in Word are **"Playback"** and **"Read That."** Playback lets you play back a recording of your voice to help you proofread. Read That is the Dragon Professional Individual text-to-speech feature. Chapter 7 provides the details of both Playback and Read That.

You can play back your text by menu command and voice command. First, select the text you want to hear. The menu command for playback is Audio ➪ Playback.

You can have Dragon Professional Individual read your selected text aloud by using the **"Read That"** command.

Natural Language Commands for Word

The worst thing about dealing with computers is that you have to learn their language. Sure, Dragon Professional Individual takes dictation, but when you want to tell it what to do with that dictation, you're back in the same old situation, right? If you don't like a 10-point font, you have to say something geeky like, **"Format That Size 12."**

If an actual human was setting type for you, you wouldn't say anything remotely like **"Format That Size 12,"** would you? You'd say, "Make it a little bigger," and the person would know what to do.

That's what a Natural Language Command is. It's a command that sounds like something you would naturally say, in your own language, rather than something you would say only because you're talking to a computer. In this section, I help you dictate Word documents in a way that might seem fairly natural to you.

Understanding Natural Language Commands

The engineers who built Natural Language Commands for Word believe in freedom of speech. They tried to anticipate any way in which you might want to command Word. I think this task is Herculean, given that people may say anything from, **"Bold That Sucker"** to **"Slice This Turkey into Two Columns."** (You're probably more restrained.)

Nonetheless, Nuance engineers do succeed in giving you a lot of flexibility with Natural Language Commands.

So, I would be crazy to try to document all the thousands of ways you can give commands, and you wouldn't be any better off. Instead, I mainly tell you what you can talk about, and tell you the best verbal commands to use.

How do you ultimately know what's best to say? Dragon Professional Individual accepts commands in so many different forms that Nuance suggests you just try speaking a command and see whether it works.

Clever as Dragon Professional Individual is, accidentally coming up with a "command" that doesn't work is still quite possible. And, to add injury to insult, if you've selected text in your document when you speak the so-called command that Dragon Professional Individual doesn't recognize, that text is replaced. If that happens, undo the error by saying, **"Undo That"** or pressing Ctrl+Z. (You may have to repeat that command to totally undo the error.)

If Dragon Professional Individual doesn't perform your command, either Dragon Professional Individual doesn't recognize it as a command or the command can't be accomplished because the context where you're trying to use it is incorrect. (See Chapter 20 to see what to do if this happens.) The following sections tell you how to perform many Word commands by using Natural Language Commands.

Dictating text

The simplest way to think about dictating with Natural Language Commands is that you can work with your favorite documents in their natural settings. Word and WordPerfect have similar commands, so for the purposes of my examples, I refer to Word.

Here are a few points to remember about dictating:

- ✔ Don't panic if **"Undo That"** doesn't seem to completely restore an error. Speak the command again. You may have to repeat the command several times to restore things as they were.

  Many Dragon Professional Individual commands are actually multiple commands as far as your word processor is concerned. **"Undo That"** undoes only one Word or WordPerfect command at a time.

- ✔ Dragon Professional Individual's idea of a paragraph isn't exactly the same as the Word or WordPerfect version. When you create a paragraph with the **"New Paragraph"** command, Dragon Professional Individual (in effect) presses the Enter key twice. That action creates two paragraphs! (In Word, click the Paragraph [¶] button on the toolbar to see the paragraph marks.) To get a single Word or WordPerfect paragraph, you must use the command **"New Line."**

- ✔ After a **"New Paragraph"** command, Dragon capitalizes the first letter of the next sentence. After a **"New Line"** command, Dragon does the same, but only if the last sentence ended in a period, exclamation mark, or question mark.

Editing with familiar commands

Natural Language Commands for editing in Word are just what you would expect. Just say something and see if it works.

Here are some familiar ones:

- ✔ **Undo/Redo:** You have the same **"Undo That"** command in Word that you have anywhere with Dragon Professional Individual. (You don't have a redo command, but you can always say, **"Press Ctrl+Y,"** instead.)

- ✔ **Selection:** The basic form of the command is **"Select <*text*>,"** where <*text*> is text you can see. You can also use **"Select All"** to select the whole document.

- ✔ **Cut, Copy, and Paste:** You enjoy the same **"Cut That," "Copy That,"** and **"Paste That"** commands you do elsewhere with Dragon Professional Individual. Likewise, you have the **"Copy All"** command for copying the whole document or **"Copy <xyz>"** to copy a specific word or words.

- ✔ **Find and Replace:** To use **"Find"** or **"Replace"** when in your document, you just say, **"Find Text"** or **"Replace,"** and the Find/Replace box opens. You can also verbally press the hotkey: **"Press Control F"** (for Find) or **"Press Control H"** (for Replace). You can also say, **"Find and Replace"** as a single command.

- ✔ **Go To:** You can "go to" places (move the cursor) just as you can in any other application served by Dragon Professional Individual. See Chapter 5 for the commands, which include such favorites as **"Go To Top," "Go To Bottom,"** and **"Go Back Three Paragraphs."**

A convenient way to go to a specific phrase is to use a Full Text Control command. First, say, **"Select <*phrase*>"** (substituting your word or phrase for <*phrase*>), then say, **"Move Right One"** or **"Move Left One."** Your cursor is now positioned just after that phrase.

One of the best editing features of Natural Language Commands has nothing to do with the Edit menu. It's the **"Move That"** command. With **"Move That,"** you can select text and then say, **"Move That Down Two Paragraphs,"** for instance.

You can replace the word **"That"** with a reference to any number of words, lines, paragraphs, sections, or pages. For instance, you can say, **"Move Next Three Paragraphs to Bottom of Document"** or **"Move Previous Three Lines Up One Paragraph."**

Inserting

Natural Language Commands can be used for anything on the Insert menu. You can use the Natural Language **"Insert *<something>*"** command for page and section breaks, by just saying, **"Insert Page Break."** You can also use the command for other whitespace features like lines, tables, and columns. (*Whitespace* refers to stuff that doesn't actually put ink on paper.)

Say the word **"Insert,"** and then immediately say one of the terms in the following list of whitespace *<somethings>*:

- ✔ **"Line"** or **"Blank Line"** (both mean the same thing)
- ✔ **"Paragraph"**
- ✔ **"Section Break"** or **"Section"** (both mean the same thing)
- ✔ **"Page Break"** or **"Page"** (both mean the same thing)
- ✔ **"Table"** (see the section on creating tables, later in this chapter)

To insert just one of any in this list, use the singular form, as in **"Insert Line."** To insert several, use the plural form and tell Dragon Professional Individual how many you want. For instance, say, **"Insert Ten Lines."**

Dragon Professional Individual makes a paragraph with two presses of the Enter key; a line is one press. In Word, that makes two paragraphs! If you want a single Word paragraph, use **"Line"** instead of **"Paragraph."**

The verb **"Insert"** can also be used for formatting borders, numbers, and bullets. See the later section "Formatting paragraphs," in this chapter.

Printing

Natural Language Commands for Word offer commands for printing. You can print any number of pages, the current page, or selected text, and you can use Print Preview.

Say, **"Print,"** then one of the following terms (substituting your chosen page numbers for *<page number>*):

- ✔ **"Preview On"** or **"Preview Off"**
- ✔ **"Document"**
- ✔ **"Selection"**

✔ "Page"

✔ "Page <*page number*>"

✔ "Pages <*page number*> through <*page number*>"

So, for instance, say, **"Print Preview On"** or **"Print Page."** You can say, **"Print This Page"** or **"Print Pages <*number*> to <*number*>,"** too, if you prefer.

Setting up page margins

Natural Language Commands have commands for margins, which are on the File (Office Button) menu. State your marginal commands by saying,

> **"Set Left, Right, Top, Bottom, Margin To <*distance*> <*units*>"**

For example, you can say, **"Set Top Margin To One Point Two Inches."** The <*distance*> in this example is 1.2 and the <*units*> are inches. Allowable units are inches, centimeters, and points.

Natural Language Commands for formatting

Formatting is where Natural Language Commands for Word really get interesting, mainly because there is so much more to talk about. You can make things larger or smaller or indent them more or less.

What, which way, how much, and where

The objects that you can talk to Natural Language Commands about are the character, word, line, sentence, paragraph, section, page, column, row, cell, table, and document. (You can also talk about the whole document or "all.") You can move any number of these objects up, down, left, right, ahead, back, backward, or forward.

You can move some number of the next, last, forward, following, back, or previous objects. You can move them a distance, measured in some number of objects. "Huh?" you say. Okay, for instance, you can say, **"Move the Next Three Words Up Two Paragraphs."** Or you can move an object to a destination: the top or bottom, start or beginning, or end of another object.

Formatting characters

In Word, you can format characters (choose basic fonts and styles, like bold) using the same commands you use in any other Full Text Control application. See Chapter 6 for instructions.

Natural Language Commands give you additional options for Word, however. I give only a few examples here, using my favorite **"Format That"** command, and point out where Natural Language Commands add flexibility:

- **Font faces:** Say, **"Format That Arial,"** for instance. Natural Language Commands recognize all the fonts in Word.

- **Font sizes:** Just as in the Dragon Professional Individual window, or in WordPerfect with Natural Language Commands, you can say, **"Format That Size 14,"** or you can add the font size to a font family by saying, **"Format That Arial 14"** or you can say, **"Format That 14"** (without the font name or the word size). Sizes are limited to the ones Word lists in the toolbar and dialog box. (So, for example, you can't use odd-numbered sizes in the 20- to 30-point range. Dragon Professional Individual types your command as text, if you try.)

- **Font styles, colors, and effects:** Say, **"Format That *<style>*,"** where *<style>* is anything in the following list. You can apply a style by itself with, for example, **"Format That Italics,"** or add the style at the end of a longer font command, as in, **"Format That Courier Italics."** Say, **"Make This,"** and then immediately follow with any of the following terms:

  - **"Black"**
  - **"Green"**
  - **"Blue"**
  - **"Gray"**
  - **"Red"**
  - **"White"**
  - **"Yellow"**
  - **"Bold,"** or **"Boldface"**
  - **"Italics"** or **"Italicized"**
  - **"Hidden"**
  - **"Superscript"**
  - **"Underline"** or **"Underlines"** or **"Underlined"**
  - **"Double Underlined"**

- **"Wavy Underlined"**
- **"Thick Underlined"**
- **"Strikethrough"**
- **"Bigger**
- **"Smaller"**
- **"With Hyphens"**
- **"Lowercase"**

You can use an imperative verb form of command for certain styles. (Remember imperative verbs from English class? No, me neither, but that's what they are!) The imperatives for fonts are a short list, as follows:

- ✔ **"Cap That"**
- ✔ **"Italicize That"**
- ✔ **"Bold That"**
- ✔ **"Underline That"**

When you format something, **"That"** refers to text you have selected or previously uttered. You can say things other than **"That"** if you like. See the upcoming bullets that talk about equivalent terms.

As with most commands in Natural Language Commands, you can say them in different ways. Here are a few of the variations Natural Language Commands allow for font commands:

- ✔ **"Make"** and **"Set"** is equivalent to **"Format."** For instance, you may say, **"Make That Blue"** or **"Format That Arial 12 Point."**
- ✔ You can also substitute **"That"** phrases with **"Next Three Words"** or **"Previous Two Paragraphs"** to avoid having to select the text first.
- ✔ You can use the command **"Make Font Blue."**

Formatting paragraphs

For formatting paragraphs in Word, I prefer (you guessed it) the **"Format That *<some formatting>*"** command. You can use **"Format That"** no matter whether you're formatting paragraphs, fonts, or anything else, and this command is easiest for my poor brain to remember.

When you format paragraphs, you can use two other types of commands. Table 9-1 gives the gory details. The top three rows give the conventional commands that work anywhere (left-, right-, and center-align). The remaining rows list commands that Natural Language Commands give you.

Table 9-1	Three Ways to Format Paragraphs in Word	
Say, "Format That" and Then	**Or Just Say**	**Notes**
"Left Aligned"	**"Left Align That"**	
"Right Aligned"	**"Right Align That"**	
"Center Aligned" or **"Centered"**	**"Center That"**	
"Justified"	**"Justify That"**	Means no ragged right edge.
(nothing)	**"Indent That"** (Also **"Outdent That"**)	Means increase indentation to the next default or user-added tab stop. (Outdenting decreases indentation.)
(nothing)	**"Indent That by** *<distance>***"**	For indenting a specific amount (for example, 1.5 inches). Substitute your indentation distance for *<distance>*.
"Bulleted" or **"Bullet Style"**	**"Bullet That"**	Say, "Unbullet That" or "Make that not bullet style" to turn off bullets.
(nothing)	**"Double Space That"**	

Dragon Professional Individual gives you no Natural Language command for setting tabs. For most purposes, though, you can use indentation or table commands instead.

For most work, I suggest my favorite command, **"Format That** *<whatever>***."**

"That" refers to paragraphs you have selected or what you previously uttered. See the bullets that follow for other words you can use instead of **"That."**

As with font formatting, Natural Language Commands let you say paragraph-formatting commands in different ways. Here are some of the variations Natural Language Commands allow you:

- You can substitute **"Justified"** for **"Aligned."** (And, as you may suspect, you can substitute **"Justify"** for **"Align,"** or **"Justification"** for **"Alignment."**)

- You can use the term **"Paragraph"** in place of **"That."** You can direct your paragraph commands to the previous or next 1 to 20 **"Paragraphs,"** **"Pages,"** **"Sections,"** **"Columns,"** **"Tables,"** **"Rows,"** or **"Cells,"** or to the **"Document."**

Formatting styles

Want a top-level heading? Say, **"Change Style to Heading 1."** Want to redefine what Heading 1 is? Format a paragraph (by voice or by hand).

If you aren't familiar with styles, here's the story in brief: Styles are combinations of font and paragraph formatting that go by a certain name, such as Heading 1. Word comes with certain predetermined styles. You, however, can change what font and paragraph formatting goes with any of the named styles.

To apply a style, first click in a paragraph or select some text. Then say, **"Set That Selection To,"** followed immediately by any of the following phrases:

- **"Normal Text"** (same as **"Normal"**)
- **"Text"** (same as **"Body Text"**)
- **"Body Text"**
- **"Body Text 2"**
- **"Body Text 3"**
- **"Plain Text"**
- **"A Quote"** (same as **"Block Text"**)
- **"Quoted Text"** (same as **"Block Text"**)
- **"A Caption"**
- **"A Heading"** (same as **"Heading 2"**)
- **"Heading 1"**
- **"Heading 2"**
- **"Heading 3"**
- **"A Heading 1"**
- **"A Heading 2"**
- **"A Heading 3"**
- **"A Major Heading"** (same as **"Heading 1"**)
- **"A Minor Heading"** (same as **"Heading 3"**)
- **"A List"**
- **"List 2"**
- **"List 3"**
- **"Bulleted List 2"**

- ✔ "Bulleted List 3"
- ✔ "A Title"
- ✔ "A Subtitle"
- ✔ "Numbered List 2"
- ✔ "Numbered List 3"

Natural Language Commands don't perform all the Word styles, just the ones I list.

To see what these styles are like, choose Format⇨Style, and the Style dialog box appears (Home⇨Styles). In that dialog box, click in the box marked List, and then choose All Styles. The area marked Paragraph Preview shows you what the current paragraph formatting for that style looks like; the Character Preview area shows you the font currently in use. The Description section lists exactly what font and paragraph formatting the style contains. Many style descriptions begin with "Normal+," which means the style is based on (uses the same settings as) Normal style, then the settings are modified from there. If you change the Normal style, all the styles that are based on Normal change.

Some of the style commands, like the ones for numbered and bulleted styles, sound very much like the paragraph formatting commands, but they really refer to named styles. The number **"2"** or **"3"** at the end of certain commands refers to how much the line is indented. A **"3"** is more indented than a **"2."**

As with paragraph and font commands, Natural Language Commands let you say it your way. Here are three ways you can say things:

- ✔ If the term **"Format"** doesn't seem natural to you, you can use **"Make"** or **"Set."** For instance, you can say, **"Quote that selection."**
- ✔ You can use the term **"Selection"** or "**It**" instead of the word **"That."**
- ✔ You can use the term **"Paragraph"** in place of **"That."** You can also substitute phrases like **"Next Three Paragraphs"** or **"Previous Two Pages"** to avoid having to select the text first. You can apply your style commands to up to 20 of the previous or next **"Paragraphs,"** **"Pages,"** **"Sections,"** **"Columns,"** **"Tables,"** **"Rows,"** or **"Cells,"** or to the **"Document."**

Editing and formatting text

Natural Language Commands bring to Word all the editing and formatting features of the Dragon Professional Individual DragonPad (described in

Chapters 5 and 6). See those chapters for the picky details. Here's an overview of those features and a couple of examples of the verbal commands each uses:

- ✔ Ordinary cursor control commands (**"Go To Top"** or **"Move Back Three Words"**)
- ✔ Ordinary selection (**"Select Paragraph"** or **"Select Previous Three Words"**)
- ✔ Through (**"Select <*beginning text*> Through <*end text*>"**)
- ✔ Correction (**"Correct That"** or **"Correct <*text*>"**)
- ✔ Insertion (**"Insert Before <*text*>"** or **"Insert After <*text*>"**)
- ✔ Cut and paste (**"Copy That,"** **"Copy <xyz>,"** or **"Paste That"**)
- ✔ Deletion (**"Delete That,"** **"Delete <xyz>,"** or **"Delete Previous Character"**)

Checking spelling and grammar

How easy can this be? Following are the commands for the two Microsoft Word tools for spelling and grammar:

- ✔ **"Check Spelling"**
- ✔ **"Check Grammar"**

On the other hand, if you truly are dictating everything in your document using Dragon Professional Individual, you should never need to run the spelling checker! Dragon Professional Individual never makes a spelling error (unless you added a misspelled word to your Dragon Professional Individual vocabulary).

Keep in mind that when you check spelling, the Word spell checker may not recognize words that are in your Dragon Professional Individual vocabulary. The two programs maintain their own lists of acceptable words.

Inserting tables

You can use Natural Language Commands to create Word tables with up to 20 rows or columns. Use the commands **"Insert,"** **"Add,"** or **"Create,"** as you prefer. I prefer **"Insert"** because it's the same command I use for other whitespace insertions like spaces, paragraphs, and page breaks. Here are the different forms of commands you can use (using **"Insert"** as my example):

> **"Insert <*n*> By <*m*> Table"**

Substitute numbers between 1 and 20 for **<n>** and **<m>.** In any of these commands, you can say the columns first and then the rows, or vice versa.

You can leave out either the rows or the columns in any of these commands and then add them later.

After you have a table, you can verbally move your cursor around in the table, referring to rows, columns, or cells. Commands use either **"Move"** or **"Go"** and take forms like these examples:

- ✔ **"Move Right One Column"**
- ✔ **"Move to Next Row"**
- ✔ **"Go Down Three Cells"**

You can move Left, Right, Up, Down, Back, Backward, Ahead, or Forward.

You can add rows or columns using exactly the same sort of command you use to create a table: **"Insert," "Add,"** or **"Create."** Place the insertion point where you want to add stuff, and speak the command.

As usual, I prefer **"Insert."** You can insert a number of rows or columns or insert a new row or column. Here are a few examples, using my favorite command, **"Insert"**:

- ✔ **"Insert A New Row"**
- ✔ **"Insert Five Rows"**
- ✔ **"Insert Two Columns"**

You can select, delete, cut, or copy rows, columns, or cells just as you would words in regular text. For instance, you can use **"Select Row"** to select the row your cursor is in. To paste a row, column, or cell you have copied, use **"Paste That."** Don't refer to a row, column, or cell in the command.

Inserting, deleting, and pasting by voice works just as it does when you insert, delete, or paste by hand. That is, rows are inserted above the current row; columns are inserted to the left of the current column.

Adjusting and viewing windows within Word

Natural Language Commands don't give you any special commands for document windows in Word. If you want to do anything in the Word Window menu — such as use Arrange All to display all open Word documents on the screen — you have to do it manually or with the **"Click View"** command. You can, however, make use of the key combination Ctrl+F6 to switch document windows (say, **"Press Control F6"**). Ctrl+F4 closes a document window (say, **"Press Control F4"**).

"Close This Document" is a command that you can use in Word to close just the document and leave Word open.

This isn't to say you can't switch between the Word window and other program windows. As in any application, you can say, **"Switch To *<program name>*"** (if that program is running) or **"Switch To Previous/Next Window."**

You can always say, **"List Windows For *<program>*"** to get to the document window you are looking for.

Choosing OpenOffice.org Writer

Want an online suite of office products that you don't have to license? If so, check out OpenOffice.org. It is an open source program that includes a word processor called Writer and several other applications that resemble the Microsoft Office suite.

People use it so they always have access to the most up-to-date version of the application. (Also, it's free.) In Dragon Professional Individual, Nuance has commands that can be used directly with OpenOffice.org Writer 3.x and 4.x

The following are some tips you should know if you want to use Writer with Dragon Professional Individual:

- ✔ With Dragon Professional Individual, Writer is a Full Text Control application. This means that you can create, edit, and format content.

- ✔ You can use the general navigation commands to edit when you dictate. For example: **"Go To," "Select," "Line Up," "Line Down," "Page Up,"** or **"Page Down."**

- ✔ You have a full range of familiar correction commands: **"Scratch That," "Correct That," "Correct *<word>*,"** and **"Correct *<x>* Through *<y>*."**

- ✔ Formatting commands are available. For example, **"Bold/Italicize/ Underline/Cap *<x>*."**

- ✔ When several instances of a word are present, Dragon will number all of them and enable you to either **"Choose All"** or choose the one you want.

Chapter 10

Working with Excel

In This Chapter

▶ Using Dragon Professional Individual with spreadsheets

▶ Working in Quick Edit or Full mode

▶ Using your cursor with spreadsheets

*E*arlier chapters explain what Dragon Professional Individual offers to word-oriented people, but what about number-oriented people, people who have a lot of data to enter, to keep track of, and to process? Left-brainers, unite!

Dragon Professional Individual enables you to work with spreadsheets. In Dragon Professional Individual you can use Full Text Control, Menu Tracking, and Natural Language Commands for Excel.

In this chapter, I cover the use of Dragon Professional Individual with spreadsheets. I also show you how to work in the Quick Edit and Full Edit modes.

Doing Excel-lent Works with Spreadsheets

Using spreadsheets with older versions of Dragon was difficult because you couldn't directly address the names of the cells. You wanted to say something like, **"Cell A5"** or **"Select Column C."** But (sigh), no dice. Your assistant had no idea what you were talking about. Well, your assistant has "up-leveled" its skills!

You now can select a cell and go right to it. After you know how to move around in your spreadsheet, you will be surprised how easy it is. If you are stumped about what command to say, you can always call on your Dragon DragonBar with, **"What can I say?"** to see the appropriate commands. You can, of course, use the mouse for these sorts of operations, and dictate only the text that goes into the cells. That decision is up to you.

You also have another option to address the cells. Spreadsheets are designed by and for geeks who regard using a mouse as a sign of weakness, so for their sake, most popular spreadsheet applications contain (at last count) bazillions of hotkey combinations that do just about anything you would ever want to do. If you know the right hotkeys, you can use **"Press <keyname>"** voice commands to have a reasonably pleasant and efficient no-hands experience with your spreadsheets.

The examples in this section are demonstrated with Microsoft Excel. It's important to show you the kinds of activities that are possible with voice, keyboard, and mouse.

Getting in the mode

Excel has two voice modes in which you work: Dictation and Edit, called Quick Edit and Full Edit mode, respectively. Unlike the Recognition modes (see Chapter 3), you don't select the Quick or Full Edit mode manually. You invoke them based on the actions you take inside the spreadsheet.

It's important to know about them because they make life easier when you want to dictate or edit the cells. On the other hand, if you aren't aware of them, you can become frustrated when your Dragon Professional Individual assistant does something you aren't expecting because of the mode it is in. Here is what you need to know about each mode:

- ✔ **Quick Edit mode:** This mode is the Dictation mode. If you dictate into a cell, you see a yellow background. This tells you that everything you say will show up in the cell. So, for example, if you say, **"Select Cell C5,"** and then started dictating, the program writes everything you say into that cell. Then you use commands to format what you say, just as you do in a text-editing application.

- ✔ **Full Edit mode:** This mode enables you to fully edit a cell by saying, **"Edit Cell <name>"** or **"Press F2."** After you do that, the background of the cell becomes blue. Then you can edit the cell in any way you want.

If you see a cell acting funny, check the background color.

- ✔ **Yellow:** If the background is yellow, you're dictating into it.

- ✔ **Blue:** If the background is blue, you're commanding it.

Adjust your words accordingly.

Having a look around

Thankfully, moving around in an Excel spreadsheet is pretty intuitive. Start by saying, **"Open Excel."** Voilà, it does! The same thing goes for creating a new spreadsheet or closing it. Say, **"Open A New Workbook"** or **"Close the Workbook,"** and it does.

If you aren't sure what to do, the Command Browser will display all the commands you can use in Excel. Saying, **"What can I say?"** while you're in Excel shows you common commands you can use. What could be easier? There are commands for the following:

- ✔ Moving around
- ✔ Selecting and inserting
- ✔ Cutting, copying, pasting, and deleting
- ✔ Formatting, saving, and printing

Selecting cells

Selecting cells or blocks of cells in a spreadsheet is a snap. You can just say, **"Cell C2"** and your cursor goes there. Or you can say, **"Select <x> Through <y>,"** and Excel does. If you want to move to the next row, say **"Next Row."** Previous column? Say, **"Previous Column."** Wow, this isn't hard at all!

You can also just click in the cell you want to select, or drag a selection rectangle over a block of cells. If you want to do the mouse thing by hand, Dragon Professional Individual won't stop you.

When you select cells by voice, consider using the International Communications Alphabet (ICA). In the ICA, the names of the letters all sound different, so you can spell aloud with confidence — if you know the ICA. For example, you can say, **"Alpha"** for A or **"Bravo"** for B. That means you say, **"Cell Bravo 12"** to move to cell B12.

You can find the ICA names of the letters listed in Chapter 5. Filling you in

If you like doing crossword puzzles, you'll really enjoy filling in your cells in Dragon Professional Individual. Here are some quick ways you can fill in your spreadsheet with the format you need.

To put in the days of the week, pick the cell you want to start in by saying, **"Cell *<location>*."** Then say, **"Sunday Through Saturday Down."** That column where the cell was now shows all the days Sunday through Saturday. You can then **"Bold That"** or format it in any other way you want.

To put in consecutive numbers, choose your cell as I explain in the preceding paragraph, and then say, **"One Through Ten Across."** Those numbers will be put in the row you chose.

The same goes for months of the year or any other grouping of numbers or letters. If you have a consecutive sequence, you can use the **"Through"** command.

Using the cursor

The **"Move Up/Down/Left/Right"** commands can also be used when you work with spreadsheets. They do exactly what you need: move the cursor from one cell to another. If the currently selected cell is B2, saying, **"Move Right Two"** moves the cursor to D2. If you then say, **"Move Down Five,"** the cursor moves to D7. Unfortunately, the highest number of steps you can move with one command is 20.

For longer trips, **"Press Page Up/Down"** displays the preceding/next full screen of the spreadsheet. In Excel, **"Press Alt Page Up"** shows you the next full screen to the left. **"Press Alt Page Down"** displays the next full screen to the right.

Return to cell A1 by saying, **"Press Control Home."** Go to the extreme lower-right corner of the spreadsheet by saying, **"Press Control End."**

Go to any cell by selecting it using the Go To dialog box described in the next section.

Boxing up a block of cells

In Excel, the F8 function key anchors a selection box in the current cell. Moving the cursor to another cell automatically selects the block of cells "between" them (in other words, a block of cells in which these two cells are opposing corners). For example, you could select the C3:E7 cell block as follows:

1. Move to cell C3.

Use any technique you want. See "Having a look around" earlier in this chapter.

2. **Say,** "Press F8."

3. **Say,** "Move Down Four."

   Now the C3:C7 block is selected.

4. **Say,** "Move Right Two."

   Now the C3:E7 block is selected.

If a block of cells is surrounded by empty cells, you can select the whole block in Excel by saying, **"Press Control Shift 8."**

Selecting rows and columns

To select an entire row or column in Excel, first move the cursor into the row or column. Then say, **"Press Control Spacebar"** to select the column, or **"Press Shift Spacebar"** to select the row.

You can also use the commands **"Select Column <*letter*>"** or **"Select Row <*number*>"** to select columns and rows.

How do you remember which does what? The words *control* and *column* both begin with the letter *C.*

Do you want column F with that?

After you select a block of cells, you can extend it by one cell in any direction by saying, **"Press Shift <*direction*> Arrow."** So, for example, if you have selected all of column E, you can add column F by saying, **"Press Shift Right Arrow."**

This command works in many spreadsheets, including Excel, but not all.

Inputting and formatting data

Spreadsheets are all about manipulating numbers, so the obvious question is how to get the numbers into the spreadsheet in the first place. The basic idea of how to get a number or date or time (spreadsheets think of dates and times as numbers) into a cell is fairly simple. Here are the steps:

1. **Select the cell.**

   See "Selecting cells," earlier in this chapter.

2. **Dictate the number.**

   There are no special commands here, so think of Dragon Professional Individual as if it were a keyboard. Whatever you want to see in the cell, say it. If, for example, you want the cell to contain the date 5/17/99, say,

"Five Slash 17 Slash 99." If you want to see 1.52E+01 in the cell, say, **"One Point Five Two Cap E Plus Zero One."** See Chapter 4, Table 4-5, for more ways to dictate numbers. A good spreadsheet should recognize any of the formats of Table 4-5 as numbers.

3. **Move to another cell.**

Spreadsheets like Excel are capable of displaying numbers, dates, and times in a nearly infinite number of ways. (You'd need a spreadsheet to figure out how many.) Your best bet is not to worry too much about how to format a number in Dragon Professional Individual. Just get the number into the spreadsheet in any old form, and then reformat it in the spreadsheet.

For example, suppose you were inputting a column of prices. You could dictate them as prices: **"Twenty-six dollars and seventy-two cents."** Or you could dictate them as numbers: **"Twenty-six point seven two."** After you dictate the column of numbers, you can convert them to prices. Here are the steps:

1. **Select the column.**

See "Selecting rows and columns," earlier in this chapter.

2. **Say,** "Click Format, Cells."

The Format Cells dialog box appears, as shown in Figure 10-1.

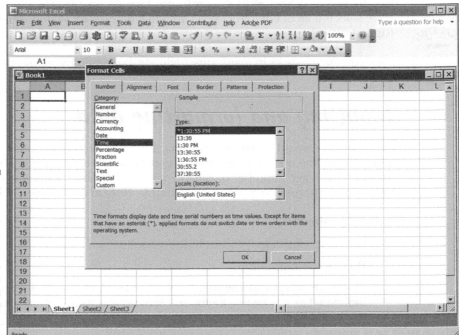

Figure 10-1:
A spreadsheet like Excel can format numbers, dates, and times in more ways than you can count.

3. **Display the Number tab in the Format Cells dialog box.**

   This tab may be on top when the box opens (or not!). Use the **"Press Right/Left Arrow"** commands to move from one tab to another.

4. **Say,** "Press Alt C."

   This hotkey moves the cursor into the Category List.

5. **Select Currency on the Category list.**

   The **"Move Up/Down"** commands are the easiest way to select items on the list.

6. **Say,** "Press Enter."

   The Format Cells dialog box disappears, and the column is formatted as dollars and cents.

 If you are using Excel 2010 to perform the previous task, you would say, **"Click Number Format,"** then say, **"Show Choices"** and then say the format you want. Or you could use a Natural Language Command and simply say, **"Change That to Currency."**

Improving Your Vocal Functions

Spreadsheets have so many defined functions these days that nobody remembers exactly what their names are or what they do. (Remembering things is for people who *don't* have access to a computer.) All you have to do is pick the function out of a list (that the spreadsheet remembers for you) or add the function name to the Dragon Professional Individual vocabulary.

All the popular spreadsheets have a menu command that brings up a dialog box listing all the available functions. In Excel, the menu choice is Formula and it produces the Function Library ribbon.

To use this feature with Dragon Professional Individual, do the following:

1. **On the Excel Menu bar, choose formulas.**

   You see the icons of the functions available.

2. **Select the cell where the function belongs on your spreadsheet.**

3. **Say the category name of the function you want (for instance, "Math and Trig").**

   A list is displayed. Pick the function by saying its letters. When the Function Arguments box opens, the cursor is in the number box.

4. Say the number you want to insert.

5. Say, "Click Okay."

If you use the same function over and over again, you can introduce it into the Dragon Professional Individual vocabulary. For example, you could introduce the "word" STDEV into the vocabulary and train Dragon Professional Individual to recognize its spoken form, **"Standard Deviation Function."** Or you could give a function a pronunciation similar to its written form, like **"Tansh"** for the function TANH (for *tangent*) because it sounds like that. See Chapter 17 for details on how to implement vocabulary tricks like this.

In the formula section of Excel, TANH is the hyperbolic tangent of a number. If you aren't solving differential equations, you probably don't need to add this voice command.

Chapter 11

Using Recorded Speech

*T*hank Alexander Graham Bell. He's the guy who figured out that you don't have to be standing there talking to your transcriptionist. Nope. Instead, you can record stuff in the privacy of your own office and hand it off to your transcriptionist later. Of course, in Bell's day, people had to yell into a big horn and their words were recorded on a wax cylinder. But the idea was a good one: Record now, transcribe later.

The idea was so good that now you can use any number of wonderful gadgets to dictate into while you're on the go. This chapter deals solely with a voice recorder.

If you want to use Dragon Professional Individual with mobile devices such as the iPhone, iPad, iPod touch, or Android, see Chapter 14.

In this chapter, I explain what you need to know about setting up your equipment, speaking into a recorder, and having Dragon Professional Individual transcribe that recording. Also, new to Dragon Professional Individual is the ability to transcribe someone else's voice recording. This chapter covers that, too.

Why Record?

Perhaps the most attractive benefit of recording first and transcribing later is the same one that Alexander Graham Bell probably had in mind. I suspect that he had no desire to master the manual skill of typing, preferring to let his assistant Watson do that job. Likewise, you can simply dictate your text and then let your assistant (if you're lucky enough to have one) handle the transcription. That way, you never have to master the intricacies of Dragon Professional Individual itself. You still have to master the intricacies of using a recording device, however.

One of the nice things about recording on a portable recorder is that you can sit there talking into a little box in your hand (a recorder). It doesn't strain your eyes or cramp your fingers.

The second advantage of recording first and transcribing later is that, surprisingly, it's often more accurate! Because your recorder provides a digital audio file, Dragon Professional Individual's transcription doesn't have to keep up with your rate of speech. It can take its time and read your speech from the file at its own rate. As a result, it will be more accurate.

The disadvantage of recording first and then transcribing is that you don't get to correct Dragon Professional Individual on the fly. As a result, you may find that you have to make the same correction repeatedly throughout your document. Subsequent documents will, however, benefit from your corrections.

One fantasy to shoot down right now is the one in which you transcribe meetings using your recorder and Dragon Professional Individual. One problem is that Dragon Professional Individual has to be trained to each speaker's voice. What's more, the acoustic environment for meetings is invariably far too poor to get a decent recording from even one person. Besides, who really wants everything he said in a meeting to appear in a transcription?!

Setting Up to Use a Portable Recorder

Hopefully, if you already own a portable recorder — it will be good enough to work with Dragon Professional Individual. Nuance lists on its website (http://support.nuance.com/compatibility/default.asp) the categories of recorders that the company has tested with its products, as shown in Figure 11-1. In general, you need a good-quality recorder that outputs digital audio files. For serious remote dictation work, you want a recorder that enables you to store multiple separate recordings. Or do you feel lucky? You can try using your existing recorder and see how well it does.

You can improve the audio quality of some recorders by plugging a separate microphone into them. Look for a microphone jack on your recorder. Of course, a separate microphone often makes the recorder significantly less convenient and portable. "Stub" microphones (microphones on a short stalk) that do not make the recorder too unwieldy exist for this purpose. Check with a good audio equipment supplier.

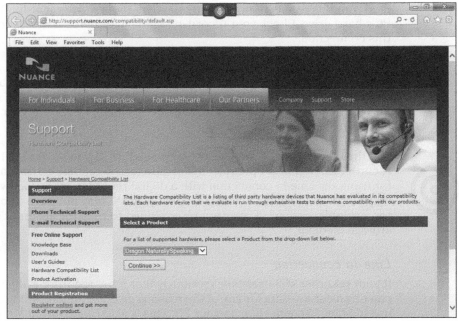

Figure 11-1:
Check the
Compatibil-
ity List on
the Nuance
website.

You have to do a few things before you can make remotely recorded dictation work, including the following:

✔ You must be able to make a physical connection between your recorder
and your PC. You can't just let the recorder play into the microphone.

✔ You must install any additional software required by your portable
recorder.

✔ You must train Dragon Professional Individual to recognize your voice
the way it sounds after being altered by the processes of recording and
transferring to your PC.

Figuring out your connection

To get started, you need a physical connection between the recorder and
your PC. If your recorder isn't digital, you'll have to use the Line-In connection discussed here.

Digital data transfer connection

Digital transfer most commonly takes place through a data cable, running
from a connector on a digital recorder to a connector (usually a USB) on your

PC. From this connection, you copy the data (your voice recording) to your PC's hard drive. Check your recorder's manual for details on how to make this connection.

Other possible ways to transfer digital data include a memory card that you remove from the recorder and place in a slot in your PC (or in a device connected to your PC). Check your PC's manual or your recorder's manual for instructions on copying the data from this memory card to your PC's hard drive.

Use the Line-In connection (see the next section), if you have a digital recorder but it doesn't provide digital data transfer. Some other reasons for using the Line-In connection with a digital recorder are as follows: You may not have the digital cable you need; your PC may not have a connector available; or your PC may not be equipped to read the recorder's digital storage medium.

Line-In connection

If your recorder still uses tape (seriously?) or if the recorder is digital but you can't transfer the data for any of the reasons given in the preceding section, use the Line-In connection on your PC. This is also called an _analog connection_ (as opposed to digital).

A Line-In connection requires a cable from the audio output jack (a round hole) of the recorder to the round Line-In jack on your PC. You can use this sort of connection with any recorder that has a Line-Out jack or a headphone jack (sometimes marked "ear" or "audio out"). If you use a stereo recorder for a Line-In connection, you need a special cable or adapter that creates a _monaural_ (single-channel) output.

To be able to create a User Profile from another audio source (your recorder), you must have Administrator privileges. If you are the licensed owner of the software, you likely also are the administrator.

Adding a dictation source to your current profile

Most people think their voice sounds pretty terrible after it has been passed through a recorder. So does Dragon Professional Individual. In fact, as far as Dragon Professional Individual is concerned, your voice is so different that it needs to train with the recorder to recognize it.

Just like the first time you used Dragon Professional Individual, you used the New User Wizard to set up Dragon Professional Individual. Additional training of Dragon Professional Individual to understand your recorded voice is just like training it for direct dictation, with one difference: You read the training material into your recorder, transfer the dictation to your PC, and then have Dragon Professional Individual transcribe it.

The process is as follows:

1. **Choose Profile ⇨ Manage Dictation Sources, as shown in Figure 11-2.**

   A window pops up and you see your current dictation sources.

Figure 11-2: Choose from the Profile menu.

2. **Choose Transcription source from the list as shown in Figure 11-3 and click Select.**

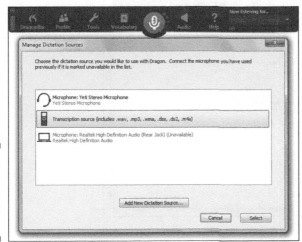

Figure 11-3: Pick the source from which you will dictate.

A screen pops up as shown in Figure 11-4 that says, "Choose a sample recording."

Figure 11-4:
Choose a
sample
recording.

3. **Click the Browse to Locate the File button to locate the file on your PC.** Find the file and choose it so that it appears in the window as shown in Figure 11-5.

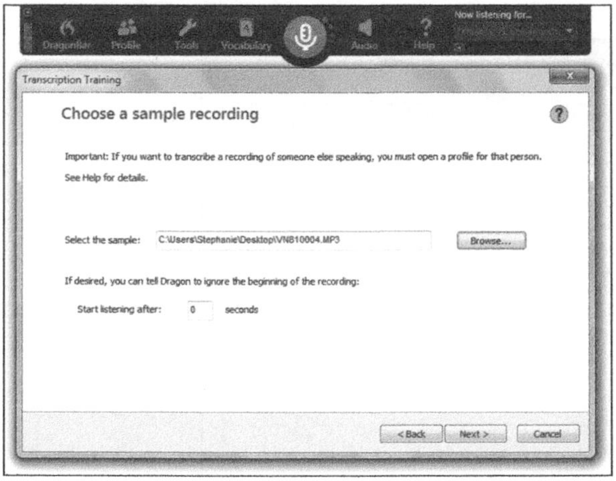

Figure 11-5:
Your file
name
appears in
the window.

4. **Click Next.**

You see a screen as shown in Figure 11-6 that says "Dragon is working on the sample recording."

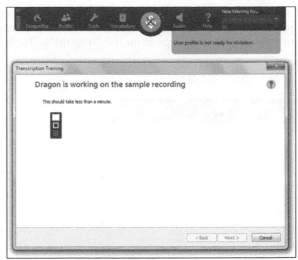

Figure 11-6:
Dragon is working on the sample recording.

5. **Click Next.**

A screen comes up as shown in Figure 11-7 that tells you that "Dragon is adapting the transcription source." (Note that the screen says there are 3 steps that it moves through.)

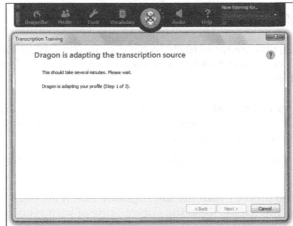

Figure 11-7:
Dragon is adapting the transcription source.

6. **Click Next.**

The training process can take several minutes, so be patient. It is recommended that you don't touch the computer keyboard or cursor until the training is complete. This gives you the opportunity to take some victory laps to refresh yourself.

When the training is complete, you see a congratulatory screen, as shown in Figure 11-8 that says "The transcription source is ready!" You can now transcribe your recordings from the DragonBar Tools menu.

7. Click Finish.

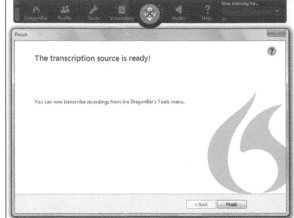

Figure 11-8: You're transcription source is ready to use.

Getting better sound quality from portable recorders

For lots of reasons, you are more likely to have sound quality problems when you use a mobile recorder than when you dictate into your PC. Here are six tips to avoid problems:

- ✔ **Avoid noisy environments.** Moving cars, traffic, machinery, wind, surf, weddings, car washes, rock concerts, or active airport runways can negatively impact sound quality and recognition.

- ✔ **Don't move your fingers around on your recorder while recording.** This causes noise.

- ✔ **Don't speak so directly into the microphone that it records puffs of breath when you speak.** Keep the microphone of your recorder off to one side of your mouth. Keep the microphone a constant distance from your mouth.

See if you can fit two fingers in between the microphone and your mouth.

✔ **Don't set your microphone's sensitivity higher than necessary.** If your recorder has different microphone sensitivity settings (or a microphone volume control), use the lowest sensitivity that still gives you a strong, clear recording. (Too high a sensitivity picks up background noise and sometimes distorts your voice.)

✔ **Choose the recorder's highest quality setting.** Make sure your recorder is set for the highest quality of recording, if it offers different quality levels. Check your recorder's instructions. Highest quality usually comes at the expense of maximum recording time, so choose the setting that gives the shortest recording time if quality level isn't an option.

✔ **Train in the environment in which you'll be dictating.** That way, Dragon knows what to expect. If you train in a quiet room and dictate in a coffee shop, the accuracy will be dismal.

Recording Your Dictation

When you record text for Dragon Professional Individual to transcribe, speak that text just as if you were dictating into Dragon Professional Individual directly. Chapter 4 tells you how to do it.

Certain aspects of recording, however, make that process a little different from dictating directly to Dragon Professional Individual. Using commands, for instance, is tricky because you can't see the transcription in progress. In addition, dictating into a portable recorder introduces some new issues that affect sound quality. The best thing to do is to limit your voice commands to dictation commands.

Because you can't see the result of Dragon Professional Individual's transcription as you dictate, using certain commands in recorded speech is risky. Dragon Professional Individual might, for instance, edit or delete the wrong text in response to a command. You wouldn't know that until you see your text on the screen.

Because of that risk, Dragon Professional Individual ignores most editing commands it encounters while transcribing your recording. Dragon Professional Individual does, however, accept dictation commands in your recorded text — the ones that control capitals and spaces. The safest procedure is to use commands that apply only to your next spoken word, such as **"Cap <*word*>."** Even though Dragon Professional Individual allows you to use the dictation commands that turn something "on," such as **"Caps On,"** Dragon Professional Individual may occasionally miss the concluding **"Caps Off"** or other **"Off"** command. You may end up making more work for yourself (or whoever does the final cleanup) by using those on/off commands.

Following are some of the commands that, in addition to punctuation, I think work most reliably in recorded speech:

- ✔ "**All Caps** *<word>*"
- ✔ "**Cap** *<word>*"
- ✔ "**New Line**"
- ✔ "**New Paragraph**"
- ✔ "**No Caps** *<word>*"
- ✔ "**No Space** *<word>*"
- ✔ "**Spacebar**"
- ✔ "**Tab Key**"

You can also use **"Scratch That"** (which deletes back to the last time you paused) if you make a mistake. Use it only if you're sure when you last paused, or you'll delete more or less than you intended! You can repeat the **"Scratch That"** command to back up through multiple pauses if your memory for pauses is very good.

To avoid having to remember your pauses, a better command for amending recorded dictation is **"Resume With *<word>*."** This command enables you to back up to a specific word within the last 100 characters and then dictate new text beginning from that point. (Of course, it only works if Dragon Professional Individual got your word right in the first place!)

See Chapter 4 for more about **"Scratch That"** and **"Resume With."** Both commands are allowed when you transcribe from a recording. They are called the "restricted command set."

Transferring Files from a Digital Recorder

When you use your recorder, you need instructions from the manufacturer for transferring audio files to your PC. It may have its own program for handling file transfers that you need to install on your PC. Check your recorder manual for instructions.

Where on your PC's hard drive should you put the digital audio files from your recorder? You can put them anywhere. If you have a digital recorder but it doesn't offer digital output or you do not have the necessary cable or software to make a digital transfer, you may be able to make an analog connection instead. See "Figuring out your connection," earlier in this chapter. Take your recorder to an electronics store and ask for a cable to connect its audio output jack to a PC's audio line-in jack.

Transcribing Your Recording

Watching Dragon Professional Individual transcribe a recording is somewhat magical. You sit there and your words (or something like them) appear on the screen.

How does it work? Dragon Professional Individual transcribes recorded speech from a sound file (a file with a .wav extension or a WMA, MP3, DSS, M4A, or DS2 format), created by a digital recorder, which you have stored on your PC's hard drive. (Oh, you haven't? See "Transferring Files from a Digital Recorder," earlier in this chapter.)

To transcribe a recording from a portable recorder, Dragon Professional Individual must be set up with a special additional source User Profile specifically trained to handle recorded speech from that recorder. (See the earlier section, "Setting Up to Use a Portable Recorder.") You don't need to choose a special user to transcribe files from the Dragon Professional Individual Sound Recorder (assuming the files were created on your PC); use the same user that you use for dictating directly to Dragon Professional Individual.

Launch Dragon Professional Individual if you haven't already, and take the following steps to transcribe:

1. **Click Profile⇨Manage Dictation Source and select the Digital Recorder source you previously created.**

   The source you created for transcribing from a recorder loads.

   If the microphone in the DragonBar is red, your headset dictation source is loaded. If the microphone is gray with an X, you already have your recorder source open.

   Make sure to change to the recorder source before moving to the next step to avoid negatively impacting your dictation source data, because you sound different when using the recorder.

   If your portable recorder uses the analog (Line-In) connection, Dragon Professional Individual will expect a certain volume from your recorder. When you transcribe text, either make sure the volume is set to the same level you used for training or run the microphone check again at this point. To run the training, choose Audio⇨Read Text to Improve Accuracy and choose the Adjust Volume Only selection.

2. In Dragon Professional Individual, choose Tools⇨Transcribe Recording as shown in Figure 11-9.

Figure 11-9:
Choose transcribe recording.

A "Transcribe a spoken recording" screen opens and asks you to select where Dragon Professional Individual can find the audio file you want to transcribe, as shown in Figure 11-10.

Figure 11-10:
Select the source of the file to transcribe.

3. Type in the file name or click the Browse to Locate File button to select the file you want to transcribe from your hard drive, as shown in Figure 11-11.

4. Click the Transcribe button.

The DragonPad begins transcribing. When it's completed a screen pops up and says your transcription is complete as shown in Figure 11-12.

5. Choose the radio button of the format to which you want to output your transcription.

6. Click Done.

Figure 11-11: Select the source of the file to transcribe.

Figure 11-12: Your transcription is complete.

Correcting Your Transcription

It's kind of exciting to watch as your words print magically on the screen. The hitch comes when you spot errors. Just like regular dictation, you need to proofread and correct your errors.

To proofread, I recommend that you transcribe into the DragonPad or your word processor and use the capability to play back your own voice if you are unsure about what you actually said. Here's a method you can use:

1. **Begin reading your text. If you spot an error, you can say,** "Select *<text>*" **and then,** "Correct That."

   The Correction menu pops up just as it does for your regular dictation. Choose the correct number of the correct version or say, **"Spell That"** and correct it that way.

2. Use Playback when you spot an error by selecting the incorrect passage and right-clicking. Choose Play That Back from the list of options, as shown in Figure 11-13.

You can alternate methods until you have corrected the entire transcription.

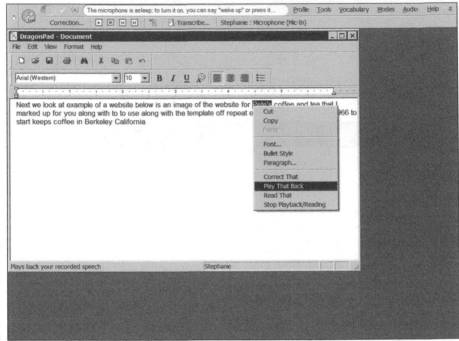

Figure 11-13: Right-click to see your transcription options.

Correct Dragon's mistakes, not yours. If you hear yourself say something incorrect and Dragon Professional Individual transcribes it, just go over it and correct it. Dragon didn't make a mistake, so it doesn't need to be corrected. (Yes, this is an operator error, not a software error! And for the record, it happens to the best of us!)

Are you lucky enough to have a staff member or other willing participant who will transcribe your recording for you? Make sure that individual transfers your User Profile to his PC before he begins. If he doesn't have your User Profile on his computer, the audio won't be recognized properly. (Of course, your faithful human transcriber also has to own Dragon Professional Individual software to hear your voice when playing it back.)

Transcribing Someone Else's Voice Recording

A great new feature in Dragon Professional Individual is the ability to transcribe a recording of someone else's voice. This is something that many users have been waiting for, and now it's here.

Imagine that you attend a training session and record the trainer's voice. You can take that recording and let Dragon Professional Individual transcribe it for you. That's very nice of your Dragon assistant to do the extra work!

Here's how to do it:

1. **In Dragon Professional Individual, click Profile ⇨ New User Profile on the DragonBar and click the New button.**

   Type in a name for that profile.

2. **Click Next and choose your speech options.**

   A screen pops up, and you are asked to select your region and your accent from the drop-down boxes, as shown in Figure 11-14.

Figure 11-14: Select your speech options.

3. **Click Next.**

   You are asked to choose an audio device, as shown in Figure 11-15.

4. **Choose Transcription source as the audio device and click Next.**

   A screen pops up and asks you to choose a sample recording, as shown in Figure 11-16. Type in or browse to the location and filename of the recording.

Figure 11-15:
Choose an
audio
device.

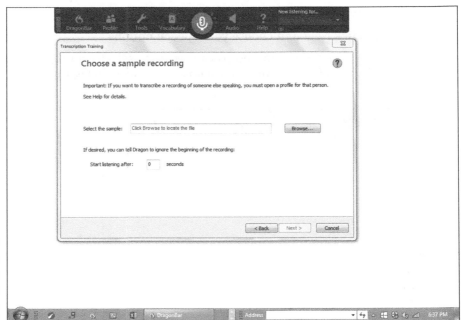

Figure 11-16:
Choose a
sample
recording.

5. Click Next.

Wait for the transcription sample to be completed. A dialog box pops up, showing you the results. Make corrections if necessary.

6. Click Next.

Wait for the configuration to be completed.

7. Click Finish.

Part III

Communicating Online

In this part . . .

- Sending and receiving email with your voice saves time. If you use Outlook, I show you how to do all your daily chores quickly, including adding appointments.

- You can launch and surf with your favorite browser. You'll learn how to work the web and use shortcuts to navigate.

- You're never without your mobile device. Discover how easy it is to dictate into mobile devices to send emails and find new locations to eat or shop.

Chapter 12

Sending and Receiving Email

*U*sing Dragon Professional Individual to command your email application is an effective way to be more productive. Nuance has made email sending a priority. Several voice commands help you get things done faster. Programs like Outlook work with some Natural Language Commands. They're easy to learn and well supported.

This chapter delves into four email programs: Outlook, Outlook.com, Thunderbird, and Gmail. If your preferred email program isn't on my list, it may work with some common commands. Try them. Now, just dive right in and start e-communicating, the Dragon Professional Individual way!

For more on web browsers, see Chapter 13 to learn about installing and enabling the Dragon Web Extension when you are using Internet Explorer, Firefox, and Chrome.

Creating and Managing Emails

As you contemplate using Dragon Professional Individual to send your emails, keep in mind these general recommendations that apply to most email programs:

✔ **Check your previous emails.** Make sure you let Dragon Professional Individual look at your previously sent emails before you send your next new email. You want to give your Dragon Professional Individual assistant a proper orientation, don't you? Your Dragon Professional Individual assistant looks at your email files to familiarize itself with email addresses. To run this process, choose Vocabulary⇨Learn from Sent Emails on the DragonBar to enable Dragon Professional Individual to look at them. See Chapter 17 for more information.

✔ **Use the Dictation Box.** If you have trouble dictating into your email program, use the Dictation Box and then transfer the dictation back into the email window. With your email program open, access the Dictation Box by choosing Tools⇨Dictation Box on the DragonBar or by saying, **"Show Dictation Box."** See Chapter 8 for more information on the Dictation Box.

✔ **Know common email commands.** Several commands work with most email programs. Familiarize yourself with them before you start. Check the Command Browser to see what other commands you can use. To do this, go to Tools⇨Command Browser and use the Context drop-down menu to access specific program commands. Many commands are specific to Microsoft Outlook.

✔ **Use the Help files.** You can always get immediate help while you dictate your emails. Say, **"What can I say?"** to bring up hints on the spot. You can also say, **"Give me help."** There is no need to become frustrated trying to think of the right commands when help is almost literally on the tip of your tongue.

✔ **Format email addresses.** You can make choices about how your email and web addresses are formatted. Go to Tools⇨Auto-Formatting Options on the DragonBar and choose your preferences. Read more information about this in Chapter 17.

✔ **Add email addresses.** If you frequently use a particular email or web address, you can add it to your vocabulary like you do other "non-words." Otherwise, you can say an address, such as *person@company. com,* much like you would in conversation. Make sure everything is lowercase by saying, **"No Caps On,"** and then say the email address. Then say, **"No Caps Off."** For the address itself (*person@company.com,* for instance), say, **"<*person's name*> at company dot com."**

✔ **Say web addresses.** Speak a web address in the form, **"w w w dot company dot com."** For a full address (such as http://www.*company*.com) say, **"h t t p w w w dot company dot com."** Don't mention the colon or slashes. Dragon Professional Individual adds the colon and slashes and recognizes the terms *com, gov, mil, net, org,* and *sys* just as you normally say them. If you prefer, you can verbally spell those terms letter by letter. Table 12-1 shows the Dragon Professional Individual commands that are generally used for email applications.

Dragon Professional Individual works with Internet Explorer, Google Chrome, and Mozilla Firefox when you use a browser with your email application.

If Dragon Professional Individual insists on capitalizing the *www* portion of a web address, correct the capitalization by using the Correction dialog box. (Dragon Professional Individual has an obsession about capitalizing initials.) Or say, **"No Caps,"** then, without pausing, speak the address. To absolutely, completely suppress all capitals within the address, say, **"No Caps On No Caps w w w dot whatever dot com No Caps Off."**

Table 12-1	Dragon Professional Individual Commands for Email Applications
To Do This	*Say This*
Launch <*program name*>.	**"Start Microsoft Outlook."**
Open your inbox.	**"Go To Inbox."**
Look at new mail.	**"Check For New Mail."**
Move to next email.	**"View Next Unread Message."**
Send email.	**"Send Message."**
Close email.	**"Close All Items."**
Mark message to follow up.	**"Flag This (or That or It) For Follow-Up."**
Open with email address.	**"Send Email To <*person's name*>."**
Add a file(s) to email.	**"Attach A File."**
Launch spell check.	**"Check Spelling."**
Print email.	**"Print Mail."**
Reply to everyone in message list.	**"Reply To All."**

You can substitute **"Message"** or **"Email"** for the word **"Mail."**

Interacting with Microsoft Outlook

Microsoft Outlook is the most widely used business email client. When used in combination with Dragon Professional Individual, it is a Full Text Control application that also provides some Natural Language Commands. Outlook keeps track of your personal information — at least appointments, addresses, and the like. Because of its extensive use in business organizations, I focus on several specifics that make using Outlook easier.

Outlook has a good collection of hotkeys that enable you to access features with the **"Press *<hotkey>*"** voice command. To see a list of Outlook's hotkeys, look in Outlook's Help Index under *keyboard shortcuts* for your version of Outlook.

Using the three-panel email application window

Outlook uses the basic three-panel window arrangement:

- ✔ **The folder list:** A vertical pane on the left displaying message folders or mailboxes.

- ✔ **The message list:** A horizontal pane in the upper-right corner that lists the messages contained in the selected message folder.

- ✔ **The reading pane:** A horizontal pane in the lower-left corner displaying the contents of the selected message.

Move from one pane to another by pressing the Tab key or saying, **"Press Tab."** Move in the opposite direction with Shift+Tab.

Like Microsoft Windows 7 and 8 and 10, Outlook 2010 and 2013 displays the Ribbon and the Office button. Use the cursor to mouse over the menu items to see what they are called. Then you can select them by saying, **"Click *<name of menu>*."** (See Chapter 15 for more about controlling and navigating in Windows 7.)

The folder list

The folder list in an email application behaves like the folder list in Windows Explorer. (See Chapter 15.) When the cursor is in this pane, use the **"Move Up/Down"** commands to select a folder or mailbox. For example, **"Move Down Five"** selects the folder or mailbox five places below the currently selected folder or mailbox. Folders that contain subfolders or mailboxes have a +/– check box next to their folder icons. To display the subfolders or mailboxes, select the containing folder and say, **"Press Right Arrow."** To hide the subfolders or mailboxes, say, **"Press Left Arrow."**

The message list

The message list is, first and foremost, a list. When the cursor is in the message list pane of the email application window, select messages in the list by using the **"Move Up/Down"** commands. To select the message three places above the currently selected message, say, **"Move Up Three."**

Reading messages

You can read a message in the reading pane of the application window, or you can get a little more reading room by opening a message window. Open a message window in Messenger by selecting a message in the message list and choosing File ⇨ Open from the menu. (Alternatively, you can say, **"Open Mail Message"** or **"Open Message."**)

Whether the cursor is in the reading window or in a message window, the **"Move"** and **"Go"** commands move the cursor through the message. However, the most useful command when you're reading a message is **"Press Page Down."** It displays the next window of text.

Switching between open mailboxes and messages

Say, **"Press Alt Tab"** to cycle through the items on the taskbar. Switch to a new mailbox by selecting it in the folder list. You can also say, **"List All Windows"** or **"List Applications"** to see what's open and select it from there.

Dictating messages

You can use some Natural Language Commands with Outlook just like when you dictate text into a word processor (see Chapter 9). In Outlook, a message composition window consists of a number of textboxes: several one-line boxes corresponding to the various parts of a message header, and one large textbox for the body of the message.

Move the cursor from one textbox to another by using the Tab key or saying, **"Press Tab."** Move in the opposite direction with Shift+Tab. You can also use the name of the field you want to access. To send your first email, launch Dragon Professional Individual and do the following:

1. **Say,** "Send Email to George Foster."

   Outlook (if it's your default email program) opens a new email form and inserts the name George Foster into the 'To' field. When you send the email, Outlook will automatically check that name against your contacts and associate the right email address to the name. If you want to check and make sure before you send the email, just say, **"Check names."**

2. **Say,** "Go to Subject."

   The cursor moves to the Subject field.

3. **Dictate your email subject.**

4. **Say,** "Body Field."

   The cursor is now in the body of the email and ready for you to dictate your complete message.

5. **Dictate your email.**

6. **Proofread your email.**

   If you find mistakes, select and correct them as you would in any other dictation process. (See Chapter 5 for more on quick correction of dictation.)

7. **After you correct all mistakes, say,** "Send Message" **or** "Click Send."

   Your message is sent. You can now move on to reading or sending other emails.

Getting your mail read to you

Your Dragon Professional Individual assistant can read your email to you. Isn't that what you'd expect from a first-rate assistant? Use the text-to-speech feature to do this. Select the text you wish read to you and say, **"Read That."** The text will be read back to you in the voice you have chosen from the options available to you. If you want to modify the voice of your assistant, go to Tools ⇨ Options ⇨ Playback/Text-to-Speech and look at the Text-to-Speech attributes. Where you see Voice, use the drop-down list to choose either American English Samantha or British English Serena.

If for any reason your application doesn't work that way, just copy the text of the message from the reading pane of your email application into the Dragon Professional Individual Dictation Box and say, **"Read Document."** The Dragon Professional Individual voice and diction won't compete with James Earl Jones's voice, but you will understand what it is saying.

Keeping track of appointments

After you send an email, you don't need to stop using voice commands in Outlook. You can schedule appointments through Outlook's Calendar window. Bring up the Calendar window (shown in Figure 12-1) by saying, **"Create a New Appointment."** Opening the Calendar window adds the Calendar menu to the menu bar. Use this menu for all of your calendar-related activities. To create a new appointment in Outlook, do the following:

1. **Make sure Dragon Professional Individual is running and say,** "Create a New Appointment."

   The Outlook Appointment Form opens and the cursor is positioned in the Subject field.

2. **Dictate your subject.**

3. **Say,** "Move to Location" **to go to the location field and dictate your location.**

4. **Say,** "Go to Start Time" **and dictate the date.**

5. **Move to time fields by saying,** "Press Tab" **and add the times.**

6. **Say,** "Move to Body Field" **and dictate details.**

   Complete your message.

7. **Say,** "Save and Close."

8. **To check if the appointment is there, say,** "Switch to the Calendar Folder" **to view it.**

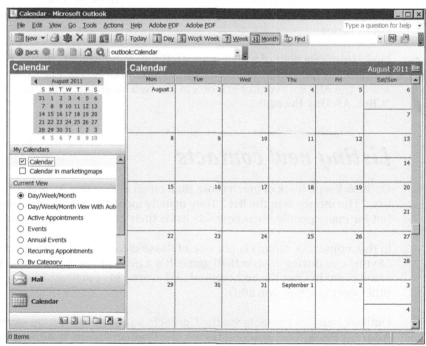

Figure 12-1:
Outlook's
Calendar
utility helps
you keep
track of your
appoint-
ments.

Six additional common commands you can use with Outlook appointments are as follows:

- ✔ **"Show Date"**
- ✔ **"View Month"**
- ✔ **"Invite Attendees"**
- ✔ **"Cancel Invitation"**
- ✔ **"Create a Meeting About <xyz>"**
- ✔ **"Create an Appointment on <date>, <time> <am/pm>"**

Outlook Tasks are visible in the Calendar window, but they are most easily added and deleted using the Task window. To open the Task window, say, **"Open, Tasks."** Opening the Task window adds the Task menu to the menu bar. To add a new task, say, **"New Task."**

Whether you add an appointment or a task, a dialog box with a number of fields to be filled in confronts you. When the cursor is in a textbox, you can dictate just as you would dictate into a word processor. Don't be afraid to use those Full Text Control capabilities (see Chapter 8) to edit or correct your entries.

Move from one field of a dialog box to the next by saying, **"Press Tab,"** or jump to any field you want by using the field's name. For example, in order to select the All Day Event check box in the New Appointment dialog box, say, **"Click All Day Event."**

Listing new contacts

Outlook keeps track of much more than email addresses. As marketers like to say, "The money is in the list." They usually mean your customer mailing list — but for many people, their contacts list *is* their customer mailing list.

In this context, a *contact* is not one of those clear round things that falls out of your eye during a basketball game. It's a person you have contacted at some point in your life and created and stored his email address (plus any other optional info you add).

Outlook handles contacts via the Contacts window. Open it by saying, **"View Address Book."** As an added bonus, the Contacts menu is appended to the menu bar. Anything you want to do with your contacts list is handled by this menu. For example, to add a new contact, say, **"Create New Contact."** Outlook responds by displaying the New Contact dialog box, shown in Figure 12-2.

The New Contact window looks intimidating because it contains spaces for
everything you may know about a person other than hat size. Nevertheless,
the only field you have to fill out is Name. Other than that, you can skip
around, using the hotkeys to pick other fields to fill. For example, to skip
to the Web Page textbox, say, **"Press Alt W."** The New Contact window
begins with the General tab on top. To switch to another tab, say, **"Press
Control Tab."**

Making notes

Outlook Notes is a great place to jot down important things you don't want
to forget. It works well with Dragon Professional Individual because its main
purpose is dictation, just like any word processor. If you want to dictate
notes in Outlook, make sure that Dragon Professional Individual is running
and then do the following:

1. **Say,** "Start Microsoft Outlook."

   The Outlook application opens.

2. **Say,** "Open Notes."

3. **Say,** "New Note."

   A note opens for you to dictate into.

4. **Dictate your note.**

   After you dictate the note, proofread it for mistakes and make corrections as you would with any other type of dictation.

5. **Say,** "Save The Note."

6. **Say,** "Close The Note."

   If you want to view your note, say, **"Click Notes List"** to select the radio button and view your missive.

Easy, huh? If you like to create sticky-note reminders, this is much quicker (and neater and environmentally friendly and cheaper, but I digress!). Instead of sticking notes on your screen, use this.

Enhancing Email

Dragon Professional Individual plays nicely with Outlook. You also get some additional commands for Outlook.com, Thunderbird, and Gmail. If you use these email applications, you'll be happy to know that voice commands are an option for them, too.

Aggregating email accounts with Thunderbird

If you use Thunderbird, Mozilla Foundation's free email client, you know that it's an open source application and works cross-platform. This means that it is created by developers who donate their time and share code. It can be used with Windows, Mac, or Linux.

If you haven't used Thunderbird, consider it if you want to aggregate emails across several email accounts. Thunderbird doesn't send email on its own. It lets you combine your accounts and work from one main source. It has several add-ons and lets you configure your email account in a way that makes sense for you.

After you set up and open Thunderbird, you notice that it looks like most other email clients. It uses the three-panel window configuration: the folder list, a message list, and a reading pane.

You will find that using Thunderbird is like using the DragonPad. If you can navigate that, you already know how to navigate Thunderbird. Thunderbird acts like a Full Text Control application. You can navigate by saying the menu and submenu names. You can use voice commands for each one by saying **"Click"** and then the menu name. For example you can say the following as you follow along the top menu:

- ✔ **"Click Get Mail"**
- ✔ **"Click Write"**
- ✔ **"Click Chat"**

When writing emails, you say, **"Go to the Address Book and Pick a Name."** Then you say, **"Go to Subject,"** and dictate the subject. Then you dictate the body of the message by saying, **"Move to Message Field."**

Choosing Gmail

In Dragon Professional Individual, Gmail can be used with the following browsers:

- ✔ Internet Explorer version 9, 10, 11 (32-bit or 64 bit)
- ✔ Mozilla Firefox, latest version
- ✔ Google Chrome, latest version

Gmail, like Thunderbird, is another Full Text Control application that doesn't work with Natural Language Commands. But it gets the job done, and if Gmail is your application of choice, fear not. It can work for you.

One secret to using Gmail with Dragon Professional Individual is to use the **"Click"** command. Doing so enables you to manage email tasks quickly. For example, you can say, **"Click Reply," "Click Delete,"** or **"Click Report Spam."**

The Gmail program doesn't have a reading pane, but closely follows the other structures of other email programs. To send mail in Gmail after launching Dragon Professional Individual and your Gmail window, follow these steps:

1. **Say,** "Click Compose Mail."

   The email window opens with the cursor in the address box.

2. **Dictate the address and then say,** "Move to Next Field."

   Move through the subject field the same way.

3. **Dictate your email.**

4. **Say,** "Click Send."

Chapter 13

Working the Web

*W*ord processing may be the most obvious application of speech recognition, but it isn't the only one. Gadgets like smartphones and iPads factor heavily into the equation, too. If you're like me, you spend more time than you care to admit on the web — browsing, tweeting, exchanging email, and trying out new apps.

Dragon Professional Individual command shortcuts for searching and dictating online are easy. The menu commands of the email and browser applications provide all the specialized commands you need, and the rest is basically just word processing and window management. Nonetheless, in this chapter, I assemble a few tricks worth knowing.

Browsing the Web

Using Dragon Professional Individual with Internet Explorer, (IE 9 or higher), or current versions of Mozilla Firefox and Google Chrome, lets you do your entire web browsing by voice, efficiently, without having to touch a mouse or keyboard. Of course, you can use them if you want — do whatever is most comfortable for you.

For use with Dragon Professional Individual, an extension is available, called the Dragon Web extension. This extension enables the browsers previously mentioned to have more complete web application support.

You will know if the extension is enabled in that version of the browser by clicking the gear icon and choosing Manage Add-ons. If you see the extension listed (Dragon Web Extension) and enabled, you can proceed.

Some features may not be available in your browser of choice. You need to experiment to see whether one that you want to use is available.

Getting started

To start browsing the web, follow these steps:

1. **Start Dragon Professional Individual.**

2. **Start Internet Explorer.**

   It doesn't matter how you start Internet Explorer. You can start it with the **"Start"** command by saying, **"Start Internet Explorer,"** by selecting a Favorite from the Start menu (not in Windows 8), or by clicking its desktop icon with the mouse. The first time you access IE after you install Dragon Professional Individual, a window pops up asking you if you want to enable Dragon in Internet Explorer. Click Proceed and follow the instructions.

That's all there is to it. Your browser opens and is immediately ready to take your commands.

Choosing Firefox or Chrome as your browser

If you enjoy using Firefox or Chrome over Internet Explorer, the Nuance folks serve you well. Dragon Professional Individual works equally well with Firefox and Chrome, so you can just select links by saying them in that browser instead of IE. If you want to use Firefox with Dragon Professional Individual, you can do it without much of a learning curve. Just remember the following when using Firefox:

✔ **Make sure Firefox is pinned to the Start menu, so that you choose Firefox from there if that's the way you prefer to launch it.**

✔ **As an alternative launch method, say,** "Open Firefox," "Launch Firefox," **or** "Show Firefox" **to launch it.**

✔ **Say,** "Go To The Address Field" **when you want to get to the address box.**

To install the extension for Firefox, the method is the same as for IE. You see the pop-up window asking whether you want to enable Dragon in Firefox and you click Proceed and follow the directions.

If you want to search something directly, use the shortcut examples in the "Using shortcuts created for the web" section later in this chapter.

To install the extension for Chrome, you will see the same pop-up window asking you to install the extension. When you click proceed, you see a screen from the Chrome web store. Just click the plus (+) sign and then click Add.

That's it. You're on your way and using the browser of your choice.

One reason people started using Firefox or Chrome was because they enjoyed using multiple tabs. You can use the following voice commands with Firefox or Chrome tabs:

✔ **"Add A New Tab"**

✔ **"Open A New Tab"**

✔ **"Click The Next Tab"**

✔ **"Click The Previous Tab"**

✔ **"Go To The Next Tab"**

✔ **"Go To The Previous Tab"**

✔ **"Close Tab"**

Giving orders to Internet Explorer

You can give Internet Explorer its marching orders in several ways:

✔ **Natural Language commands:** See Chapter 9 for a discussion of Natural Language.

✔ **Keyboard commands:** See Chapter 8 for a discussion of levels of control.

✔ **Menu commands:** See Chapter 15.

As mentioned in Chapter 3, Dragon Professional Individual enables you to have more control over when you need to say **"Click"** when issuing commands. This is particularly important with web browsing. To see what you have your commands set at now, go to Tools ⇨ Options ⇨ Commands.

See the check boxes that say: Require Click to Select Hyperlinks in HTML Windows, Require Click to Select Menus, and Require Click to Select Buttons and Other Controls, and see what your settings are. If you want to say **"Click"** with web browser commands, then leave them selected. If not, deselect them. As you go through the commands in the rest of the chapter, say **"Click"** before each command if you have them selected.

In addition, you can use the same **"Move"** and **"Go"** commands that work in the Dragon Professional Individual DragonPad, like **"Go To Top/Bottom"** or **"Move Down Three Paragraphs."** You can also use the mouse voice commands (see Chapter 15) to click toolbar buttons or links on web pages, but usually one of the other techniques achieves the same result more easily. Table 13-1 shows how to replace the Internet Explorer toolbar buttons with Natural Language, menu, or keyboard voice commands.

Table 13-1		Substitutions for the Toolbar Buttons	
Toolbar Button	*Voice Command*	*Menu*	*Key Combination*
Back	**"Go Back"**	Choose View ⇨ Go To ⇨ Back	Press Alt + Left Arrow
Forward	**"Go Forward"**	Choose View ⇨ Go To ⇨ Forward	Press Alt + Right Arrow
Stop	**"Stop Loading"**	Choose View ⇨ Stop	Press Escape
Refresh	**"Refresh"**	Choose View ⇨ Refresh	Press F5
Home	**"Go Home"**	Choose View ⇨ Go To ⇨ Home Page	Press Alt + Home
Search	none	Choose View ⇨ Explorer Bar ⇨ Search	Press Ctrl + E
Favorites	none	Choose View ⇨ Explorer Bar ⇨ Favorites	Press Ctrl + I
History	none	Choose View ⇨ Explorer Bar ⇨ History	Press Ctrl + H
Mail	none	Choose Tools ⇨ Mail and News	none
Print	none	Choose File ⇨ Print	Press Ctrl + P
Edit	none	Choose File ⇨ Edit	none

Going Places on the Web

Web browsers provide multiple ways to open a web page or move from one web page to another. Your home page opens when you start Internet Explorer (unless you start it by selecting an entry from the Start➪Internet Explorer➪Favorites menu). From there, you can move around on the web by choosing links; clicking toolbar buttons (refer to Table 13-1 for menu and keyboard equivalents); entering a web address into the Address box; or jumping to a page for which you have stored its location on the Favorites menu.

Linking from one web page to another

One useful feature you can use while browsing is the capability to click a link on a web page by saying all or part of its text label. For example, suppose that you are viewing the web page shown in Figure 13-1, the "What's next" page of the Nuance blog, and you want to click the link labeled Connected Living. All you have to do is say, **"Click Connected Living."** IE searches the links visible in the Internet Explorer window to see if any of them contain that text. Because one and only one such link appears on the page in Figure 13-1, the linked page is chosen.

Link

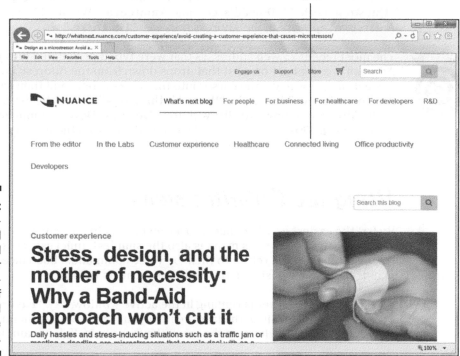

Figure 13-1:
Dragon Professional Individual checks for the occurrence of Connected Living on the page.

Pick whatever part of the link's text label is easiest to say.

If the link is an image, say, **"Image."** Dragon Professional Individual selects all the images visible in your viewing window and numbers them. Then simply choose the number of the image you want by saying, **"Choose <*image number*>."** If you know the text label of the image (it is displayed while the image loads), select it by name, just as you would any text link.

When you're clicking links that have the same words in them (for example, "Learn more") you will find that Dragon places a green number to show you its selections. Choose the number that corresponds to the one you want. It works the same way as your Correction menu does by giving you numbered choices.

Dictating to the Address box

The Address box is the textbox at the bottom of the browser's toolbar, the one that shows the web address of the current page. Say, **"Go To Address"** to move the cursor into the Address box. Then dictate the address you want and say, **"Go There."**

You can start a web search by dictating, **"Question mark <*search terms*>"** into the Address box and then saying, **"Go There."** For example, if you are looking for articles about McDonald's franchises in Antarctica, say, **"Question mark, McDonald's, comma, Antarctica."** When "?McDonald's, Antarctica" appears in the Address box, say, **"Go There."**

The most recent 25 web addresses that were typed or dictated into your Address box are kept on a list that drops down from the Address box. To make it drop down, get the cursor into the Address box, and then say, **"Press Alt Down Arrow."** Naturally, **"Press Alt Up Arrow"** makes the list retract again. Move up or down the list with the **"Move Up/Down"** commands, like **"Move Down Three."** After you select an address from the list, say, **"Press Enter"** to tell your browser to go there.

Using the Favorites menu

By far, the easiest way to connect to a web page is to store its location on the Favorites menu. Using this menu is also the simplest, quickest way to keep track of websites and return to them by voice commands. Use voice commands to go to a website on the Favorites menu as follows:

✔ If Internet Explorer is running in the active window, say, **"Favorites,"** then say the name of the favorite item you want from the menu. It doesn't matter where on the menu the favorite is. If, for example, you have a favorite called CNN in a folder called News Sites on the Favorites menu, you just have to say, **"Favorites,"** then say, **"CNN."** You don't have to say the name of the News Sites folder.

✔ Use the Favorites menu on the Internet Explorer menu bar, just as you use Start ⇨ Internet Explorer from the menu. If Internet Explorer is the active window, say, **"Click Favorites, News Sites, CNN."**

When you are at a site or page that you want to bookmark in your Favorites menu, say **"Add To Favorites,"** and it will be placed on that menu list.

When you create favorites, give them short names that are easy for you to pronounce and easy for Dragon Professional Individual to recognize. If the names of the favorites you already have are too long or too difficult, you can change them. Follow these steps:

1. **Open Internet Explorer.**

   Don't select the favorite itself, because you don't want to open it right now. In the CNN example earlier in this section, you would say, **"Click Start, Favorites, News Sites."** The menu expands so that you can see the CNN favorite, but it is not selected.

2. **Use the Move Up/Down commands to highlight the favorite.**

   If CNN is the fifth entry in the News Sites folder, say, **"Move Down Five."**

3. **Say,** "Right Click, Rename."

   A Rename dialog box appears.

4. **Dictate the new name.**

5. **Say,** "Click OK."

Pinning websites or pages to the Start menu

If you are using Internet Explorer or Firefox and running Dragon Professional Individual, you can use voice commands to pin shortcuts to the Start menu. This is an added benefit when you are working quickly and want to grab something to look at later. A simple voice command will capture it. To pin it, do the following:

1. **Say,** "Pin this *<web page or website>* to the Start menu."

   You will see a dialog box with the web address (also known as One Box).

2. **If you want to edit the box, say,** "Go To The One Box," **and edit accordingly.**

3. **To finish say,** "Click."

Moving around a Web Page

Dragon Professional Individual has an automatic scrolling feature that I find very convenient for reading long articles. Just say, **"Start Scrolling Down,"** and the text of the current web page starts moving up your screen like the credits at the end of a movie. Adjust the scrolling speed by saying, **"Speed Up"** or **"Slow Down."** (I love it — no computerese nonsense like, "Set Scrolling Speed Up Five," or something equally obscure.) The **"Stop Scrolling"** command (and I bet you already figured this out) stops the scrolling. To go backward, say, **"Start Scrolling Up."**

If automatic scrolling makes you feel like you're in a speed-reading test, you have other options for moving through a web page. Perhaps you are accustomed to using the scroll bar on the right edge of your browser's window to move through a web page. As always, mouse-oriented techniques don't translate to speech as well as keyboard-oriented techniques do. The simplest way to scroll through a web page by voice is to say, **"Press Page Down"** when you want to display the next screen's text.

The **"Move"** and **"Go"** commands (see Chapter 5) also work with a browser, but predicting what they're going to do is sometimes hard. The "lines" that Dragon Professional Individual moves when you say, **"Move Down Four Lines"** don't precisely correspond to the lines of text that you see on your screen. (They're usually a little bit larger than the lines of text. Don't ask me why.) And on web pages that have several frames, images, animations, or other advanced features, what a "paragraph" means is anybody's guess. "Top" and "bottom" are still meaningful terms, though, and you will find that **"Go To Top"** and **"Go To Bottom"** are good commands to remember when you're reading long documents on the web.

Entering information on a web page

Many web pages contain forms for you to fill out or textboxes into which you can dictate longer messages. Dragon Professional Individual has special commands for entering such information or messages.

Before you can dictate text into a textbox, you must first move the cursor there. You can, of course, move the cursor by clicking the mouse in the box, just as you would if you weren't using Dragon Professional Individual. Alternatively, you can say, **"Click *<the name of the text box>*"** to move the cursor to the textbox on the page.

For example, say, **"Click Name."** When the cursor is in the box, you can dictate, edit, and correct, just as you would in any Full Text Control application. (See Chapter 8.) When you finish with that textbox, repeat the process to move to a different box. Say, **"Click *the name of the textbox*"** to move on to the next textbox, and so on. Go back to an earlier textbox by saying its name. You can also move to the next textbox by saying, **"Next Control."** You can also say, **"Edit Box,"** and Dragon will number every available edit box on the page so you can choose it.

To click a radio button or check box on a web page, just say, **"Radio Button"** or **"Check Box."** Dragon will number the available check boxes or radio buttons. Say **"Choose *<n>*"** and Dragon will act as though you clicked it with your mouse. If it was a check box, for example, it will now be unchecked.

To cycle through the objects on a web page, say, **"Press Tab."** Say, **"Press Shift Tab"** to cycle in the opposite direction. This technique is useful when you want to go from one kind of object (like a textbox) to a different kind of object (like a radio button).

Here are some additional commands you can use to move around with tabs:

- **"Open New Tab"**
- **"Switch To Last Tab"**
- **"View The Next Tab"**
- **"View The Previous Tab"**
- **"Close Tab"**

Using shortcuts created for the web

Many of the activities you normally perform on the Internet are supported by special shortcuts created by Nuance. Take advantage of these shortcuts because you can use them no matter where you are. Check the Command browser to see a complete listing, which includes the following commands:

- **Searching the web:** Use Google, Bing, or another search tool to find anything (well, not your misplaced car keys!). For example, say, **"Search Google For Patio Furniture,"** and your browser opens the search and displays the results.
- **Searching using specific search categories:** These include images, video, news, maps, or products. For example, say, **"Search Video For Fossils."**

✔ **Searching a specific well-known site:** Find exactly what you want at a specific website. Speak the website name, such as Google, Yahoo!, Bing, Amazon, and eBay, in your command. For example, say, **"Search Amazon for Dragon Professional Individual For Dummies."**

✔ **Searching using a web address:** If you want to go to a specific website, say, **"Go To Address Bar"** and then say the URL you want to go to, as in **"Red Cross Dot Org."**

View the shortcut options for the web and other commands by choosing Tools ⇨ Command Browser.

Chapter 14

Dictating the Mobile Way

. . . .

In This Chapter

▶ Dictating messages for Facebook and Twitter on your iPad

▶ Creating reminder notes via voice with your iPad

▶ Correcting what you say

▶ Searching the web with Dragon Search

▶ Turning your smartphone into a microphone

▶ Speaking Dragon on your Android phone

▶ Looking at the new Dragon Anywhere app

. . . .

*I*t was inevitable that after we started talking into mobile phones, we'd want to use Dragon Professional Individual to talk *to* them as well. Now, thanks to Dragon, have your phone or other mobile device take over the pesky task of typing your emails. If speed is your goal (and whose isn't?), you can dictate and email to your mobile device — iPhone, iPad, iPod touch, or Android — and quickly dispatch it to your waiting minions. It's (at least) five times faster than typing on that little keyboard!

This chapter covers the use of Dragon Professional Individual dictation apps for your mobile devices. Typing with your thumbs makes most people feel like, well, "all thumbs." Now, a way to forget all furious fumbling is close at hand (pun intended).

This chapter starts by looking at the free mobile applications available from Dragon, and then I tell you about a great new application created for use with Dragon Professional Individual called Dragon Anywhere.

Dictating with Free Dragon Apps on Apple Mobile Devices

Nuance's mobile apps for Apple devices, including the iPhone, iPad, and iPod touch, are incredibly easy. Mostly, you tap, speak, and send. If you like having to figure out how complex applications work, you're out of luck. The integration with Apple products is nothing short of dead simple. You'll be up and running as fast as you can download them.

Dragon Professional Individual enables you to use these apps with your Apple devices, and I give you the highlights in the sections that follow:

- ✔ **Dragon Dictation:** Dictate directly into your Apple mobile devices, send email, and post to Facebook and Twitter.

- ✔ **Dragon Search:** Easily search the most popular web search engines.

- ✔ **Dragon Recorder:** Use your iOS device as a digital recorder to take notes on the go and have Dragon transcribe them later.

- ✔ **Dragon Go!:** Makes searching the mobile web with your mobile device almost too easy — and it's available for Android devices as well.

Discovering Dragon Dictation

What's great about Dragon Dictation is that it turns your mobile device into a mini-Dragon Professional Individual hub, and it's free. You get the same quality dictation with the added benefit of bypassing the mini keyboard for email functions.

To get the Dragon Dictation app, go to www.nuancemobilelife.com/apps/dragon-dictation and click the Download for iOS button, shown in Figure 14-1. Or you can download it from iTunes.

Dictating email on your iPhone

This section explains how to dictate emails on the iPhone. Then I show you how to use Dragon Dictation with your iPad to post to Facebook and Twitter and create notes.

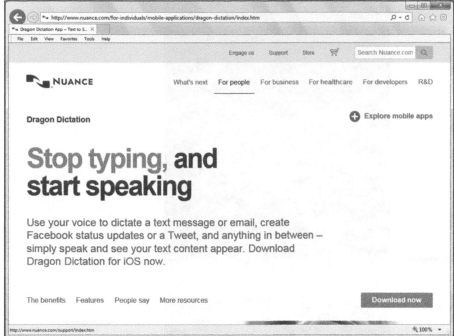

Figure 14-1:
Dragon
Dictation
app on the
Nuance
website.

To use the app after you've installed it on your device, do the following:

1. Look at the icons present on your home screen.

You see a Dragon icon and the caption "Dictation."

2. Tap the Dragon icon.

On the screen, you see a red Recording button with the words "Tap and Dictate" above it, as shown in Figure 14-2.

3. To begin recording, tap the red button.

The screen indicates that you are recording, as shown in Figure 14-3.

4. When you are finished, tap the Done button.

If you are dictating into your iPhone or iPod touch and are not using a wired headset, remember that the built-in microphone is located on the upper-left corner. Speak in that direction. On your iPad, you will see a message indicating where to speak when you dictate.

It is easy to end a recording. Tap the arrow icon (see Figure 14-4) on the bottom-right corner of the screen and choose Settings. Tap on the "Detect end of speech" setting to turn it on. Then, when you stop dictating, the recording stops without having to tap it. In that window, you also see other options for your dictation: SMS, Email, Copy, Facebook, Twitter, and Settings.

Figure 14-4:
The arrow icon in Dragon Dictation.

Arrow icon

5. **To send the message in an email, tap the Email icon, shown in Figure 14-5.**

An email form pops up, complete with your message. Send it as you would any other email.

Extending dictation with the iPad

Like Dragon Dictation for your iPhone, you can use your iPad to send email, and you can also

✔ **Post to social networks.** Without leaving the app, you can post directly to Facebook and Twitter.

✔ **Create notes.** Nuance has added a feature that allows you to dictate notes that you can store and use in a variety of ways.

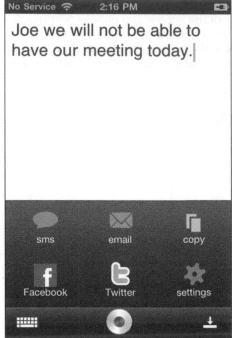

Figure 14-5:
Use the
email icon
to send
emails on
your iPhone.

To post to Facebook and Twitter, do the following:

1. **Launch Dragon Dictation from your iPad home screen by tapping the icon.**

   You see the recording screen.

2. **Dictate the message that you want to post to Facebook or Twitter.**

3. **Tap the down-facing arrow icon on the upper-right corner of the screen.**

   A window opens, showing you several choices (see Figure 14-6).

Figure 14-6:
Choices for
sending to
Facebook or
Twitter on
the iPad.

4. **Choose either the Facebook or Twitter icon.**

   A sign-in screen pops up, asking you to input your screen name and password.

5. **Enter your log-ins.**

   You're asked if you want to send your message.

6. **Tap Send.**

After you set up your logins, you'll be able to seamlessly post your message.

To create notes with Dragon Dictation, follow these steps:

1. **With the Dragon Dictation app open on your iPad, tap the Notes button on the upper-left corner of the screen.**

   You see a split screen. On one side, you see your list of notes. On the other is the dictation of your last note, as shown in Figure 14-7.

2. **Tap the plus sign (+) to start recording, and then tap it again when you are done.**

   You see that your dictation is recorded and will be in your list of notes until you either delete it or do something else with it. With the Notes app, you can record and save passages of text, send them as an email, or post to a social network.

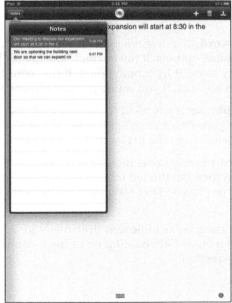

Figure 14-7:
The iPad
Notes
screen.

Notes you dictate are automatically saved and put in your notes list. To manually delete a note, use the Trash icon. Your note will also be deleted if you send it as an email or cut it.

Correcting what you say

The correction process is a bit different when you dictate with your mobile device versus working on your PC. On your PC, you have the luxury of correcting on a good size screen where you can employ several ways to make corrections. You can select Copy from a list of options, spell it, or type it. You can do that with the small screen (not the spelling function), but the experience is different because of the touchscreen.

If you have Dragon Professional Individual on your PC, you will quickly become familiar with all the different ways to command your assistant. Use this book and other Nuance training resources to build a backlog of knowledge and understand how the application works and what your options are. It becomes second nature, so that when you add a mobile device, you're more than halfway there. You'll instinctively know what to do.

On the flip side, if your first introduction to Dragon Professional Individual is on a mobile device, you don't have the benefit of already knowing how things work in the PC version. You're starting from scratch. Given the high quality of the mobile apps, it's still easy to get things up and running. Form a frame of reference for how dictation corrections work. Following are four ways to make corrections that are specific to the Apple mobile devices:

- ✔ **Correcting/deleting a word:** To correct a specific word, tap it. You are presented with possible options. If the correct spelling of the word is there, you can quickly select it by tapping on it. If the word has no options, a delete option appears. If you want, you can choose that.

- ✔ **Correcting/deleting a phrase:** If you want to correct a phrase, instead of tapping one word, drag your finger to select the phrase. It will be highlighted. Then you can select from the list or delete the phrase.

- ✔ **Voice correcting a word/phrase:** Do as indicated previously to select the word or phrase, and then tap the red icon at the top of the screen to record a different word or phrase. That recording replaces the one you highlighted.

- ✔ **Typing over a word/phrase:** Do as indicated previously to select the word or phrase, and then tap the keyboard icon at the bottom of the screen. Type in your correction.

Finding your way around with Dragon Search

Whether you're on the go or multi-tasking, your iPhone can be a real life-saver. You can search the web to locate the nearest restaurant, find a new oven, or get sports equipment. The hitch is that it's hard to navigate on a tiny screen. Dragon Search simplifies the effort in two ways:

- ✔ **You can speak your search commands.** If your arms are loaded down with a briefcase or papers or you are in a room full of people, you can still do your search.

- ✔ **You can easily access several search locations without lots of extra navigation.** Dragon Search has a Search Carousel that is set up to go to Google (or Yahoo! or Bing, if one of them is your default search engine), YouTube, Twitter Search, iTunes, or Wikipedia.

To download the Dragon Search app, go to www.nuancemobilelife.com/apps/dragon-search and click the Download for iOS button. Or you can download it from iTunes.

To perform a search and customize the app for your own searches, follow these steps:

1. **Launch Dragon Search by tapping the icon on your home screen.**

   You are presented with a screen that reads Tap and Speak.

2. **Tap the red Record button in the center of the screen and say your search term.**

   It will be placed into the Google search box just as if you typed it.

   In this example, say, **"Best iPad Apps."**

   Up pops the search results in Google. You can either tap a link or select one of the other icons above the search from the Search Carousel, as shown in Figure 14-8. The choices are YouTube, iTunes, Google, Wikipedia, and Twitter Search.

3. **To see what people are saying about the subject, tap the Twitter icon.**

   This shows you what Twitter users are saying about "Best iPad apps."

4. **Scroll through to see whether there's anything interesting that you want to tap.**

   You can continue to do this or start a new search. Dragon Search makes it very easy to find what you're looking for — hands free.

Figure 14-8:
The Search
Carousel in
the Dragon
Search app.

Having Fun with Dragon Go!

If you like using Dragon Search, you'll love using Dragon Go! Nuance created this free downloadable app for use with the iPhone 3GS, iPhone 4, iPhone 5, iPhone 5S and 5C, iPhone 6, iPhone 6 plus, iPhone 6s, iPhone 6s plus, iPod touch (3rd generation), iPod touch (4th generation), iPod touch (5th generation), iPod touch (6th generation), and iPad.

Dragon Go! makes searching with your mobile device almost too easy. (Read: *almost.*) If you haven't tried any of the other Dragon Professional Individual mobile apps, this is the one to start with. You don't need any other Nuance software on your PC, and there is absolutely no software to train. You can use this app to find entertainment and shopping venues, or you can use it to find something serious and important. The choice is yours.

For this example, I use the iPad and do something fun. To get started, do the following:

1. **To learn more about Dragon Go!, go to** www.nuancemobilelife.com/
   apps/dragon-go **or** http://itunes.apple.com/us/app/dragon-
   go/id442975871?mt=8&ls=1 **and download and install the app.**

   Sync it as you would any other iPad app.

2. **Launch Dragon Go! by tapping the icon from your home screen.**

   You're asked if you would like to use your current location with this app.

   Nuance asks this question so that it has permission to use your personal
   location to search for things in your area and get driving directions.

3. **If you agree, click OK.**

   After you click OK, you're asked to select the region in which you live
   and are asked to accept the end user license agreement.

4. **Select the region and click Accept.**

   The main title screen appears, as shown in Figure 14-9.

Figure 14-9:
Tap the
Record
button to
make your
search
request.

5. **To start a new search, tap the record button that is displayed on the screen.**

   In this example, I said, **"Who delivers coffee in my neighborhood?"** A search is returned that shows my local shops, as shown in Figure 14-10.

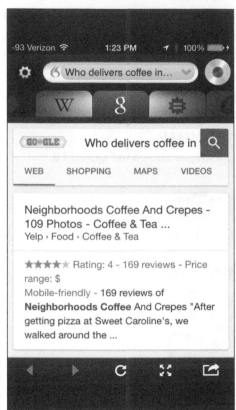

Figure 14-10:
Search results.

The searches are enhanced with the use of the Dragon Search Carousel (refer to Figure 14-8).

Carousel choices include: YouTube, iTunes, Google, Wikipedia, and Twitter Search.

You can also click the following links found below the search box to do further searching. The links include web, maps, shopping, images, video, news, books, flights, apps, and search tools.

If you want to share what you've found with friends, all you have to do is tap the "up arrow icon" as shown earlier in Figure 14-4, and choose one of the icons for sharing, as shown in Figure 14-6.

Dictating with Android Devices

There are lots of exciting new developments for Android devices. Android developers have improved the operating system's dictation capabilities. Following are some additional applications that you can use with your Android device.

Are you jealous of all the questions that iOS users get to ask their virtual assistants? Now you can have your own assistant on your Android device, and it's free. It's called Dragon Mobile Assistant and it lets you ask questions and make requests of your own. Want to make a call? How about send a text message? Yes, you can. In fact, you can now send and receive text messages completely hands free.

One of the really fun uses available in the latest version is your ability to share your location. You tell the assistant, **"Tell *<person>* where I am."** The person gets a Google Map showing where you are. They can tell you where they are if they're using Dragon Mobile Assistant too.

You can download Dragon Mobile Assistant from Google Play by going to `https://play.google.com/store/apps/details?id=com.nuance.balerion&hl=en`.

Swype for Android

Swype is a Nuance application for the Android smartphone. It provides very exciting keyboard functionality as well as dictation. You can download it at `http://www.nuancemobilelife.com/apps/swype/`. On this page, you'll also find the list of supported languages.

For support on Nuance Mobile applications, go to `www.nuancemobilelife.com/support`.

Swype is a booster shot for your Android keyboard. It lets you communicate by tracing on the keyboard with your finger to form words. Tracing is just like it sounds. You use the keyboard with continuous motion and you can actually see the tracing your hand is creating. As you begin tracing a word, you're given choices. If you see the right choice, tap it and save yourself the trouble of finishing the word. Over time, you can move pretty quickly by working this way.

You can also use your finger to write as you do when you just can't find anything digital to write with. Then magically it becomes digital — whew, that was close! It recognizes what you write and turns it into text. What's interesting is that it takes handwriting recognition to the next level. The reason is that it takes advantage of the predictive nature of the Dragon Professional Individual application. In order for Dragon to be able to pick the right word when you dictate, it has algorithms that predict which words most likely go together. By using those same statistics for handwriting recognition, it can be more accurate in the choices it presents to you.

But what about dictation? When using Swype, you can dictate into open windows, and your speech becomes text, just like in applications you use with Dragon Professional Individual on your PC. This means that you can dictate emails, post to social media, send instant messages, and pretty much do anything that involves a text window, like web searching.

Here are some features you may want to try:

- ✔ **Swype Editor:** When you dictate, Swype looks for the word that would fit the context best and suggests it to you. If you would rather use that word, you tap it, and it's inserted. This is a great help when you're making corrections.

- ✔ **Living Language:** This is a feature that you have to opt into. It adds words that are currently popular online and incorporates them into the vocabulary available to you. That way, you don't have to introduce the application to new words that explode in the popular culture.

Considering Dragon Anywhere

Dragon Anywhere is a new mobile application to consider if you need a professional-grade voice recognition tool to accomplish your work on the road. It's available for both iOS and Android and requires a subscription. Key to its value is that it sync with your desktop.

Here are some of its main features:

- ✔ You get the same dictation accuracy you get with Dragon Professional Individual. You can correct your work using editing features, which are similar to what you have on your desktop product.

- ✔ There is no time limit to your dictation. You can speak as long as you like to get the job done.

✔ You can create custom vocabulary to support your specific work documents.

✔ You can import and export to your favorite cloud sharing applications like Dropbox and notetaking apps like Evernote, giving you the same flexibility that you have with any other shared document.

The systems requirements are

✔ **For iOS devices:** iOS 8.1 + (iPad 3+, iPhone 5+, or iPad mini1+)

✔ **For Android:** Android 4.4+ phones and tablets

✔ **An active Wi-Fi or cellular connection**

So what are some of the main ways to dictate and get help in the application? In Figure 14-11, you see the main dictation screen.

Menu

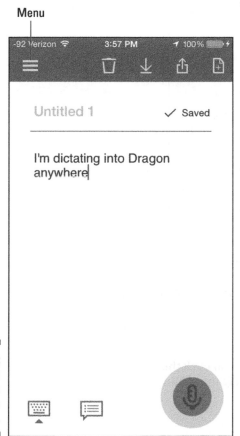

Figure 14-11:
Dragon
Anywhere
dictation
screen.

It uses the same easy record button and sharing icons. If you click the menu icon in the upper-left corner of the screen, you see the menu items available to you, as shown in Figure 14-12.

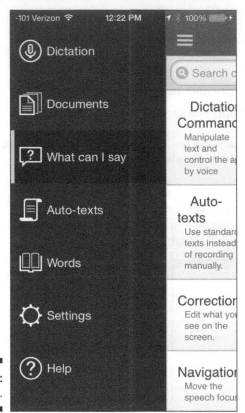

Figure 14-12:
Menu items.

The menu items are as follows:

- **Dictation:** You dictate from this main dictation screen. Click the Record button on the lower right.
- **Documents:** This is where you see a list of the documents you are working on.
- **What can I say:** When you click this menu item, you see the What Can I Say, screen, shown in Figure 14-13.

Figure 14-13:
What Can
I Say
command
links.

✔ **Auto-texts:** This is where you find a list of the auto-texts you set up.

✔ **Words:** In this section, you manage the words you have added to your vocabulary.

✔ **Settings:** This is where you manage your login, account, and other settings.

✔ **Help:** If you click the Help menu, you are taken to Figure 14-14. Here you see links to a variety of help items.

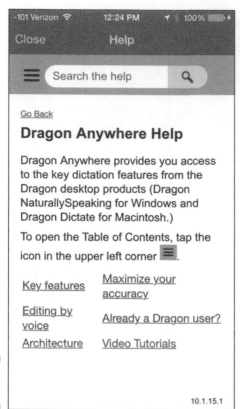

To find out more about the app and the subscription details, go to `http://www.nuance.com/for-business/by-product/dragon/dragon-anywhere`.

Part IV
Working Smarter

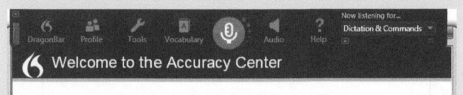

Welcome to the Accuracy Center

You can use the tools below to refine your profile to help Dragon best hear and execute what you say. Be sure to explore them by clicking them or saying "Click" and the link that interests you.

Personalize your vocabulary

Add a new word or phrase

Open the Vocabulary Editor
View or edit words, phrases and dictation commands, their pronunciations and Properties (capitalization, spelling, spacing).

Import a list of words or phrases

Learn from specific documents
Let Dragon analyze what words you often use and list words you may want added.

Learn from sent e-mails
Let Dragon find and learn the names you use often.

Set options and formatting

Open the Options dialog
Includes Speed vs. Accuracy, Correction, Hotkeys, Commands to enable or disable...

Open the Auto-Formatting options dialog
For dates, times, phone numbers, prices, units of measure, contractions...

Adjust your acoustics

Check your microphone

Launch Accuracy Tuning now
Accuracy Tuning makes your profile more accurate by analyzing the dictation, corrections, and training you have done.
To schedule accuracy tuning to run periodically, choose Administrative Settings from the Tools menu.

Read text to train Dragon to your voice
This option will display all the text at once without prompting and also allow you to print out the text.

Find or train commands

Open the Command Browser
Explore the commands available in different contexts and applications.

Get more information

How to manage and personalize your vocabularies

How to increase your performance

Visit the Nuance website for the latest tips and documentation.

Discover some quick ways to improve your speech online at www.dummies.com/extras/dragonprofessionalindividual.

In this part . . .

✔ Have you discovered that you aren't speaking to your assistant as clearly as you thought? See how to clear up speech issues that arise.

✔ Even though you've done some preliminary training, see why additional training for accuracy is a good idea.

✔ If you are concerned about improving audio output, learn when you need to run the microphone check again.

✔ Find out how to handle multiple users or computers so that you and others can work more productively.

✔ You'll want to create your own commands to work faster. I show you how to create new commands and use the Command Browser.

✔ There's lots of help if you need it. I highlight where to get help from your desktop and online.

Chapter 15

Controlling Your Desktop and Windows by Voice

*P*eople have been talking to their operating systems since the very early days of computing, but most of what they've been saying is not repeatable in public. Using voice recognition software, though, you can talk to your operating system and have it *do* something in response: run an application, switch to another window, move the mouse pointer, or choose a command from a menu.

You probably are used to controlling Windows's windows and applications through the keyboard and/or the mouse. You can easily imitate keyboard commands with the voice command **"Press"** — **"Press Right-Arrow,"** for example. You can also imitate mouse actions that click buttons or choose items from a menu with the voice command **"Click"** — for example, **"Click OK,"** or **"Click File, Save."** (Unfortunately, this technique doesn't apply to toolbar and Ribbon buttons like Back. See Table 15-1 later in this chapter for keyboard and menu equivalents for the Computer and Windows Explorer toolbar and Ribbon buttons.)

By contrast, mouse actions that involve maneuvering the mouse pointer to click some tiny, nameless object (like the +/– boxes in Windows Explorer or the arrow that nets a drop-down list box) are less convenient to do by voice. You *can* maneuver the mouse pointer by voice (see "Do Mice Understand English?" later in this chapter), but doing so is seldom the most efficient way to accomplish your purpose. Fortunately, these mouse actions almost always have keyboard equivalents that you can use with the **"Press"** command.

And so, in addition to the obvious theme of this chapter — learning voice commands to control Windows — a secondary theme appears: learning keyboard commands for tasks that you may be used to doing with the mouse.

Ya Wanna Start Something?

Plenty of people talk to their desktops, particularly when they are under great stress or have forgotten a loved one's birthday. Unfortunately, up until now, most of that talk has been unproductive. Desktops have seldom responded, and those that did respond came up with very few ideas that were worth putting into practice.

Dragon Professional Individual, however, lets you talk to your desktop and actually see results. Now your desktop responds to your commands by starting applications, opening windows, and giving you access to menus, including the Start menu.

You can start applications or open files or folders by saying, **"Start <*name of application, file, or folder*>."** For example, say, **"Start WordPad,"** to open the WordPad application. You can also use voice commands to access anything on the Start menu — Pictures, Documents, the Control Panel, or anything else.

Operating tips for Windows 8

If Windows 8 is your operating system, fear not: Dragon works right along with it. But, you will have to experiment a bit when you first get started. Until then, the key to making Windows 8 work is to bypass some of the new interface conventions, like the tiled Start screen. (In Windows 8.1, the Start menu has returned.)

Navigation for Windows 8 is best done by using commands to replicate keyboard actions or move actions, such as **"Press Enter"** and **"Move Right Five."**

Below is a list of some commands specific to the Windows 8 Modern User Interface:

- ✔ "Open Start Screen"
- ✔ "Show All Applications"

- ✔ "Charms Bar"
- ✔ "Open *<charm name>* Charm"

You may want to use these new commands to leverage Windows new search charm function. Do this by saying, **"Charms Bar," "Open Search Charm"** and then dictate your search and say, **"Press Enter."**

Operating tips for Windows 10

If you are using Windows 10, you will be happy to know that Dragon works with it. Below is a list of some commands specific to the Windows 10 Modern User Interface that you can use to navigate:

- ✔ **"Start screen"**
- ✔ **"Switch to screen mode"**
- ✔ **"Start Windows settings"**
- ✔ **"Open task view"**

Starting applications by voice

Dictating text is nice, but the first feeling of real power you get from Dragon Professional Individual is when you say, **"Open Microsoft Word."** The screen blinked, the hard drive growled, angels sang hosannas (okay, maybe I imagined that part), and the Word window appeared in all its glory.

The **"Open"** command opens any application whose name appears in one of the following places:

- ✔ **The desktop:** For example, if a Microsoft Excel shortcut is on your desktop, you can start it up by saying, **"Open Microsoft Excel."**

- ✔ **The top of the Start menu:** If you see the name of an application when you click the Start button, you can run it with the **"Open"** command.

- ✔ **In the Programs folder on the Start menu, or in any of the subfolders of the Programs folder:** For example, saying, **"Open WordPad"** opens it, even though it lies inside the Programs folder hierarchy (in Start/ Accessories — unless you moved it).

In general, use whatever name is on the menu or shortcut. Dragon Professional Individual does recognize a few nicknames, though. If you say, **"Open Word,"** for example, it runs Microsoft Word. Saying **"Open Firefox"** opens Mozilla Firefox. Try opening your programs with the name you use to see if a shortcut exists.

You also aren't stuck with the names on the Programs menu. You probably didn't create most of those entries yourself. Some of them have been there since you unpacked your computer, while others have been created by the setup wizards that installed your applications. Delete them. If you have a long-winded, hard-to-remember entry on your Programs menu — something like "WinZip 15.0" — you can change it to something catchy, like "Zip." Then you can start it by saying, **"Start Zip."** Right-click any icon on your desktop, choose Rename, and give your program an easier moniker.

Using the Start menu in Windows 7

Anytime that Dragon Professional Individual is running, you can say, **"Click Start"** to pull up the Start menu. (This specifically refers to Windows 7 or earlier.) You can then say the name of any object on the Start menu like: **"Shut Down," "Log Off," "Restart," "Help And Support,"** or any individual applications, files, or folders that you have added to the menu. The resulting action is the same as if you had clicked the mouse on that entry in the Start menu:

- ✔ If the object is itself a menu, it expands when you click it. (For example, Documents expands to a listing of the names of about the 15 most recent objects.) Select one of those objects by saying its name. If the object is another menu, it expands, and so on.

- ✔ If the object is an application, it runs. (Run the application more easily by saying, **"Start <*application name*>."**)

- ✔ If the object is a file or folder, it opens. The files could be documents or even web pages.

For example, if Skype appears on your Start menu, then you can access your Skype account online by saying, **"Click Start, Skype."** (The commas represent short pauses; don't say, "comma.") To open the Control Panel, say, **"Click Start, Control Panel."**

In addition to using the Start command, you can use the **"Launch"** or **"Show"** commands. For example, instead of saying **"Start Word,"** you can say, **"Launch Word"** or **"Show Word."**

When using Windows 8, you can say **"Show Start Screen,"** but from there you are better off navigating by touch if you have a touch display or mouse. The lack of accessibility options in the Modern UI makes mastering it difficult for Nuance, but they plan to continue improving the experience in the future.

Don't shut down the computer by voice, unless you have challenges that prevent you from doing it any other way. In general, shutting down Windows with a lot of applications running (especially robust applications like Dragon Professional Individual) upsets the system. At the very least, it causes an application to do something illegal that makes Windows shut it down in an unnatural way. Some data could be lost in the process. Of course, some Windows operating systems run better than others, and you may get lucky. But why take the chance?

Does It Do Windows?

Yes, Dragon Professional Individual does windows. Open them, close them, move them, resize them, switch from one window to another, use their menus, and interact with their dialog boxes — all without using your hands.

Listing all applications

If you want to know which applications are open on your computer, you can use the **"List"** command to say, **"List All Windows."** A list pops up, showing what is running (see Figure 15-1). You see a numbered list of the applications. Choose it as the active window by saying, **"Choose <*number*>."** If you are not good about closing applications after you have used them, this is a very handy feature.

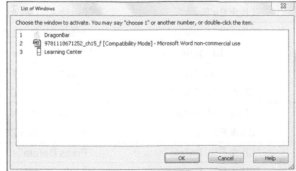

Figure 15-1: List of open windows on your desktop.

Opening Computer and other folder windows

You can open any folder on your desktop with the **"Start"** command. For example, say, **"Start My Computer,"** or, more generally, **"Start <*folder name*>."** In this example, the Computer folder opens in a window, just as if you had double-clicked its icon on your desktop.

After a folder window is open, you can select any visible object inside the window by saying the object's name. You can then work on the object by using the menus. For example, open the Control Panel folder as follows:

1. **Say,** "Start My Computer."

   The Computer window opens.

2. **Say,** "Open Control Panel."

   The Control Panel folder is selected.

3. **Say,** "<*name of icon*>."

After you have a folder window open, you can use the subcommands from its menu. You can also drag and drop within a folder window or from one window to another. (See "Dragging until you drop," later in this chapter.) Unfortunately, no direct way exists to use the toolbar buttons other than to maneuver the mouse pointer over one and say, **"Click."** The toolbar buttons in Computer or Windows Explorer have keyboard and menu equivalents that you can access by voice. You can duplicate the toolbar button functions with the keyboard and menu commands shown in Table 15-1.

Table 15-1	Voice Commands for Toolbar Button Functions	
Toolbar Button	*Voice Menu Command*	*Voice Key Combination*
Back	**"Click Go Back"**	**"Press Alt Left Arrow"**
Forward	**"Click Go Forward"**	**"Press Alt Right Arrow"**
Up	**"Click Go Up One Level"**	**"Press Backspace"**
Cut*	**"Click Edit, Cut"**	**"Press Control X"**
Copy*	**"Click Edit, Copy"**	**"Press Control C"**
Paste*	**"Click Edit, Paste"**	**"Press Control V"**
Undo	**"Click Edit, Undo"**	**"Press Control Z"**
Delete*	**"Click File, Delete"**	**"Press Delete"**
Properties*	**"Click File, Properties"**	none*
Views*	**"Click View"**	**"Press Alt V"**

Commands marked with an asterisk (*) are also on the right-click menu.

Giving orders to Windows Explorer

Windows Explorer is an obedient application. If you say, **"Start Windows Explorer,"** it pops up, ready to take your orders. As with Computer, the Windows Explorer menus are available to your voice commands, but the toolbar and Ribbon buttons are not. (Refer to Table 15-1.)

Windows Explorer has a Ribbon of great tools that can all be controlled with Dragon by saying, **"Click <button>."** You can also say things like **"Open Documents,"** then say the folder name of the file you want to select, and say, **"Open," "Rename," "Move To," "Delete," "Copy," "Share,"** and many more.

Windows Explorer has three main components, which are shown in Figure 15-2: the Explorer bar, the Contents window, and the Address box. How Windows Explorer responds to your commands depends on what component the cursor is in.

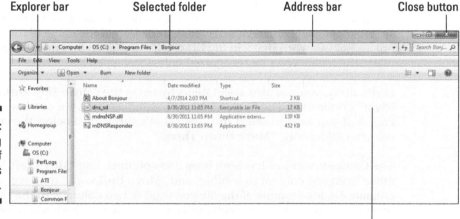

Figure 15-2: Exploring the parts of Windows Explorer.

Contents window

Moving the cursor from component to component

Windows Explorer opens with the cursor in the Explorer bar. That's the left pane of the main window, the one that displays the overall structure of your file-and-folder system. Press the Tab key (or say, **"Press Tab"**) to cycle the cursor through the following three components of the Windows Explorer window:

✔ **Contents window:** The right pane of the main window, which displays the contents of the folder selected

✔ **Address box:** Displays the address of whatever file or folder is currently selected

✔ **Explorer bar:** The left pane of the main window that can contain a variety of things, depending on your choice in View ⇨ Status Bar

Depending on how Windows is set up on your system, a fourth component may exist — the Explorer bar's Close button, that little X in the upper-right corner of the Explorer bar. (It's kind of a silly thing to make a component out of, but what can I say — it's Windows.) When the Explorer bar's Close button is selected, you can make the Explorer bar go away by saying, **"Press Enter."** To get the Explorer bar back, say, **"Click View, Explorer Bar, All Folders."**

The Shift+Tab key combination moves the cursor through these components in the opposite order. Say, **"Press Shift Tab."**

Selecting and opening files and folders

The Explorer bar and the Contents window are each a list of folders and files. Select an item from the list by saying its name. That sounds great, but a few complications exist: You have to say the complete name, and if the file extension is displayed, you have to say it as well. Also, if the name of the item is not an English word that's in the Dragon Professional Individual active vocabulary, the name won't be recognized unless you spell it.

Fortunately, you can also select items by using the **"Move Up/Down/Left/ Right"** commands. The Explorer bar is treated as if it were one long vertical list. If you want to select the folder that's three lines below the currently selected folder, say, **"Move Down Three."**

The Contents window has both lines and columns. Use **"Move Left/Right"** to move from one column to another, and **"Move Up/Down"** to move within a column. So, for example, if the file you want is two columns to the right and three lines up from the currently selected item, say, **"Move Right Two, Move Up Three."**

After you select an item, open it by saying, **"Press Enter."**

Expanding and contracting lists of folders

Those plus (+) and minus (–) signs in little boxes next to the folders on the Explorer bar control whether a folder's subfolders appear on the list. You may be accustomed to clicking these little boxes with the mouse, but you *don't* want to try that technique with the vocal mouse commands. It's possible, but much too time-consuming.

Instead, select a folder on the Explorer bar, and then use the right- and left-arrow keys to expand and contract the list of subfolders. If the folder is contracted (that is, the + is showing), say, **"Press Right Arrow."** The folder expands. If it is already expanded (the – shows), say, **"Press Left Arrow."** The folder then contracts.

Switching from one application to another

If you have several application windows active on your desktop, you can switch from one to another just by saying so. You can do this in five ways:

✔ If the window represents an application or a folder, you can call it by the name of the application or the folder. For example, say, **"Switch To Word"** or **"Switch To Documents."** (Windows Explorer is an exception. Switch to an open Windows Explorer window by saying, **"Switch To Exploring."**)

✔ Return to the previously active window by saying, **"Switch To Previous Window."** This command is equivalent to pressing Alt+Tab. Repeating this command several times switches back and forth between two windows.

✔ Cycle through all the active windows (even the ones that are minimized) by repeating, **"Switch To Next Window."** This command is equivalent to pressing Shift+Alt+Tab on the keyboard.

✔ If the name of a document appears on the title bar, you can use the name of that document in a **"Switch To"** command. For example, if you're using Microsoft Word to edit a document called My Diary, the title bar of the window says "Microsoft Word — My Diary." (The block on the task-bar corresponding to this window says the same thing, though the block may not be large enough to accommodate the full title.) Switch to this window by saying, **"Switch To Word"** or **"Switch To My Diary."**

✔ As described earlier in "Listing all applications," you can use the **"List Programs"** or **"List All Windows"** command. For example, you can say, **"List Open Windows,"** and a list of the programs that are open on your desktop appears. Just select the program you want by choosing the number shown in the window.

Do Mice Understand English?

Once upon a time, you had to go to Disney World to find a mouse that under-stood English. Now, of course, you have one attached to your computer. The Dragon Professional Individual voice commands let you move the mouse pointer anywhere on your screen and give you access to the full range of mouse clicks: right, left, and double. You can even drag and drop objects within a window, or from one window to another.

Telling your mouse where to go

Dragon Professional Individual gives you two methods to move the mouse pointer. **"MouseGrid"** breaks up the screen (or the active window) into a series of squares, letting you zero in on the location you want to move the pointer to. The mouse pointer commands let you make small adjustments by saying things like, **"Mouse Up Five."**

How does it work? Surprisingly well, after you get used to it. Naturally, you have to adjust your expectations: Voice commands are not a high-performance way to move the mouse, so you won't break any speed records the next time you play a game. But your virtual, voice-commanded mouse, like the physical mouse attached to your computer, is remarkably intuitive. It makes a good backup system for those times when you can't remember the right hotkey or voice command.

Making your move with MouseGrid

In days of yore, before the invention of *GameBoy,* children amused themselves on long driving trips with number-guessing games. Here's a simple one: One kid picks a number and another makes guesses. The number-picker responds to each guess by saying "higher" or "lower." The guesser narrows down the range where the number can be until eventually he knows what the number is.

"MouseGrid" is like that, but in two dimensions. You pick a point on the screen where you want the mouse pointer to go, and Dragon Professional Individual guesses where it is. Start the game by saying, **"MouseGrid."**

The MouseGrid is not supported in Windows 8 Modern UI.

Dragon Professional Individual's first guess is that you want the mouse pointer to be in the center of the screen. But just in case it's wrong, it turns your screen into a tick-tack-toe board, as in Figure 15-3. The nine squares are numbered like the keypad of a touch-tone phone: The square on the upper left is 1, and the square on the lower right is 9. The pointer is sitting on square 5. Look closely to see the numbers in the centers of the squares.

Now it's your turn: If you want the mouse pointer in the center of the screen, tell Dragon Professional Individual that the game is over by saying, **"Go."** The squares vanish and the mouse pointer stays in the center of the screen.

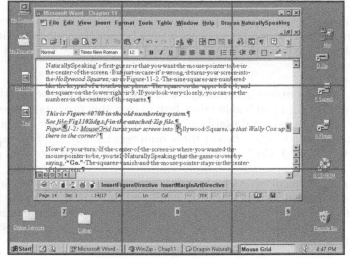

Figure 15-3:
MouseGrid
turns your
screen into
a tick-tack-
toe window.

If the center was not the point you had in mind, say the number to tell Dragon Professional Individual the square your chosen point is in. For example, you may say, **"Nine,"** indicating that the point is in the lower-right part of the screen. Dragon Professional Individual responds by making all the squares go away other than the one you chose. Now Dragon Professional Individual guesses that you want the mouse pointer to be in the center of that square. But just in case it's wrong, it breaks that square into nine smaller squares (see Figure 15-4). These squares are numbered 1 through 9, just like the larger squares were.

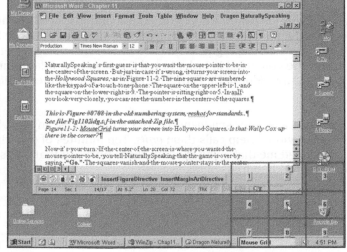

Figure 15-4:
Dragon
Professional
Individual
closes in
on the
destination
you have
chosen for
the mouse
pointer.

Again, either you say, **"Go"** to accept Dragon Professional Individual's guess and end the game, or you say a number to tell it which of the smaller squares you want the mouse pointer to be in. It then breaks that square up into nine really tiny squares, and the game continues until the pointer is where you want it.

This description makes it sound as if you'll be old and gray before the mouse arrives at the point you had in mind, but, in fact, this process happens very quickly after you get comfortable with it. If you are aiming for something like a button on a toolbar, two or three numbers usually suffice. You say, **"MouseGrid 2, 6, 3, Go,"** and the mouse pointer is where you want it.

You can use **"Cancel"** as a synonym for **"Go."** (This situation may be the only one in human history where "cancel" and "go" are synonyms.) I choose between them according to my mood: If I succeed in putting the mouse pointer where I want it, I say, **"Go."** If I just want out of the game, I say, **"Cancel."** It makes no practical difference.

If you want to move the mouse pointer to a place within the active window, you can restrict MouseGrid to that window by saying, **"MouseGrid Window"** instead of **"MouseGrid."** Now only the active window is broken up *Hollywood Squares* style. The process of zeroing in on the chosen location is the same (for example, **"MouseGrid Window 2, 7, Go"**).

You can also get out of MouseGrid by giving a click command (which is probably why you were moving the mouse pointer to begin with). So rather than saying, **"MouseGrid 5, 9, Go"** and then **"Click,"** say, **"MouseGrid 5, 9, Click."** This trick works with any of the click commands, and also with **"MouseGrid Window."** See "Clicking right and left," later in this chapter.

Nudging the mouse pointer just a little

If the mouse pointer is *almost* where you want it and just needs to be nudged a smidgen, use the mouse pointer commands **"Mouse Up," "Mouse Down," "Mouse Left,"** and **"Mouse Right."** You need to attach a number between one and ten to the command in order to tell the mouse how far to move. So, for example, say, **"Mouse Up Four,"** and the mouse pointer dutifully goes up four.

"Four what?" you ask. Four smidgens, or four somethings, anyway. Dragon Professional Individual Help calls them *units*. Ten minutes of experimentation has convinced me that a *unit* is about three pixels, if that helps. (Your computer screen is hundreds of pixels wide.)

All you really need to know about units is

- They're small, so **"Mouse Right Six"** isn't going to move the pointer very far. (For big motions, use **"MouseGrid."**)

- They're all the same size, so **"Mouse Down Three"** is going to move the pointer three times as far as **"Mouse Down One."**

As with **"MouseGrid,"** you can combine the mouse-pointer commands with the click commands. Instead of saying, **"Mouse Left Ten,"** and then **"Double Click,"** you can say, **"Mouse Left Ten Double Click."**

Clicking right and left

You don't usually move the mouse pointer just so that you can have a little arrow displayed on your screen in an aesthetically pleasing location. You move the mouse pointer so that you can *do* something, and doing something usually involves clicking one of the mouse buttons.

Dragon Professional Individual gives you a full squadron of click commands:

- **"Click"** or **"Left-Click,"** which presses the left mouse button

- **"Right-Click,"** which presses the right mouse button

- **"Double-Click,"** which presses the left mouse button twice

If Dragon Professional Individual has trouble understanding your **"Click"** commands, add the word **"Mouse"** to the command: **"Mouse Click," "Mouse Double-Click,"** and so on. The longer command is easier to recognize.

Dragging until you drop

When you know how to maneuver the mouse pointer and click, you're ready to drag and drop. Drag-and-drop voice commands enable you to do almost everything that you can do with hand-and-mouse commands: Move objects from one window to another, rearrange objects within a window, select a number of objects within a window, resize windows, or move windows around on the desktop.

Perform all of these actions with the **"Mark"** and **"Drag"** commands (if you already put your cursor where you want it), following these steps:

1. **Move the mouse pointer until it's over the object that you want to drag.**

   This object could be an icon on your desktop or in a window, the title bar of a window that you want to move, or the lower-right corner of a window that you want to resize. It could even be an empty place in a window or on the desktop that you're using as one corner of a selection rectangle.

2. **Say,** "Mouse Mark."

3. **Move the mouse pointer until it's at the point where you want to drop the object.**

4. **Say,** "Mouse Drag."

You can combine **"Mark"** and **"Drag"** with the **"MouseGrid"** command. For example, instead of saying, **"MouseGrid 4, 5, Go"** and then **"Mark,"** you can just say, **"MouseGrid 4, 5, Mark."**

Suppose that your Computer icon is in the top-left corner of your desktop, and you want to move it to the bottom-right corner. Follow these steps:

1. **Say,** "MouseGrid 1, 1, Mark."

   From my screen, **"MouseGrid 1, 1"** was sufficient to get the mouse pointer over the Computer icon. Depending on your screen settings, you may need to say more than two numbers. For fine control, use mouse-pointer commands like **"Mouse Up Two."**

2. **Say,** "MouseGrid 9, 9, Drag."

   The Computer icon disappears from its old location and reappears at the 9, 9 location, which is in the lower-right corner of the screen.

The **"Mark . . . Drag"** combination mimics certain familiar mouse actions, but it isn't precisely equivalent to any of them. For example, selecting an icon (either with a mouse click or by saying the icon name) doesn't mark it. Also, a marked object stays marked until something else is marked. You can, for example, mark an object on your desktop, go edit a document in your word processor, and then go back to your desktop to complete the drag-and-drop. The object is still marked, so all you have to do when you return to the desktop is move the mouse pointer to the appropriate location, and say, **"Drag."** Dragging and dropping by hand is not nearly so flexible.

"Mark . . . Drag" doesn't drag and drop text or illustrations within a word-processing document. Use **"Cut That . . . Paste That"** instead. (See Chapter 5.) Another deficiency of the **"Mark"** command is that it doesn't mark collections of objects. For example, if you have selected four objects inside a folder window (possibly by using **"Mark . . . Drag"** to drag a selection rectangle over them), you cannot now move them all by marking them as a group and dragging them elsewhere. Instead, choose Edit ⇨ Cut from the folder window, and then Paste from the Edit menu of the window where you want them (or Paste from the context menu of the desktop).

Dialoging with a Box

After you start talking to your desktop, it's only a matter of time before you find yourself conversing with a box. In fact, you may have been talking to Dragon Professional Individual dialog boxes even before you started dictating to other applications. Don't fight it; dialog boxes are where Windows does its dirty work.

Dialog boxes are more difficult to deal with than menus, because dialog boxes can contain almost anything: radio buttons, drop-down lists, text boxes, check boxes, tabs, browsing windows — sometimes all in the same dialog box. How the dialog box responds to a voice command depends on where the cursor is: If the cursor is in a text box, the dialog box interprets spoken words as text that otherwise might select a file or change a radio button. Consequently, you must always pay attention to where the cursor is in a dialog box. The cursor location tells you what kind of input the dialog box is expecting, which determines how it will deal with any command that you give it.

These keys are hot!

People who don't have voice-recognition software (you may have been one of them until quite recently) use the mouse a lot when they are confronted with dialog boxes. Click here, click there, type something, double-click somewhere else, then click OK, and it's over.

Dragon Professional Individual has mouse commands (see "Do Mice Understand English?" earlier in this chapter), but moving the mouse pointer around by voice is not as quick as moving it by hand. And hitting a tiny target like the down arrow on a drop-down list requires patience.

Fortunately, you don't have to do things that way. Most actions that are performed with a mouse can also be done through the keyboard,

by using what are called "hotkeys." The Tab and Shift+Tab keys, for example, cycle the cursor through the various components of a dialog box.

The Alt key is used in most hotkey combinations. The Alt+↓ key combination makes a drop-down list, uh, drop down. Alt+↑ retracts a drop-down list. The **"Press"** command lets you use these key combinations by voice, as in **"Press Alt Down Arrow."**

Buttons and check boxes have hotkeys as well. You can find the hotkey by looking for the underlined letter in the accompanying text. Select or deselect the check box by saying, **"Press Alt S."**

Moving the cursor around a dialog box

A dialog box may have any number of windows, text boxes, buttons, and so on. Before you can deal with any particular component, you usually have to get the cursor into its window. (Buttons are an exception. If the box has a Cancel button, for example, **"Click Cancel"** closes the box no matter where the cursor is.)

When you're working by hand, the simplest way to put the cursor where you want it is to move the mouse pointer there and click. You can do the same thing by voice if you want (see "Do Mice Understand English?" earlier in this chapter), but often you will find it simpler to cycle through the components of the dialog window with the Tab key. Say, **"Press Tab"** to move from one component of a dialog window to another. Repeat the command to cycle through all the components of the box. Say, **"Press Shift Tab"** to cycle in the opposite direction.

To see exactly how this works, go through some of the examples in "Looking at a few of the most useful dialog boxes," later in this chapter.

Dealing with dialog box features

Many menu commands lead directly to dialog boxes. For example, in the Dragon Professional Individual window itself, the menu selection Tools ⇨ Options ⇨ View opens the dialog box shown in Figure 15-5, which illustrates a number of the simpler standard features of dialog boxes: buttons, radio buttons, check boxes, and tabs:

- ✔ **Buttons:** Click a button by saying, **"Click <*button name*>."** You can make the dialog box (refer to Figure 15-5) go away by saying, **"Click Cancel."** You can also say, **"Press Enter"** as an alternative way to click the OK button or whatever button is currently selected (the one that has the darkest outline).

- ✔ **Radio buttons:** Choose an option by saying its text label. Saying, **"Docked To Bottom"** changes the placement of the DragonBar to be at the bottom of the screen (refer to Figure 15-5), for example.

In general, this technique works when you have a single set of radio buttons (that is, a setup in which selecting one button deselects the others). More complicated multi-radio-button configurations require a **"Click"** command.

Figure 15-5:
The Options
View dialog
box.

✔ **Check boxes:** Check boxes are on if they are selected and off if not. Change from On to Off or Off to On by saying the text label. In Figure 15-5, saying, **"Anchor"** anchors your Results box. Saying, **"Show Extras"** removes the check mark from the Show Extras check box.

✔ **Tabs:** Switch to another tab by saying its name. Using Figure 15-5 as an example, you could say, **"Click Correction Tab,"** to switch to the Correction tab.

The Open dialog box shown in Figure 15-6 has a more complex set of features: drop-down lists, a text box, toolbar buttons, and a list of files and folders. Although I obtained this dialog box by choosing File ➪ Open from the Dragon Professional Individual DragonPad window, it's typical of a type of Windows dialog box. It also illustrates a standard problem: The Open dialog box first appears with the cursor in the File Name text box. Any text you say other than **"Click," "Press,"** or **"MouseGrid"** will be interpreted as the name of a file.

Figure 15-6:
The Open
dialog box
illustrates a
common
problem:
How do you
get the
cursor out
of the File
Name text
box?

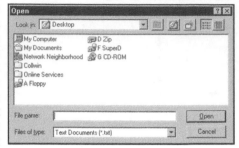

Deal as follows with the features exemplified in this box:

✔ **Drop-down lists:** The Open dialog box has two drop-down lists: Look In and Files of Type. You can recognize them as drop-down lists because of the little down arrow at the right edge of the text. To bring the cursor into the list say, **"Click <*text label*>."** For example, say, **"Click Look In."** In some cases, this command also causes the list to drop down, but if it doesn't, say, **"Press Alt Down Arrow"** to display the list. After the list drops, change the selected item on the list by saying its name or by using the **"Move Up/Down"** command. Say, **"Move Down Five,"** for example. To retract the list and lock in the new selection say, **"Press Alt Up Arrow."**

✔ **Text boxes:** The Open dialog box opens with the cursor in the File Name text box. Enter text into this box by saying it. To get the cursor out of this box, use the **"Click"** command to click a button or a drop-down menu; use the **"MouseGrid"** command to click the mouse inside some other part of the dialog box; or say, **"Press Tab"** or **"Press Shift Tab"** to move the cursor into Files of Type or the file and folder list in the main window, respectively.

✔ **Toolbar buttons:** Unlike the big buttons (OK, Cancel, and so on), tool-bar buttons in dialog boxes usually don't respond to their names. If you want to use them, you must click them with the mouse.

✔ **Lists of files and folders:** The tricky thing about using the list of files and folders is getting the cursor into its window. That's because there is no **"Click"** command that puts it there unless you maneuver the mouse pointer into the window. Instead, say, **"Press Shift Tab,"** if the cursor is just below the window in the File Name text box, or **"Press Tab"** if the cursor is just above the window in the Look In drop-down list. After the cursor is in the main window, select files and folders either by name or by using the **"Move Up/Down/Right/Left"** commands. Open a selected file or folder by saying, **"Click Open"** or **"Press Enter."**

When you open a folder from a list of files and folders in a dialog box, either **"Click Open"** or **"Press Enter"** does the job. However, **"Click Open"** returns the cursor to the File Name text box, and **"Press Enter"** leaves the cursor in the main window, which now displays the contents of the opened folder. I prefer **"Press Enter."**

Looking at a few of the most useful dialog boxes

Now to get down and dirty and slug it out with a few of the dialog boxes that you're going to run into again and again. These are "Look Ma, no hands" examples. Everything is done with voice commands. Naturally, sometimes you can accomplish the task faster by pecking a key or moving your mouse, but I assume you know how to do that already. Over time, you'll work out your own compromises between voice commands and mouse-and-keyboard commands. By giving these pure-vocal examples, I leave the compromising to you.

For the following searches, Dragon Professional Individual supports these search engines: Google Desktop, Windows 7 Search, Windows 8 Search, and Windows 10 Search.

Searching documents

Suppose that a couple of days ago you found a great article about Mind Maps somewhere on the web, and you know you saved it somewhere. Probably you used "mind map" somewhere in the filename, but in the heat of the moment, you aren't sure what you called it. It's bound to be somewhere on your hard drive. Find it by following these steps:

1. **Say,** "Search Documents For Mind Map."

   The dialog box opens. The search engine shows you all the indexed items that have "mind map" in the title.

2. **Choose the one you want by saying,** "*<document name>*."

   The document is selected. Say, **"Press Enter"** to open it.

Searching your computer

If you think you misplaced an important spreadsheet from the Widget Co. somewhere on your hard drive, find it by doing the following:

1. **Say,** "Search The Computer For Spreadsheets."

   A list of all the items that match that search are listed.

2. **To choose the one you want, say the name of the spreadsheet.**

Finding and replacing text

Suppose your daughter has used the Dragon Professional Individual window to dictate a report for Show-and-Tell about your new dog Spot. The report is excellent, except for one small problem: She believes that Spot is a cat. How can she repair this error in her report?

1. **Say,** "Click Edit, Replace."

   The Replace dialog box opens. The cursor starts in the Find What text box.

2. **Say,** "Cat."

3. **Say,** "Press Tab."

   The cursor moves to the Replace With text box.

4. **Say,** "Dog."

   You're almost done. But unless you want the word "Category" replaced with "Dogegory," you need to do one more thing.

5. **Say,** "Click Match Whole Word Only."

   The corresponding check box is selected.

6. **Say,** "Click Replace All."

Chapter 16

Speaking More Clearly

· ·

In This Chapter

▶ Deciding what speech issues to worry about

▶ Doing what Dragon Professional Individual needs for clarity

▶ Improving enunciation

▶ Differentiating words

▶ Knowing when to run the microphone check again

▶ Deciding on additional training

· ·

Say, "I want a Fig Newton and a glass of milk." Go ahead. Say it the casual way you would in a diner. (Presuming, for the moment, that you like Fig Newtons and milk.)

If you're like me, you probably said something like, "Eyewanna FigNew'n 'na glassa milk." You probably skip the final "t" of "want" and slur "want a" ("wanna"), omit the "to" of "Newton," skip the "a" and "d" of "and" ("n"), and don't really pronounce either letter in the word "of."

North Americans commonly don't waste time or effort. Often, we ignore short words, initial vowels, and the final consonants of many words. And we unnerstan 'chother perfeckly, raht? Riot. So whah cain't t' dang computer unnerstan goodol 'merican English?

Most Americans would understand the Fig Newton line perfectly because of our love affair with cookies and milk. The computer, on the other hand, is rarely fed Fig Newtons and milk, except for what you drop into the keyboard or what your kids stuff into the DVD drive for the dog to lick out. The result? A computer relies on all those little things you normally skip but that distinguish one word from another. Without them, Dragon Professional Individual may translate the line something as like, "I have Fig Newton awesome milk." That translation may inspire a popular new dairy or fruit beverage, but it wouldn't be exactly what you had in mind for your computer activity.

So, should you learn to speak better, or should you train your Dragon Professional Individual assistant to love you just the way you are? As with most things in life, the answer is "yes" — to both questions

Do You Need to Speak Better?

You probably do need to speak a bit better. Improving your speech habits is one of the best and cheapest ways to cut down on errors in Dragon Professional Individual.

On the other hand, don't go nuts. For instance, try to pronounce that example sentence about Fig Newtons *without* slurring any consonants or dropping any a's. (Say, "I want a Fig Newton and a glass of milk," being sure to speak all the underlined letters.)

Hard work, huh? You'd probably get tired of speaking like a BBC announcer after a very short while, or else develop an urge to go to cricket matches. Moreover, Dragon Professional Individual still may not perform perfectly. For instance, you may get, "I want a Fig Newton in a glass of milk." If you try too hard to enunciate phrases like "Fig Newton," you get "Fig a Newton." Go fig ewer.

So, the first question is: Should you try to speak better than you do normally? If you suspect that your speech is naturally a bit sloppy, or if you've never thought about it much, you probably should try to do better.

If you find yourself working too hard to get better accuracy, stop. You will get tired quickly, start making even more errors, and your Dragon Professional Individual assistant will never learn to recognize your natural speech.

If you have an accent (and who doesn't?), don't worry much about it. Dragon Professional Individual adapts to your accent during training. What it has most trouble adapting to is missing words and sounds. If your accent is particularly strong, certain words may sound like other words to Dragon Professional Individual. (You can correct it using word training. See Chapter 17.)

If you aren't sure whether you'd know good speech if you heard it, listen to some professional broadcast journalists on the radio or television. But listen to people hired specifically as news readers (as opposed to disk jockeys, "personalities," and retired sports heroes now working as sportscasters). News readers — particularly news readers at larger radio stations or broadcasting companies — are hired partly for their careful speech.

If your speech is pretty clear, but you continue to get recognition errors, consider some of the other remedies in this part of the book. Training (Chapter 17) and better audio input (Chapter 18) can make a big difference. For example, Figure 16-1 shows that the correct placement of the microphone is crucial for accuracy.

Figure 16-1:
Correct
placement
of the
microphone.

If Dragon Professional Individual misrecognizes special phrases, words, or acronyms in your vocabulary, for instance, the solution is more likely to be training or vocabulary work than improving your speech.

How Do You Do It?

Changing any habit is hard, and speech is one of the most habitual activities any of us do. (Well, besides drinking coffee.) Apart from taking our thumbs out of our mouths, most of us talk the way we have since childhood. How does a person improve his or her speech? Following are some fairly painless tips for speaking better:

- **Avoid skipping words.** Speak every word, without fretting at first about the enunciation of the word itself. Dragon Professional Individual relies on the adjoining words to help figure out a word. If you skip or slur words, Dragon Professional Individual will make more mistakes.

- **Speak long phrases or full sentences.** The more words in an utterance, the better Dragon Professional Individual can figure out your words from context.

✔ **Make sure you pronounce even small words like "a" and "the."** If, like most people, you normally pronounce the word "a" as "uh," keep doing so. Don't switch to "ay," as in "hay."

✔ **Avoid running words together.** The tiny breaks between sounds help distinguish one word from another.

✔ **Focus your effort on pronouncing words differently that *should* sound a little different,** and which Dragon Dragon Professional Individual may otherwise confuse. Trying to pronounce "hear" differently from "here," for instance, won't gain you much: They are supposed to sound alike. (They are homonyms.) Nor will you benefit from trying to pronounce the "t" in "exactly," because that word won't be confused easily with any other word, even if you pronounce it "zackly." But pronouncing the "th" in the word "the" — even if you do it very lightly — will help Dragon Professional Individual distinguish that word from the word "a."

✔ **Enunciate.** If you're speaking every word and still have problems, work on your enunciation of words themselves. Pay attention to how a word is spelled. Try to speak all the consonant and vowel sounds in a word, especially ones that begin and end the word — unless they make the word noticeably awkward or the word sounds wrong as a result. ("Psychology" comes to mind. Don't pronounce the *P*, of course.)

✔ **Position the microphone appropriately.** If you're getting small words in your text that you didn't say, like "a" or "and," the microphone may be picking up small puffs of breath. Try moving the microphone more to the side. Then run the microphone check by clicking the Audio button on the DragonBar. Select the Check Microphone option. You are forced to run both the volume and quality checks. (See Chapter 17.)

✔ **Sit with good posture, not bent over.** Relax. Breathe freely. Think peaceful thoughts. Visualize twirling stars. You are getting very sleepy. . . .

✔ **Don't speak too rapidly.** You don't have to speak slowly, but in today's high-pressure environment, many people begin to sound like a chipmunk with a Starbucks habit.

✔ **If your throat gets dry or scratchy, drink water or warm tea.** (Creamy, cheesy, or overly sweet foods or drinks can goo up your throat. They can make you sound murky or cause you to clear your throat a lot.)

✔ **Check your microphone.** If your voice changes volume over time, and errors increase, run the microphone check process again (Audio ⇨ Check Microphone), choosing to adjust volume. If you have a cold or allergies, or any other long-term change to your voice, consider doing some more general training, discussed in Chapter 17.

✔ **Speak the way you trained.** When you trained Dragon Professional Individual, you read text aloud. Use your reading-aloud voice when you dictate text for highest accuracy.

✔ **Talk to a voice trainer or singing instructor.** A single session with a professional can give you a lot of tips about speaking more clearly. Who knows, you may find a whole new career.

If all else fails and accuracy does not improve, consider choosing Audio⇨Reset Audio Calibration. This makes Dragon forget everything it learned about how you sound. It still knows what words you use and when, but it will need to relearn your unique voice characteristics.

Shouldn't Dragon Professional Individual Meet You Halfway?

Despite all the tips in this chapter for speaking better, Dragon Professional Individual is pretty adaptable to a wide variety of speech habits. The only speech flaws that can't be compensated for, in some way, are these two:

✔ Skipping or slurring words

✔ Pausing between each word (not using continuous speech)

Nearly every other speech peculiarity can be compensated for by training. On the other hand, it may take a lot of training, and maybe you can improve your speech, instead, with less effort. See Chapter 17 for more about word training, general training, and vocabulary work.

For instance, if Dragon Professional Individual consistently gets the same word wrong, the problem may be that your pronunciation is a bit unusual. I, for instance, thought I heard a reference to a "9 o'clock chicken" when riding to the airport in New Zealand. I thought it was a colorful Kiwi phrase for a small commuter plane. The speaker was referring to a "check-in." Chickens aside, rather than retrain yourself, you can word-train Dragon Professional Individual, or enter a phonetic spelling for the "spoken form" of the word using the Vocabulary Editor. (Of course, if you say "chicken" for "check-in," what will you say for "chicken"?)

For the most part, Dragon Professional Individual is not sensitive to how fast you talk. But very rapid or slow speech may require adjusting Dragon Professional Individual settings for better accuracy. Dragon Professional Individual looks for a pause as a cue that the next text may be a command. Normally it works best using a quarter-second (250-millisecond) pause, but you can adjust it. Choose Tools ➪ Options, and then click the Commands tab. Drag the slider for Pause Required Before Commands to the right for longer pauses, left for shorter. If this setting is too short, words may get chopped up. If it is too long, Dragon Professional Individual may translate commands as text.

Chapter 17

Additional Training for Accuracy

- -

In This Chapter

▶ Using the Accuracy Center

▶ Recognizing when and how to train words

▶ Knowing when and how to add vocabulary words

▶ Adding the words you want in vocabulary building

▶ Creating shortcuts

▶ Doing more training

▶ Deciding when and how to train commands

- -

*I*f your Dragon Professional Individual assistant doesn't appear to be quite as sharp as you'd like it to be, you can teach it to do better. Dragon gives you a central place — the Accuracy Center — from which to improve its skills. If you start there, you will find all the tools you need at your fingertips. You can also find training options in other DragonBar menus, but if you are new to the software, this is the best place to start.

Using the Accuracy Center

Training and improving Dragon Professional Individual is the key to an almost flawless experience over time. Take the time to work with the software and train it to understand your special way of communicating.

Go to the Accuracy Center from DragonBar ➪ Help ➪ Improve My Accuracy, or say, **"Open Accuracy Center"** from the Help menu. You'll see the following sections, as shown in Figure 17-1:

✔ **Personalize your vocabulary:** Use the Vocabulary Editor to build your personal library of words and let your assistant build your special vocabulary by "reading" your documents and emails.

✔ **Set options and formatting:** Here you see how to set the Options menu to personalize your settings.

✔ **Adjust your acoustics:** Launch your Accuracy Tuning and check your microphone.

✔ **Find or train commands:** This section shows you what commands are available to you in a variety of different contexts.

✔ **Get more information:** Here you find information directly from the Dragon Professional Individual Help menu pertaining to vocabularies.

Yikes, lots of choices! Nobody said that educating software was effortless, but this chapter familiarizes you with what to do, and when and how to do it.

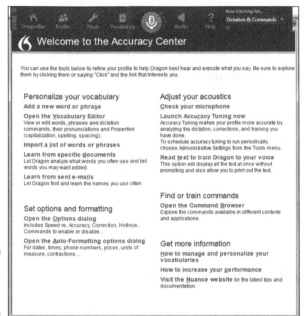

Figure 17-1:
The Accuracy Center.

Personalizing Your Vocabulary

Personalizing your vocabulary involves two functions. The first is vocabulary editing, which lets you add words to the Dragon Professional Individual vocabulary and, optionally, train Dragon Professional Individual in how you say those words. It also lets you add custom phrases that translate into text.

For example, you can say, **"My Address,"** and Dragon Professional Individual types your address. The second function is vocabulary building, which uses documents and emails to build your existing vocabulary. I cover both of those in the following sections.

Vocabulary editing

You can directly add words to the Dragon Professional Individual active vocabulary. The Vocabulary Editor is your tool to add or delete any word you have added but no longer use. It also has special features that allow you to do any of the following:

- ✔ Train Dragon Professional Individual in your own, personal pronunciation of a word, for better recognition.

- ✔ Add special words or phrases to the vocabulary, like your company name, properly capitalized or hyphenated, or jargon that you use in your profession.

- ✔ Give awkward words or phrases a different "spoken form" to make dictation easier, like saying, **"My Email"** for voiceguy@yourcompany.com. These are called *shortcuts.*

- ✔ Come up with alternative ways to say words, punctuation, or whitespace characters, like saying, **"Full Stop"** for a period.

Although I talk about mouse commands here, you can use voice commands to control the Vocabulary Editor, too.

Adding a new word or phrase

Adding a word tells Dragon Professional Individual that you want to include something new to its vocabulary. The accompanying Word training also teaches Dragon Professional Individual how *you* say a word.

No matter whether you say the word *bear* as "beer," "beyah," or "bayrrr," word training can tune Dragon Professional Individual's ear to your pronunciation. If Dragon Professional Individual is having trouble recognizing specific words, word training may be your solution. Word training is most helpful when your pronunciation of a word is unique or not at all like its spelling. For example, in New York, Houston Street is pronounced "Houseton." In Texas, it's pronounced "Hueston."

To add a new word or phrase, from the Accuracy Center click Add a New Word or Phrase. Up pops the Add Word or Phrase box, as shown in Figure 17-2.

TIP

You can train words without going to the Accuracy Center, too. Just say, **"Select <*word or words*>"** to select a word in your document, and when the Correction menu comes up, say, **"Add That to Vocabulary"** and the same dialog box appears. Note the option will be grayed out if the word is already in your vocabulary.

Figure 17-2:
Use the Add
Word or
Phrase box
to add new
words or
phrases.

To add words, follow these steps:

1. **Spell or type the word you want to add in the left prompt box.**

2. **In the right prompt box, type or spell the spoken form of the word.**

   Dragon Professional Individual uses a pronunciation guesser to figure out how most terms sound from the spelling. However, lots of jargon, acronyms, and other terms don't conform to standard rules of English pronunciation. Sometimes you can type a spoken form that gives Dragon Professional Individual something better to guess from.

   But whether you enter a written and spoken form or just a written form, if the pronunciation you're going to use isn't obvious from the spelling, you should train Dragon Professional Individual in how you pronounce the word. That's why you see a check box that lets you choose to train the pronunciation of the word or phrase. You can use the word training feature to make sure Dragon Professional Individual recognizes your word or phrase.

TIP

   For example, you may want Dragon Professional Individual to write "Boston and Maine Railroad" when you speak the phrase **"B&M."** Enter the written form Boston and Maine Railroad and the spoken form B and M or it could be bee and em for example.

3. **After you type in the word or phrase, click OK.**

   The Train Words dialog box displays in large type the spoken form of the term (or the written form if you haven't entered a spoken form), as shown in Figure 17-3. I chose to train the word "prewash."

4. **Click Go.**

   Speak the phrase into your microphone exactly as you always say it.

5. **Click the Done button after you've spoken the term.**

What if word training isn't enough? Perhaps you speak your newly trained word, and Dragon Professional Individual still gets it wrong. If two terms sound alike, Dragon Professional Individual chooses one by looking at how you have used the term in the past, in context.

Figure 17-3:
Training words in the Train Words dialog box.

If you have recently added this term (say, in the Vocabulary Editor), Dragon Professional Individual has little or no context for the term. You haven't used it in a phrase, so Dragon Professional Individual is more likely to choose the term with which it has more experience. The solution is to dictate your new term in context and then correct Dragon Professional Individual with **"Correct That"** when it chooses the wrong term. If you dictate the new word and correct Dragon Professional Individual with the Correction dialog box, it will catch on and use the new term.

Adding shortcuts in the Vocabulary Editor

To add custom terms to the Dragon Professional Individual active vocabulary, click the Open the Vocabulary Editor link from the Accuracy Center (or you can launch the Vocabulary Editor by choosing Vocabulary ➪ Open Vocabulary Editor from the DragonBar menu or speak the commands). Then follow these steps:

1. **Enter the term in the Search For box at the top of the Vocabulary Editor.**

   In Figure 17-4, for example, I entered an email address, `info@ SavvyExecutiveInstitute.com`.

   To see what's in the vocabulary, you can either scroll the list in the Vocabulary Editor or type the term in the Search For box. As you type, the list scrolls to match your typing.

   If you want to speak something other than what's typed, first add the word by clicking Add. In the Add New Word or Phrase dialog box that appears, enter the way you want to say the word in the text box labeled Spoken Form (If Different). For example, if I enter *My Email* there, I can simply say, **"My Email"** and have Dragon Professional Individual type `dragon@gurus.com`. If you use a term in the Spoken Form box that Dragon Professional Individual doesn't already have in its vocabulary, a dialog box lets you know that fact. It also asks whether you want it to assign an approximate pronunciation. Click OK.

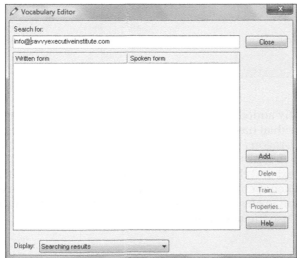

Figure 17-4:
Email address typed into the Vocabulary Editor.

2. **After you enter a written (and, if different, spoken) form of the term, click the Add button.**

   If you think the pronunciation will be difficult, select the I Want to Train check box before clicking the Add button and record the word as directed. The Vocabulary Editor adds the term to the vocabulary list and marks it with a plus sign (+). You can delete any custom term you add. Just click the term, and then click the Delete button. You can also select multiple terms to delete by holding down the Ctrl button as you click.

3. **Click the Close button.**

Creating different ways to say the same thing

The period at the end of this sentence has more aliases (alternative names) than most criminals. The words *period, decimal point, dot, point, stop,* and *full stop* are all valid names for that same symbol in different contexts. Dragon Professional Individual doesn't currently recognize all those alternative spoken names, but you can add them to the vocabulary.

If you have an alternative spoken name you would like to use for a word, phrase, or symbol, use the Vocabulary Editor to add that name. Unfortunately, you can't change any of the existing names, even if you don't like them. You can only add an alternative.

To add aliases, whether for symbols, numbers, or other terms, launch the Vocabulary Editor (choose Vocabulary ⇨ Open Vocabulary Editor) and then do the following:

1. **Type the term or symbol that needs an alias in the Search For text box.**

   The list scrolls to show the current written and spoken forms.

   To see all the currently defined symbols and dictation commands in the Vocabulary Editor, you must scroll up above the terms beginning with "a."

2. **Click the Add button.**

   The Add New Word or Phrase dialog box appears.

3. **Type a new term in the Spoken Form box, and then click the Add button.**

   A second copy of the word appears in the vocabulary list, with your new alias and a plus sign (+) to mark the alias as a custom term. (If the alias doesn't work out, you can delete it. Just click the line and then click the Delete button.)

When you change the spelling of a word, the new word does not have the same context data assigned to it as the original — which can be good or bad. For example, if you add a new version of the word *center* spelled *centre,* Dragon loses the context data that tells it what words appear near it. To have alternate written forms of words, you should change the properties of existing words by choosing DragonBar ⇨ Vocabulary ⇨ Open Vocabulary Editor, select the word *center,* and then click the Properties button.

Import a list of words or phrases

If you're likely to use terms from some specialized vocabulary in the documents you dictate, you can make a list of such terms and give them all to Dragon Professional Individual in one fell swoop. For example, Queen's Gambit Declined is the name of a chess opening. Each of the three words is surely already in the Dragon Professional Individual General English vocabulary, but Dragon Professional Individual doesn't know that these three words have a special capitalization pattern when they appear together. If you were to dictate documents about chess, you would want to include Queen's Gambit Declined on one line of your list.

You can create a list and use the Import List of Words or Phrases box, as shown in Figure 17-5.

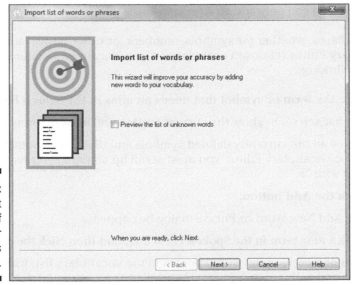

Figure 17-5:
The Import List of Words or Phrases box.

Import list of words or phrases

Import list of words or phrases

This wizard will improve your accuracy by adding new words to your vocabulary.

☐ Preview the list of unknown words

When you are ready, click Next.

< Back   Next >   Cancel   Help

Follow these steps:

1. **Create a text file in which each line is the written form of a vocabulary entry you want to add.**

2. **At the end of any line where you want a different spoken form, add a backslash (/) and then the shorthand alias you want to speak.**

3. **From the Accuracy Center, click the Import a List of Words or Phrases link or use the mouse or commands, and from the DragonBar go to Vocabulary ➪ Import List of Words or Phrases.**

   A screen pops up with the words "Import List of Words or Phrases." You also see the option to "Preview the list of unknown words." If you wish to do that, select the box.

4. **Click Next.**

   You are asked to add the file.

5. **Click the Add File button.**

   The file is analyzed.

6. **Click Finish.**

   A Summary box shows you how many words were added to your vocabulary.

A few wise ideas can save you time and trouble while adding words by using the Import method:

- ✔ Review the list of words to make sure they are real words that you really want.

- ✔ Don't add words that you use infrequently. This is especially true if they sound like some other word that you use often.

- ✔ Sometimes individual proper nouns that you want from a document are actually common words, except that their capitalization (or lack of capitalization) makes them special for you — a sports team named Bingo, for example, or an Internet domain that uses a person's name.

Learning from specific documents

At this step, you provide your Dragon Professional Individual assistant with documents so that it can look at them and pick out any words or capitalized phrases it doesn't recognize. (In essence, it's automatically building a list like the one you may have provided, as the preceding section describes.) The more documents you give the vocabulary building function, the better. In particular, give it documents that resemble the documents you want to dictate — your previous best-seller, for example, or a collection of your office memos.

TIP

Giving the Vocabulary Builder documents that resemble other documents is a great way for Dragon to add words and learn when you use those words — which updates your language model. Dragon looks at words before and after every word you say and uses context knowledge about how certain words are used. This increases accuracy and helps Dragon tell the difference between words like *ice cream* and *I scream*. It is also a good idea to run the Vocabulary Builder on documents that have words Dragon does not know. In this way, you are adding words to the vocabulary and teaching Dragon when and how you use those words.

TIP

Spell-check the documents before you analyze them. The vocabulary-building function looks for words it doesn't already know, and it thinks it has found one whenever it runs into a misspelled word. You save yourself some time if you spell-check your documents and correct any misspelled words before giving the documents to Vocabulary Builder.

To add words from specific documents in Word, WordPerfect, plain text, RTF (Rich Text Format), and HTML (web) documents, follow these steps:

1. **From the Accuracy Center, click the Learn from Specific Documents link or choose Vocabulary ⇨ Learn from Specific Documents from the DragonBar.**

   A Learn from Specific Documents screen pops up, as shown in Figure 17-6. On this screen, you have the option to Find Unknown Words (in various forms) or Adapt to Writing Style.

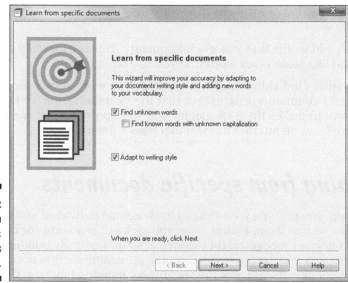

Figure 17-6:
Learn from Specific Documents screen.

2. **Select the check box next to each option you want to add and then click Next.**

   A new screen appears with buttons to add either folders of documents or single documents to analyze.

3. **Click the buttons to add your files.**

   Your Windows Browse window opens, allowing you to choose the files as you normally do. Next, the files show up in the window of the Learn from Specific Documents screen.

4. **Click Next.**

   Your documents are analyzed. A check mark appears next to the names of the documents analyzed. All the words that were new to your vocabulary are shown with check marks and the frequency with which they occurred.

5. **If you want to add all the words on the list, click Next.**

   You see a list of the words, and the screen asks you to check the words you want to train.

6. **Check the ones you think should be trained for pronunciation.**

   The Train Words dialog box displays, in large type, the written form of the term.

7. **Click Go.**

   Speak the phrase into your microphone exactly as you always say it.

8. **Click Next.**

   A Summary box shows you how many words werc added to your vocabulary.

9. **Click Finish.**

Adding words from somebody else's documents

Normally, you use your own documents to teach Dragon Professional Individual about your vocabulary. What can you do, however, for a subject that you have not written much about?

Answer: Grab words from documents other people have written. The web, for example, is full of documents about nearly any subject you can name. The trick is to have Dragon Professional Individual pick up on the words, but not the writing style, of this other author (unless you intend to write just like him or her).

To use someone else's documents, first you must get the documents! Dragon Professional Individual can read Microsoft Word or WordPerfect documents if you have Word or WordPerfect installed. It can also read plain text, RTF, and HTML documents. To get documents from the web, browse to the page you want, and then save the page as an HTML file. In Internet Explorer, for example, choose File ⇨ Save As, enter a filename in the dialog box that appears, and click Save.

Use these documents in the Add Words from Documents box as you would any other documents. When you get to the Adapt to Writing Style check box, deselect it so your Dragon Professional Individual assistant won't assume that you write like that other writer.

Learning from sent emails

Analyzing emails is another way for your Dragon Professional Individual assistant to build your vocabulary. This process helps in two ways. It learns from the style of your emails and it can automatically add email addresses you currently use. It works with Microsoft Outlook, Outlook.com, Lotus Notes, Gmail, Yahoo!, and Windows Live Mail.

From the Accuracy Center, click Learn from Sent Emails or go to Vocabulary ⇨ Learn from Sent Emails from the DragonBar. The Learn from Sent Emails Wizard appears, as shown in Figure 17-7.

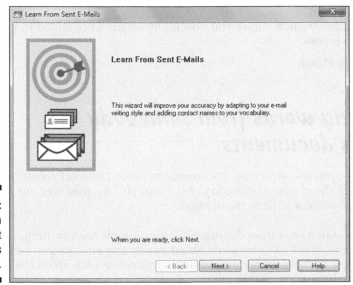

Figure 17-7:
The Learn from Sent Emails Wizard.

Follow these steps to complete the process:

1. **Click Next.**

   Choose from the options presented by selecting the check boxes.

2. **Click Next again.**

   The emails are analyzed.

3. **Click Next one more time.**

   Any new words will be displayed for you to train (see the section "Learning from specific documents," earlier in this chapter).

4. **Click Finish.**

Setting Options and Formatting

This section of the Accuracy Center is key. It contains several ways for you to customize Dragon Professional Individual to make your assistant do things your way. Remember to revisit your Options settings periodically when you are using Dragon Professional Individual. You may want to alter the settings you chose when you first started.

Opening the Options dialog box

It's important to set personal options from Options on the Tools menu. From the Accuracy Center, access it by clicking in the Open the Options dialog box. This is where you set up preferences for the Dragon Professional Individual assistant to work your way. See Chapter 3 for a full discussion.

Opening the Auto-Formatting dialog box

Auto-formatting is important so don't skip it. Access it from the Open the Auto-Formatting Options dialog box in the Accuracy Center or go to Tools ⇨ Auto-Formatting Options.

If you get overzealous and regret some of the changes you made, click the Restore Defaults button shown in Figure 17-8.

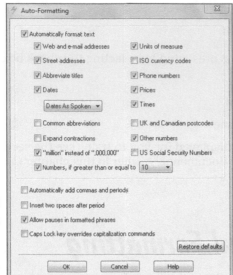

Figure 17-8:
The Auto-
Formatting
dialog box.

To save time, consider setting these default options:

- ✔ **Format Street Addresses, Phone Numbers, Prices, and Times Automatically:** These check boxes allow typical formatting without your attention.

- ✔ **Dates:** You have the option to set a specific date format from a drop-down menu.

- ✔ **Format Web and Email Addresses Automatically:** To set this option, select the check box. If you have to do these a special way and can't use auto-formatting, you may want to train them individually.

- ✔ **Allow Pauses in Formatted Phrases:** A nice feature, because you often pause to check numbers when speaking phone numbers. If you deselect this check mark, Dragon Professional Individual may put spaces where you pause.

For more details about how auto-formatting relates to the new Smart Format rules, check out Chapter 6.

Adjusting Your Acoustics

The Accuracy Center provides three ways to help your Dragon Professional Individual assistant improve your acoustics. They are as follows:

- ✔ Checking your microphone
- ✔ Launching Accuracy Tuning
- ✔ Reading text to train Dragon to your voice

I discuss these in the following sections.

Checking your microphone

Obviously, the microphone is an all-important part of your software. Make sure your Dragon Professional Individual assistant doesn't have a "hearing" problem. Does Dragon Professional Individual make errors on lots of words and phrases, not just a specific few? Your problem could be with speaking unclearly, with your microphone position or quality, with your sound card quality, or with the microphone volume set by Dragon, as shown in Figure 17-9.

Figure 17-9: The Microphone Volume setting.

To rule out a hearing problem, rerun the microphone check from the Check Microphone link in the Accuracy Center. You can also access it from the Audio ⇨ Check Microphone menu option on the DragonBar. If Dragon thinks your audio is fine, and you still get errors on lots of words after running the microphone check, try the voice tips in Chapter 16. If all else fails, you can reset your audio by choosing Audio➪Reset Audio Calibration. You may want to try checking the microphone and doing more training before going that route though because you lose all your audio training to date.

Launching Accuracy Tuning

Here's where the correction and fine-tuning of your dictation really pay off. From the Launch Accuracy Tuning Now link in the Accuracy Center (or from Audio➪Launch Accuracy Tuning), you'll be presented with the Acoustic and Language Model Optimizer screen. Don't be intimidated. Your Dragon Professional Individual assistant does all the heavy lifting.

As shown in Figure 17-10, the Perform Acoustic Optimization and Perform Language Model Optimization check boxes are selected by default. Leave them selected, then do the following:

1. **Click Go.**

   You are given an estimated time for completion of this process. Don't be shocked if the initial estimate says 450 hours! It quickly changes to a couple of minutes while it's working. Perhaps your Dragon Professional Individual assistant has a weird sense of humor.

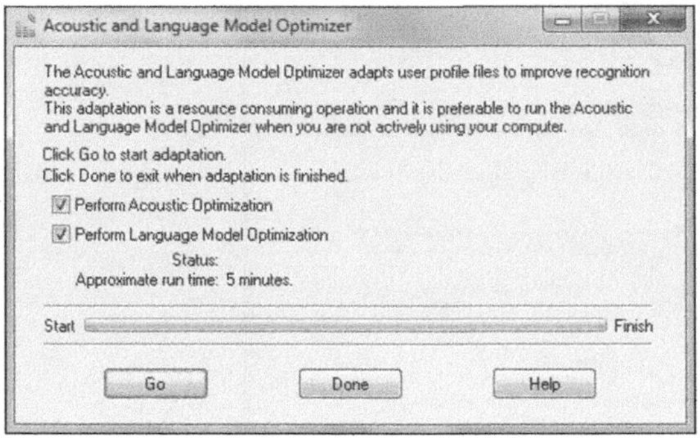

Figure 17-10:
The Acoustic and Language Model Optimizer screen.

2. **After the process completes, click Done.**

   You'll be asked to save the newly optimized files.

3. **Click Yes and you're done.**

See? Your Dragon Professional Individual assistant does all the work. (Isn't that why you pay it the big bucks?)

Reading text to train Dragon to your voice

If Dragon Professional Individual seems to be making more mistakes than it used to, ask yourself if *you* have changed since you first trained Dragon. Has your voice, manner of speaking, or working environment changed?

For example, are you getting more experienced at dictation? Have you changed your office or changed something that makes or absorbs sound in your office? If so, try running the Training Wizard. (To access it, go to the DragonBar menu and choose Audio⇨Read Text to Improve Accuracy.) Training helps Dragon Professional Individual get a more accurate picture of your voice and speech habits.

Running the Training Wizard after you've had some experience with Dragon Professional Individual is a good idea. Often, you speak differently after a few days.

The plan for training is to read something to Dragon Professional Individual so that it can figure out how you speak.

A fundamental problem with training is that many people read differently than they dictate. Try to speak the way you would if you were the author and were thinking this stuff up for the first time.

Don't say, **"Cap"** or any other dictation commands during training. Don't say any punctuation, either. Don't go back and reread something you think you read wrong. Just push forward and keep moving. It might be easier to print the story out, hold it, and read from there.

Finding or Training Commands

In Dragon Professional Individual, Nuance gives you some ways to identify commands. Because "What can I say" is context-sensitive, you will always see the commands that are helpful for the application you are in.

If Dragon Professional Individual isn't obeying your commands, it may not be recognizing your pronunciation. You can improve its recognition for many commands exactly as you would for word or phrase training. See the steps in the preceding sections for instructions.

Make sure you capitalize the words of the command properly. Check the documentation that comes with Dragon Professional Individual for proper capitalization. Most words in Dragon Professional Individual command phrases are initial-capped except for articles, prepositions, and other short words.

You can't, however, train "dictation commands" this way. These commands are the ones that control capitalization and spacing, like **"No Caps On."** To train those commands, use the Vocabulary Editor. Scroll to the top (above the "a") of the list of words in the Vocabulary Editor. Click a command and then click the Train button.

Before you try command training, make sure that you pause correctly before and after a command. If Dragon Professional Individual gets the words right but types them instead of doing them, pausing is more likely to be your problem than pronunciation. Chapter 4 talks about solving this problem.

To access the Command Browser from the Accuracy Center, click the Open the Command Browser link. Or you can choose Tools ⇨ Command Browser.

You can also add a new command by choosing Tools ⇨ Add New Command. Here you can easily type in and train a new command.

When using the Command Browser, as shown in Figure 17-11, you have several options:

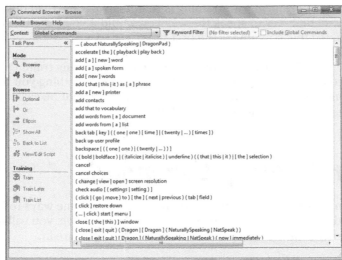

Figure 17-11:
The
Command
Browser
window.

✔ **Find specific applications:** Click the Content drop-down menu to see if the particular application you're using has specific commands in Dragon Professional Individual. Then you can peruse them to see what you need.

✔ **Train commands:** By clicking a particular command, you can use the Train icon on the left side to train that command to understand your pronunciation.

TIP

> ✔ **Look at scripts:** By choosing the Script icon on the left side, you switch from Browse mode to Script mode. Here you can directly create, delete, edit, or copy commands.
>
> Unless you know what you're doing, stay in Browse mode.

Getting More Information

This section of the Accuracy Center is where you find information about your vocabulary and a link to the Nuance website, shown in Figure 17-12.

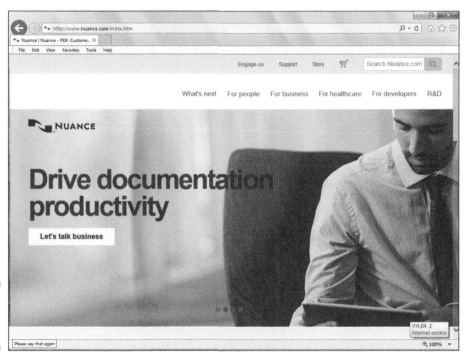

Figure 17-12:
The Nuance
website.

When you click the How to Manage and Personalize Your Vocabularies link, you are taken to an explanation of the types of vocabularies available. Recall that when you installed your Dragon Professional Individual software, you were asked several questions about your accent and what region of the world you live in. This Help section gives you more information about those vocabulary choices.

The Nuance website is chock-full of information, training, help, and tech support. Chapter 21 covers this extensively.

Chapter 18

Improving Audio Input

· ·

· ·

*T*he old expression "garbage in, garbage out" takes on a different twist when you talk about speech recognition. If garbage goes in, Dragon Professional Individual reconstructs it into perfectly good words. It acts like a trash compactor: It makes garbage look better.

Of course, you aren't talking trash. Nonetheless, your words may be trashed on their way to the laptop. The microphone or audio hardware may not be quite right. Or the microphone may have moved when you chugged your coffee. Or your office mates, appliances, or kids may be contributing background garbage of their own to your audio. The result may sound okay to your ears if you play it back, but Dragon Professional Individual assistants have very sensitive ears.

It isn't likely that you'll encounter a hardware problem when using Dragon Professional Individual, but I include some ideas here in case you do.

Figuring Out Whether You Have an Audio Input Problem

If Dragon Professional Individual misinterprets lots of words, your second thought is probably, "Something's wrong with my microphone or sound card." (Your first thought is probably uncharitable toward your new assistant. Shame on you.)

Dragon Professional Individual may be messing up for lots of reasons, however. As with a puppy that messes up, one reason may be inadequate training. Before you go looking for an audio input problem, make sure you have done some additional training. One symptom of a need for additional training or vocabulary building is that Dragon Professional Individual makes the same error repeatedly: "cheese" for "trees," for instance. See Chapter 17 for help with that.

If, however, Dragon Professional Individual gives you different text each time you say the same thing ("wheeze," "sneeze," and "breeze" for "trees"), you may have an audio input problem. One dead-simple way to test for serious audio input problems is to listen to your PC play back your voice. You can use a Nuance-approved sound recorder, if you have one, or you can use the Windows Sound Recorder:

✔ For Windows 7, access the Sound Recorder by choosing Start ⇨ Control Panel ⇨ Sound ⇨ Recorder tab. Click the red-dot button in Sound Recorder and speak into the microphone to record. Click the red-dot button to stop and save the recording to a location of your choice.

✔ For Windows 8, access the Sound Recorder by going to Search on the Charms bar and typing Sound Recorder. The recorder appears on the left side. Click it to show the recorder. To record, click the red-dot button in Sound Recorder and speak into the microphone to record. Click the red button to stop and save the recording to a location of your choice.

✔ For Windows 10, access the Sound Recorder by going to All Apps and then clicking Voice Recorder. A screen opens with a microphone. Click the microphone to start and then click again to stop, and save the recording to a location of your choice.

The most common cause of recognition errors is muttering through your coffee cup, or otherwise not speaking clearly. See Chapter 16 for tips on speaking clearly. Does your diction qualify you for the British Broadcasting Company? Then read on.

Running the microphone check

If Dragon Professional Individual has been working okay to date and only now has begun making errors, your microphone may have moved a bit, or you may be speaking more or less loudly than before. If you were using the internal microphone and changed locations, the echo and background noise may have changed drastically, too. In that case, you only need to adjust the way Dragon interprets your microphone. A microphone check can be very helpful at this point. Access it by choosing Audio ⇨ Check Microphone. Doing so adjusts the volume *and* checks the quality of the audio. Whether you pass, the audio is acceptable, or the quality check fails, you can click the Play button to listen to a playback of the audio that Dragon heard.

 Some PCs have more than one sound system installed. For instance, you may have installed a better sound card than the one your PC came with, but the original is still present. If you're using a USB microphone, you almost certainly have two sound systems. If you have more than one sound system, choose Profile ⇨ Manage Dictation Sources and make sure the correct source is selected. You must choose the system your microphone is connected to: USB Audio Device if you're using a USB microphone, for instance.

Checking your microphone

Many a slip happens between the PC and the lip. Following are some of the problems you may be having on the microphone end of things, and what to do about them:

- ✓ **Your microphone needs adjustment.** Make sure the microphone is positioned to the side of your mouth, about a half-inch away from one corner of your mouth. You may have to bend the plastic tube that holds the microphone into an S-shape to get this right.

- ✓ **You have chosen the wrong sound system in Manage Dictation Sources.** You can make the correction by choosing Profile ⇨ Manage Dictation Sources.

- ✓ **You're trying to use the cheap microphone that came with your PC.** Give it up! Buy a serious microphone from the list of Nuance-certified devices on its website in the Support area. You are likely better off using the built-in microphone *on* your PC, as long as your computer is not very old.

- ✓ **The microphone connection is loose.** Look at where the plug fits the jack in your PC; make sure it isn't wiggly. Try playing back some of your dictation. (Select text and say, **"Play That."**) If it has loud, scratchy noises, you may need to replace the microphone or get someone to test and fix its cable. Some background noise also comes from the PC (not exactly a high-end sound system) and is unavoidable.

- ✓ **The microphone cable is plugged into the wrong jack in the PC.** If the microphone is plugged into a really wrong jack, like the speaker output, it won't work at all. If you have no alternative but to plug it into the IN or LINE-IN jack on your PC (you have no microphone jack), it may work, but the volume may be low.

- ✓ **A battery is failing in the microphone or adapter.** Some microphones do have batteries. I'm willing to bet that battery-powered adapters do, too.

Should you get a better microphone or just use your built-in microphone? Many voice-recognition professionals swear by getting a better microphone, which can run up to several hundred dollars. A better microphone will generally improve your results, but only up to the limits of your PC's sound card. Both microphone and sound card are links in the chain that brings your voice to your PC, and whichever is the weakest link will limit your sound quality. Those professionals who recommend better microphones also tend to have very good sound cards. Your results will probably not improve in proportion to the money you spend. Check the list of Dragon-certified microphones on Dragon's website for options. But before you go laying out big bucks for a new microphone and sound card, read the next section on USB microphones.

Getting a USB microphone

One great way to get better quality audio and bypass all this microphone/sound-card stuff entirely is to get a Universal Serial Bus (USB) microphone. It's probably the best way to deal with a laptop that doesn't have good audio.

A USB microphone plugs into a USB connector on your PC and delivers digital sound right to the PC. You no longer use the audio input features of your PC's sound card. Because the USB mic removes all the variables that the regular microphone and sound-card system present, it's one of the better solutions to audio input problems. Some users have even reported that their words are transcribed faster when they use the USB mic. (Your mileage may differ.)

If you want the very best, a USB solution may not be the answer. Some users report that some USB microphones aren't as good as the combination of a very good separate microphone and a very good sound card.

Playing your best card

Your microphone plugs into a chunk of your PC loosely called the "sound card" or the "audio card." The sound card is responsible for converting what comes out of your microphone into computer bits. Are some sound cards sounder than other sound cards? The answer is a resounding "Yes!"

How do you know whether your sound card is your problem? It's hard to be certain. Because replacing a sound card is a pain, most people try to improve other aspects of their audio first, like speaking more clearly or adjusting the microphone position. If those efforts don't work, they get a new sound card (or buy a USB microphone).

Being of sound mind, or are you certifiable?

Dragon systems makes a point of certifying audio (sound) hardware, including microphones and sound cards. Check out Nuance's website at `http://support.nuance.com/compatibility/` for the list of compatible products. While you are at Nuance's website, explore the Knowledgebase in the Support section. You can also go to `www.facebook.com/dragonnaturallyspeaking`.

What is a sound card?

Inside your PC is a large board full of electronics that do the essential functions of your computer. Less-essential stuff is on smaller boards, also called cards, whose rear-ends are typically decorated with various connectors. These small boards are designed so that their connectors stick out the back of your PC or laptop, where you plug stuff in. Depending on the whim of the engineers who built your PC, the sound (audio) features may either be on the big ("mother") board or on one of these cards. If your audio features are on a card, changing to a Dragon-certified card is generally easier than if they are on the motherboard. So many sound cards work with Dragon Professional Individual that it is unlikely you will have a problem. Make sure to look at the list of compatible sound cards listed on the Nuance.com site in the Support area.

Try all the preceding suggestions first, before buying anything new.

Finding out whether you have a Dragon-certified sound card is a good idea. If you have one, and audio input is poor anyway, you'll know to look elsewhere for the cause.

Check out the list and see what suits you. The best way to see what you have is to check your PC's or laptop's sound card.

If you are using Windows 7, do the following:

1. **On the Windows taskbar, choose Start ⇨ Control Panel.**

2. **In the Control Panel, double-click the Hardware and Sound icon.**

    A screen with several icons pops up.

3. **Click the Sound icon.**

   You'll see the following tabs at the top: Playback, Recording, and Sounds and Communications. See which Default Devices are listed for Recording and Playback. If the ones you want are not the defaults, click them to make them the defaults.

If you are using Windows 8, do the following:

1. **On the Start Screen, use the keyboard shortcut Win+X to open the Start menu.**

2. **From the list, choose Control Panel.**

   A screen with several icons pops up.

3. **Click the Sound icon.**

   A screen pops up showing the volume mixer for your Speakers and System Sounds.

4. **Double-click the icon for System Sounds.**

   You'll see the following tabs at the top: Playback, Recording, and Sounds and Communications. See which Default Devices are listed for Recording and Playback. If the ones you want are not the defaults, click them to make them the defaults.

If you are using Windows 8.1, do the following:

1. **On the Start Screen, use the keyboard shortcut Win+X to open the Start menu.**

2. **From the list, choose Control Panel.**

   The Control Panel opens.

3. **Click the Hardware and Sound icon.**

   The Hardware and Sound window opens.

4. **Click the Sound icon.**

   The Sound window opens. You'll see the following tabs at the top: Playback, Recording, Sounds, and Communications. See which default devices are listed for Playback and Recording (they'll have a green checkmark). If the devices you want are not the default, click on them to make them the defaults.

If you are using Windows 10, do the following:

1. **Click the Windows 10 icon in the taskbar and type** Sound **in the Find a Setting window.**

   A screen with several icons pops up.

2. Click the Sound icon.

A window pops up. You see the following tabs at the top: Playback, Recording, and Sounds and Communications. See which default devices are listed for Recording and Playback. If the ones you want are not the defaults, click them to make them the defaults.

What about the rest of you who don't have a Dragon-blessed sound card, or have no idea whether you do and aren't about to spend the money to get one anyway? The best solution is to try to improve your speaking, run the microphone check regularly, do lots of training and vocabulary building, and make sure you work in a quiet environment.

Ensuring a Quiet Environment

In general, Dragon Professional Individual, like the rest of us, works best in a quiet environment. Noise from an open window, kids, dogs, appliances, fans, air conditioners, ringing phones, shredders, coffee machines, or a loudly growling stomach can make Dragon Professional Individual inaccurate. So this is a perfect excuse to shoo away the dog and kids, shut off the phone, and drink the last of the coffee (and spit out the gum). If you're at work, it's an excuse to close the door to your office. (Lucky you, if you have one.)

Nuance recommends that the best way to do all your training is in the environment in which you plan to use Dragon Professional Individual. If it's a loud, busy place, do it there. If you change environments, rerun your audio tests.

Dragon Professional Individual also works best where the environment deadens sound, such as areas with carpets, heavy drapes, or blinds. Hard surfaces such as hard floors, glass windows, granite counters, and metal furniture cause echoes that you don't notice but that Dragon Professional Individual may.

If your environment has become noisier than it was when you trained Dragon Professional Individual, you may do well to revisit some training. See the discussion in Chapter 17.

Besides acoustical noise — noise that you can hear — you may be surrounded by the hum of electrical noise. Electrical noise is the result of electricity and magnetic fields zinging around near your microphone or sound card. PCs, laptops, and monitors generate a lot of these fields, so try backing a bit farther away from your PC and monitor when you dictate.

Chapter 19

Having Multiple Computers or Users

....

....

*H*eraclitus, the Greek philosopher, is famous for his ideas about change. He is quoted as saying, "You could not step twice into the same river; for other waters are ever flowing on to you." Computer systems change faster than almost any other part of life: If something works, it must be obsolete. If you become a regular user of Dragon Professional Individual, you and your Dragon Professional Individual assistant will probably go through a number of changes together — new operating systems, new versions of the Dragon Professional Individual software, or even whole new hardware. New users may come into your life as family members or officemates and decide that they want to start dictating, too.

I address some of the potential changes elsewhere in this book. In Chapter 18, for example, I talk about hardware upgrades that may improve the performance of Dragon Professional Individual: a better sound card and microphone.

In this chapter, I look at how Dragon Professional Individual solves the problem of multiple people, computers, environments, microphones, or hats. I show you how to use these features for better accuracy. (Hold onto your hat!)

Creating and Managing Users

Dragon Professional Individual can't always understand strangers well, and sometimes it can't even understand you well if something about you changes, such as the way you use words or the way you sound. Consider it this way: Many people wear several hats. They are doctors and administrators, too; they are accountants by day and poets by night; or they are brain surgeons on weekdays and drill sergeants on weekends. Whichever hat they wear, they write and speak very differently in those roles. People may also sound different because of their environments or the microphones they work with at any given time.

If you dictate using different words or writing styles, you may need multiple users. Here's why and how to create and manage those users.

One person, different users

Dragon Professional Individual understands only those who have officially introduced themselves as *users* and created a *User Profile.*

Here are four reasons why you may want to make more than one User Profile for yourself:

- ✔ You use different vocabularies or writing styles for different tasks.
- ✔ You use different microphones for different tasks.
- ✔ You want to use different Dragon Professional Individual options for different tasks. For instance, you may want to turn off certain features to save memory when using Dragon Professional Individual with big applications. (See Chapter 3 for instructions.) Option choices are part of the definition of a user.
- ✔ You have a laptop or other hardware and use it in two or more distinct environments (noisy/quiet, outdoors/indoors, in bed/in the pool, and so on).

The drawback of having more than one user per person is the extra vocabulary training of Dragon Professional Individual that the person must do. Each user maintains his own training and experience, starting with the initial microphone check (Audio ⇨ Check Microphone) that you must repeat for each user. The same holds true for ongoing training. If you use the phrase "boogie-woogie" in both your personal and professional lives, for instance, not only do you have a very interesting life, but also you have to train both users so that Dragon Professional Individual recognizes the phrase.

You can change or broaden Dragon Professional Individual's definition of a user, however. You don't have to have a separate user for, say, when you have a head cold. Instead, you can choose Read Text to Improve Accuracy from the Audio menu and Dragon Professional Individual will add its "head cold" experience to its previous experience of your voice. (See Chapter 17.) It will do better the next time you are sneezy (or grumpy or both). Likewise, if you run the microphone check, Dragon Professional Individual changes the microphone volume to adapt to any change in microphone position. (See Chapter 18.) You can train a single user to broadly cover all the types of writing you do, too. The problem with broadening a user definition is that overall accuracy will go down to the same degree that you have distinctly different situations.

Adding a new user

Setting up a new user is a lot like setting up the original user: You're off to see the New User Wizard. Invoke the wizard's name in either of the following ways:

- ✔ Click the New button in the Open User dialog box when Dragon Professional Individual starts up.
- ✔ From the Dragon Professional Individual DragonBar, choose Profile ⇨ New User Profile from the menu.

After the New User Wizard starts up, it takes you through the same series of steps that you (may) remember from the original installation. (See Chapter 2.)

Adding an old user to a different computer

What if the user you want to add isn't really new to Dragon Professional Individual but is new just to *that copy* of Dragon Professional Individual on a different (or new) computer? Getting a new computer can be fun. Everything runs faster, the hard drive is bigger, it may cause you to get a bunch of fun, new apps that you can play with, and the screen is cleaner than your old screen ever was. But just like moving to a new neighborhood, moving to a new machine means going through a period of uncertainty as you wonder whether all your possessions will make it in one piece or whether you have to leave anything behind.

Or maybe it isn't a brand-spanking-new machine. Maybe you've just decided that your Dragon Professional Individual assistant should follow you onto your office computer or home computer, or vice versa.

What is a user, really?

The Dragon Professional Individual idea of a user is probably not quite the same as yours. To you, a user is . . . you. A human with dreams and aspirations, hopes and fears. But Dragon Professional Individual doesn't know that. All it knows about users is that they make this wiggly electrical signal in its little electronic ear, and that it is responsible for choosing the right words from a vocabulary to match that wiggle.

If you do anything to change that wiggle, Dragon Professional Individual won't recognize you. Or if you try to use a word that isn't in the vocabulary that Dragon Professional Individual associates with that user, Dragon Professional Individual chooses the wrong word.

In other words, a "user" in Dragon Professional Individual is more than just you. It's you, plus your microphone or portable recorder, the environment you're speaking in, the sound card in your computer, your laptop, and your vocabulary. It's also the options you've chosen in Tools ➪ Options, and the microphone volume set by the microphone check (Audio ➪ Check Microphone).

In either case, the two main possessions that you would like to wrap in plastic and move to the new machine are your Dragon Professional Individual software and your user files.

Owning a copy of Dragon Professional Individual entitles you to have multiple User Profiles of your own voice (for example, from different sources) on your computer. You can also install it on your other computers if you use profiles for yourself. When you install Dragon Professional Individual, the activation process will follow how many computers you install it on. If you run over your allotted amount, you will have to uninstall one to load it onto a new one. See the Nuance website for more information on licensing users and activation.

Transferring your User Profiles to a new computer

If you're installing from a DVD, the files don't remember whether they've been read before, so installing Dragon Professional Individual on the new machine is just like installing it the first time. (See Chapter 2.) I assume you have done this.

If you are transferring your User Profiles, you'll be prompted to Import a User Profile.

One of the easiest ways to transfer the files from one computer to another is to use a USB flash drive. This way, you can easily copy the files from the first computer and move them to another. Of course, if you have a preferred method for moving files, use that.

You always move the User Profile from the original machine you created the profile on to the machine you are moving it to. This means that you use the Export function on the original machine and the Import function on the new machine.

Transferring your user files to a new machine involves a few basic steps. You have to go through this process for each user that you want to move to the new machine. Use the following steps:

1. **Choose Profile ⇨ Manage User Profiles from the DragonBar or say,** "Manage User Profiles" **on the original computer.**

   A User Profile window opens up, showing the names of the User Profiles on your computer.

2. **Select your username and click the Advanced button.**

   A submenu displays.

3. **Click the Export menu.**

   A Windows browser screen opens and asks you to click on the location where you want to save the User Profile files you want to move.

4. **If you are using a USB flash drive as recommended earlier, connect the drive to the computer, double-click Computer, and locate the drive.**

   Make a new folder on the flash drive so you'll have no trouble finding the files you transfer.

5. **Click OK.**

   The files are copied automatically to your flash drive. You should get a message that says the export was successful.

6. **Close the User Profile window. Remove the flash drive and go back to the computer you are moving the profile to.**

7. **With Dragon Professional Individual running on that computer, insert the flash drive.**

   You see a message on the DragonBar that says No User Profile Is Loaded.

8. **Choose Profile ⇨ Manage User Profiles on the DragonBar or say,** "Manage User Profiles" **on the new or alternate computer, and click the Advanced button.**

9. **Choose Import.**

   The browser screen opens and asks you to select the username you just set up when you installed the software in Step 2.

10. **Locate the USB drive and click on the file you copied onto it.**

11. **Click OK.**

    The files are copied and you have successfully moved your User Profile from your original computer to your new computer.

 The point of moving the old user files to the new machine is to avoid vocabulary retraining. You don't want to train the new user files that the wizard sets up. Rather, you just want the file structure to be set up so that you can replace the wizard's generic files with the files you copied from your old machine.

Because you already ran the New User Wizard when you installed Dragon Professional Individual on the new machine, you don't need to do it again. The next time you start Dragon Professional Individual, it knows about the existence of your newly transferred user. What it hasn't done is calibrate the audio system of this machine for your voice.

Open your new User Profile from the Open User dialog box that appears when Dragon Professional Individual starts. (If you don't see the Open User dialog box, it means that your new user is the only one Dragon Professional Individual knows about, so it opened that user without asking.)

Dragon Professional Individual realizes on its own that the audio setup hasn't been run for this user. When it offers you the opportunity to run the microphone check, click Yes. For a more detailed look at the microphone check and the screens it presents, see Chapter 2.

Managing User Files

If you aren't sure what users you have, you can find them listed in the Open User Profile dialog box, shown in Figure 19-1. If your copy of Dragon Professional Individual has more than one user, the Open User Profile dialog box shows up spontaneously when you open Dragon Professional Individual so that you can identify which user you are. You can also ask to see it by choosing Profile ⇨ Open User Profile from the Dragon Professional Individual DragonBar.

When you look at the Open User Profile dialog box, you may be surprised to realize just how many users you have.

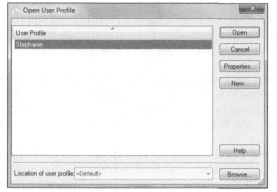

Figure 19-1:
The Open
User Profile
dialog box.

Deleting a user

User files take up space on your hard drive, so deleting user files that are no longer needed is good practice. Whatever your reason for wanting to delete a user, however, don't do it rashly. All the backups for that user are deleted, too, so you can't undo it. If you delete your girlfriend's user files when you break up, she'll have to retrain from scratch when you get back together. (She may get annoyed with you all over again.) Perform the following steps to delete a user:

1. **Choose Profile ⇨ Manage User Profiles from the menu in the Dragon Professional Individual DragonBar.**

   The Manage User Profiles dialog box appears.

2. **Select the name of the user you want to delete from the list in the dialog box.**

   You can't delete *yourself.* That is, you can't delete the current user. Among other things, this safeguard prevents you from deleting the last user on the system. (If you want to do that, you should uninstall Dragon Professional Individual.)

3. **Click the Delete button in the Manage User Profiles dialog box.**

4. **When the confirmation box appears, click Yes.**

Backing up and restoring User Profiles

Dragon Professional Individual keeps a backup copy of each user's speech files. It automatically makes this copy every fifth time you save Dragon Professional Individual's speech files — which most people do when they are prompted to as they exit Dragon Professional Individual. (You can make this backup more or less frequent by using the Options dialog box discussed in Chapter 3. Or, go to Tools ⇨ Options ⇨ Data and change the setting to Automatically Back Up User Profile Every <*xx*> Saves.)

The backup speech files lag behind any changes you make by correcting or training Dragon Professional Individual. So, if you make a mistake and save speech files when you shouldn't have (perhaps you vocabulary-trained using the wrong documents), you can restore from an earlier version of those files.

You can tell Dragon Professional Individual to update the backup copy at any time by choosing Manage User Profiles ⇨ Advanced ⇨ Backup. To restore from the backup copy, choose Profiles ⇨ Advanced ⇨ Restore. (The files are located in the folder where you installed Dragon Professional Individual, in the Users folder there, in the folder that goes with your particular username.)

Chapter 20

Creating Your Own Commands

. . . .

In This Chapter

▶ Creating new commands

▶ Editing custom commands

▶ Using the Command Browser

▶ Deleting commands

. . . .

*D*ragon Professional Individual is a great productivity tool along with its other virtues. In this chapter, you see how to save time when you compose emails, reports, and other materials. "How?" you ask. Get your Dragon Professional Individual assistant to type all the boilerplate text you normally have to type over and over again!

By working with the Command tools built into the program, you can have your Dragon Professional Individual assistant furiously type in all the text you want by stating a simple command. If everything in life was that simple, you would have time to finish all the great literature you keep promising to read.

In this chapter, I introduce you to the auto-text command feature that makes setting up frequent text in Dragon Professional Individual easier. It also allows you to more easily add variable fields to set up auto-texts that may help you fill out a form in which only the fields change.

Creating Commands That Insert Text and Graphics

If you tried counting all the voice commands in Dragon Professional Individual's vocabulary, you would be amazed at the final tally. They are the commands that Dragon Professional Individual comes with: the built-in commands and the Natural Language Commands. Even though Dragon provides hundreds, you will still want to add some that are specific to you, either in your job or in your personal life.

For example, if you have a long address that you need to put into your business emails, you can create a command to do it. If you have more than one signature for your emails, you can create them, too. How about several paragraphs? It's kind of fun to see how many you can create to save time. Just don't get too carried away!

Creating a new command

Adding a new command is easy using the MyCommands Editor, shown in Figure 20-1. Fill in the dialog boxes and click Save. But, before getting started, you need to ask yourself an important question. "In what application will I use this command?" Consider the following choices:

- ✔ **Global:** If you want to use the same command when working in different applications, you create a Global command.

- ✔ **Application-specific:** If you plan to use the command in a particular application, like Microsoft Word, you create an Application-specific command.

- ✔ **Window-specific:** If you're going to use the command in a specific window, like your email program, you create a window-specific command.

Figure 20-1:
The
MyCom-
mands
Editor dialog
box.

If you're ready with that answer, you're ready to create a command. From the DragonBar, choose Tools ⇨ Add New Command. Then follow these steps:

1. **Type (or say) the new command name where prompted.**

   In this example, I call it **Catalog Sent.**

   It's best if you name the command something distinctive that you can remember. You may also want to format it using title caps or all caps so that you can spot it easily.

2. **Click the Train button so that your command will be recognized easily.**

   A Train Words screen pops up, as shown in Figure 20-2, so that you can dictate the name.

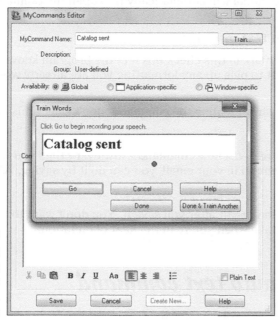

Figure 20-2:
The Train Words dialog box.

3. **Click Go.**

4. **Speak the command as you would normally.**

5. **Click Done.**

   Leave the Group as User-Defined.

6. **If you choose, you can enter a description in the Description box.**

   Below that, where you see Availability, select the radio button for the type of command you create. (See the beginning of this section for Global, Application-specific, and Window-specific.)

For this example, choose Application-specific.

You see a drop-down menu with a prompt box to type in your open application (or say it) or click the Browse button to select the application from your hard drive.

7. Type the application name.

Leave the Command Type as Text and Graphics.

8. Type or dictate the content into the large dialog box.

For this example, I dictated: **"Thanks for your request. We are sending our catalog overnight for your review. We hope this will give you a clear understanding about the value of our products."**

You can also cut and paste boilerplate text into the window of the dialog box or highlight it and say, **"Make That A Command."** Dragon Professional Individual will automatically pop open the Command Editor and paste it in.

9. Select the Plain Text check box.

Putting a check mark in this check box lets the program know that you want the content to pick up any formatting you are already working with in Word.

If you format it while creating the command, don't select this box.

10. Click Save.

You did it! You created a new command. Now every time you want to insert that paragraph in your email, you can do it by saying, **"Catalog Sent."**

Test your new command right after you save it. You don't want to find out that you made a mistake when you're in the heat of dictation.

Adding an auto text command

In case you're wondering, you can use the command you just created with any combination of other commands and dictation. For example, you can dictate a second paragraph on-the-fly that pertains to that specific addressee. In the same email or document, you can put in additional commands, like your signature or address. You can mix and match them to customize it.

Nuance has also added a great new feature that will make you even more productive when using your commands. It's the ability to use a variable in your auto-text command.

So how can you use it? Earlier in the chapter, in "Creating a new command," you see how to create a new command and dictate its contents so that you don't have to retype the same text over and over. Now you can put a variable in an auto-text command and use it on the fly.

You can use this function to do such tasks as fill out specific fields in form letters or invoices. Follow these steps:

1. **Choose Tools⇨Add New Auto-Text.**

   You are presented with a New Auto-Text Command screen, shown in Figure 20-3.

Figure 20-3:
The New
Auto-Text
Command
screen.

2. **Say or type the name of the command in the When You Say dialog box.**

   Choose a name. In this example, I entered New Online Catalog, as shown in Figure 20-4.

   After you have put in the name, dictate your message. Then position your cursor where you want to insert the variable.

3. **Click the Insert Field button.**

   The field is now inserted as a default value, as shown in Figure 20-5.

Figure 20-4:
Add a name
to the When
You Say
dialog box.

Figure 20-5:
A [default
value] field
is added
when you
click the
Insert Field
button.

Insert Field button

4. Replace "[default value]" with a prompt for the variable that you will insert, as shown in Figure 20-6.

In this example, I inserted the word *type* to prompt me to put in the type of catalog I am sending. In this case, I would say "engineering" as the type.

Prompt

Figure 20-6:
Replace the words *default value* with your prompt.

5. Click save.

When you use that command in the future, you will be able to dictate that variable.

Creating commands for new applications

When you create a command, you have to decide what type of command it will be — Global, Application-specific, or Window-specific. But what if you are using a program that hasn't been introduced to your Dragon Professional Individual assistant? You need to have them meet! That process is a snap. Follow these steps:

1. **Open the application you want to use.**

2. **From the DragonBar, choose Tools ⇨ Add New Command.**

3. **At the MyCommands Editor dialog box, fill in the name of the new command.**

4. **When you reach the Availability section, select the Application-specific radio button.**

   The name of your new application will be listed in the box, as shown in Figure 20-7.

   Continue to create the new command and remember to select that application from the Command Browser if you want to edit it.

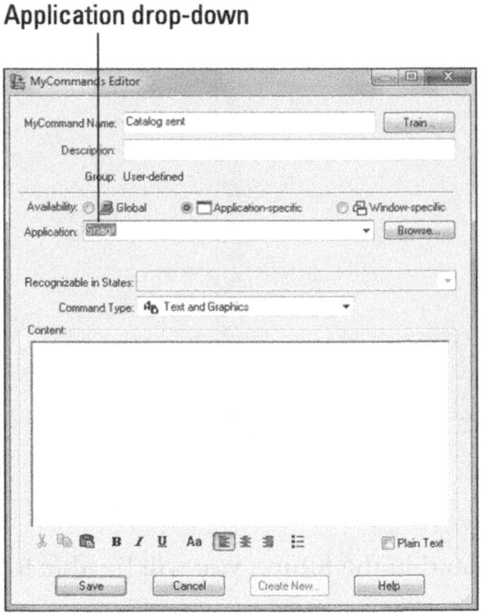

Application drop-down

Figure 20-7:
The application appears in the MyCommands Editor dialog box.

Introducing the Command Browser

After you create a command, you can edit it with the Command Browser. Don't be intimidated when you open the Command Browser screen. It looks like there is a lot going on. But it's easy to use once you know what you're looking for. (See Chapter 17 for more on the Command Browser.) Look around the Command Browser to make it less scary to browse.

Locating commands using the Keyword Filter

Just like searching on the web, you can find commands in the Command Browser by using keywords. The Keyword Filter makes it easy to find the actual command for a function you would like to perform. For example, if you want to locate a footnote in your Word document, your first inclination might be to say, **"Find Footnote."** When you look in the Keyword Filter, you find the correct command for that action is, **"Open The Footnote,"** as shown in Figure 20-8. Then you know that you should type that exact phrase in the dialog box. This is a good way to find exactly what you want. Of course, you can also use the Dragon Learning Center to find commands.

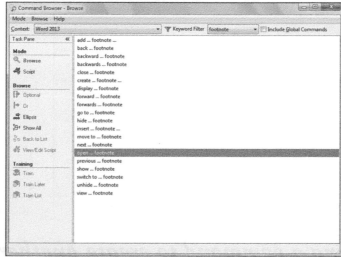

Figure 20-8: Using the Keyword Filter in the Command Browser to find the correct command.

To use the Keyword Filter to find commands, do the following:

1. Choose Tools ⇨ Command Browser from the DragonBar.

Look at the Context box in the upper-left corner and make sure you are in the application that applies to this command.

Use the drop-down menu to pick the application.

2. Select the Keyword Filter menu option next to the Context box.

The Keyword Filter box pops open and you see the list of words along the left side.

3. **Type in words that contain the command you are looking for.**

   In this example, type **Footnote** into the Choose Word dialog box.

4. **(Optional) After you type in a word(s), click the Add button so that the word is placed on the right side under the current list of filter words.**

5. **Click Done.**

   The Command Browser displays all the commands that pertain to the word *footnote* as shown in Figure 20-9. Now you can choose and use the right one!

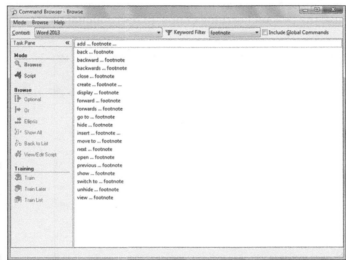

Figure 20-9:
Commands related to the word *footnote.*

Cloning a command to create another

Because you are in a time-saving mood, how about using the command you just created to create another one with a modification? You don't want to start all over again. The Command Browser is a bit different from the Command Editor. Instead of dictating information, you select the command name from a list. To launch the Command Browser, do the following:

1. **Choose Tools ⇨ Command Browser.**

   You are presented with a big list of commands. Scroll down the list until you find the exact name of your command. Check the Context dialog box to be sure you are in the right type of command. In this case, you need to be in Microsoft Word to edit the command you created for Word. In this example, it is **Catalog Sent.** See Figure 20-10.

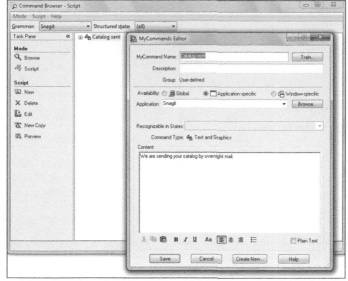

Figure 20-10:
The Command Browser and MyCommands Editor.

2. **Say or click the name of the command.**

3. **Make sure that you are in Script mode and then choose New Copy.**

   The Command Editor pops up with the command information you created. You can use the Create New button at the bottom of the dialog box. In this example, you use the Create New command as the basis for a new command.

4. **Click the Create New button.**

   Notice that the name is incremented by one. For example, if the name was "Catalog Sent," the new one becomes "Catalog Sent 2." You can modify the contents of the command and change the name to something else more memorable. In this example, I changed the MyCommand Name to "Product Docs" and edited the text accordingly by changing "Catalog Sent" to "Product Docs," as shown in Figure 20-11.

5. **Click Save.**

   You now have a new command based on an earlier one, without having to start from scratch.

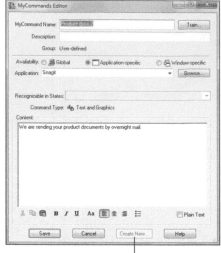

Figure 20-11:
Use the Cre-
ate New
button to
modify a
previously
created
command.

Create New button was clicked

Inserting graphics into commands

If you can stand even more timesaving, look at how you can insert a graphic with a command. To get started, find a graphic that you want to insert into documents. This could be maps, scanned images, and so forth. For this example, I use a logo:

1. **Copy your logo from your files using Windows, right-click Copy, or say,** "Select That" **and then say,** "Copy That."

2. **To create a new command, follow Steps 1 through 6 from the earlier "Creating a New Command" section and choose a memorable name.**

   In this example, call it "Digital Logo."

   When you are at the open window, paste the logo into the window by saying, **"Paste That,"** as shown in Figure 20-12.

3. **Click Save.**

4. **Test the logo command you made by opening a document and saying,** "Insert Digital Logo."

   The logo should be pasted into your document.

If you are pasting a very large graphic into the window, it helps to first enlarge the window into which you are pasting the graphic, so that you can see the whole item you are pasting.

Figure 20-12:
Making a
logo
available for
insertion
into
documents.

Deleting commands

If you find you have created a command that doesn't save time or that confuses you, delete it. (Just be sure you want to delete it because you can't get it back. You'll need to create it again.) To delete a command, do the following:

1. **Choose Tools ⇨ Command Browser.**

2. **Click the Script button under Mode on the left side of the screen.**

3. **Use the drop-down Grammar box to select the application your command is in.**

4. **Click on the name of the command you want to delete.**

5. **Choose the Delete menu item on the left side.**

6. **Click Yes to confirm that you want to delete it.**

   Your command is deleted.

Even if you don't use them, you can't delete built-in commands.

Chapter 21

Getting Help from Your Desktop and Online

. . . .

In This Chapter

▶ Looking for help on the desktop

▶ Calling or sending messages to Nuance Technical Support

▶ Searching for answers on the Nuance website

▶ Finding training on the Nuance website

▶ Using social media to connect with other Dragon users

. . . .

*E*very once in a while, you run across a problem that stands far above its colleagues. What to do? You can't find anything like it in this book or in the Dragon Professional Individual Help files. Even when you bring the problem to your local know-it-all, the one who makes you feel stupid even if you only say hello, he just smiles and says, "No kidding? It does that, huh?"

In other words, you need one-on-one attention from somebody who isn't just smart in a general way, but who really knows Dragon Professional Individual. Where do you find such people? One obvious place to look is on www.nuance.com. You can call or send messages to its Technical Support department.

Another place to look is among other Dragon users. By posting a question on a social media site or its online forum, you can get your question to the attention of Dragon users all over the world. Some of them are pretty darn smart, and a few of them may have seen exactly the same problem you are encountering.

Of course, the Dragon Professional Individual software includes various types of Help files, and that's where I begin my coverage of how to get help with the software.

Getting Help from the DragonBar

As does any good software product, Dragon Professional Individual has help files that are installed with the software. In addition, Nuance Communications has done quite a bit of work on the interface to provide help for Dragon Professional Individual. Nuance also has a new Help Center so that you can search on help topics when you need them. Here are some of the ways that you can find help directly from the DragonBar on your desktop:

- **Help menu:** To find help for Dragon Professional Individual from the DragonBar itself, start with the Help menu. Here you will find major content areas, an index, and a keyword search area. To reach it from the DragonBar, go to Help ➪ Help Topics and type or say what you are looking for. For example, you can say, **"Search Dragon Help For <*topic*>."**

- **Improve My Accuracy:** This place is where you can be guided to improve the performance of your software and your total experience. Periodic visits to the menu choice "Improve my accuracy" are critical, and I devote an entire chapter to it. (See Chapter 17.) Access it from the DragonBar by going to Help ➪ Improve my Accuracy.

- **Help:** Help is a specific Help device that is available whenever you say, **"What can I say?"** (Yes, this is actually a command that Dragon Professional Individual responds to.) Because of its importance, I explain it in more detail later in this chapter.

- **Interactive Tutorials:** The tutorials can be accessed both from the Install files when you are setting up and from the Help ➪ Interactive Tutorial.

- **Check for Updates:** This link takes you onto the web to check for updates to your current product.

- **Dragon on the Web:** From this link, you are taken to the Nuance.com website where you can find information about Dragon.

- **User Documentation:** Here you find user guides, Bluetooth wireless headset guides, and user workbooks.

- **Technical Support:** This link takes you to technical support, which I tell about in more detail in "Talking to tech support on the phone."

- **Register Online:** Click here to register your product if you haven't already done so.

- **About Dragon:** Click here to find your product ame, version number, and serial number.

You can always access the Help Center when you're dictating. Go to the DragonBar and choose Help ➪ Help Topics, or say, **"Show Help Topics"** or **"What can I say?"**

The Dragon Help Center has links directly to several main topics and subtopics. Make sure to scroll down to the end of each subtopic link to find related procedures and additional information. In Figure 21-1, you see the links for the following:

Figure 21-1:
Help Center
links.

✔ **Get started:** This is where to go to get help when you are starting to dictate with Dragon.

✔ **Edit:** For editing help, go here to see the exact commands you can use.

✔ **Move:** Click here to find commands to move around you documents, use your voice to move around your keyboard and mouse, and navigate Dragon with your keyboard.

✔ **Use applications:** Here you find help with a variety of applications such as Microsoft Word, Excel, Google Docs, and the DragonPad. You also find help with Windows controls.

✔ **Manage Dragon:** This section provides help for Dragon functions such as improving accuracy and working with user profiles.

✔ **Dictate:** Go here to find help with all aspects of dictation, including a dictation overview and how to dictate numbers and lists.

✔ **Correct:** You get help for all types of corrections here. See the Correction menu and help with spelling words and phrases.

✔ **Format:** Here you find help with formatting fonts and other elements, and see how to work with auto-formatting.

✔ **Browse the Web:** This help area covers such topics as web basics and working with browsers, email, and search.

✔ **Get Trained:** Here you find the links to interactive training modules that help you learn about Dragon's capabilities and improve your skills.

You can also open the Table of Contents menu for the Help Center by saying, **"Click Menu."**

When you look at the Help Center, you are never far away from exact commands you can use.

Getting Help from Nuance

Nuance offers many ways to help you learn how to use Dragon Professional Individual. You can ask questions on the support portal, call tech support and speak to an expert, and search the Nuance Knowledgebase for answers. Table 21-1 and the following sections provide more details.

Table 21-1	Where to Find Nuance Communications, Inc.
To Contact Them	*Try This*
Customer Service (Phone)	800-654-1187
Technical Support (Online)	Create email account for support
(Phone)	770-702-6014
Headquarters Address	1 Wayside Road, Burlington, MA 01803
Phone	781-565-5000
Fax	781-565-5001
Web	www.nuance.com

Murphy's Law dictates that companies will reorganize their websites as soon as anyone writes about them, so don't be terribly surprised if particular features of the Dragon website are not exactly where I say they are. (Odds are that the features I mention are still there somewhere.) Nuance does a very good job of structuring its website, so if you look around, you should be able to find things, even if they've recently moved.

Asking your first question on the Customer Service & Support portal

To access the support portal, you need to set up a free account. From this account, you can register your products, access your stored serial numbers, send a message to the Technical Support department, learn about new Dragon products, or order upgrades.

In general, the better you define your question, the more likely you are to get satisfaction from your email message. If you can say, "When I do *this and that*, I get such and such error message," the technical support staffers have a better chance to figure out what's wrong and give you a written answer. They also can do a good job with "How do I make Dragon Professional Individual do *X*?" questions, though I believe I answer almost all those in this book. And questions like "Where can I find more about improving my accuracy?" can be easily handled in writing.

For the first 90 days after you register your Dragon software, you get your questions answered free. After the 90-day warranty expires, there is a fee. See the later section "Talking to tech support on the phone," for specifics. In Dragon Professional Individual, you can also find a Technical Support link in the Help menu.

To set up an online account and ask your first question, do the following:

1. **Click the Support link on the Nuance.com home page.**

2. **Choose the Get Support link under the picture of Dragon NaturallySpeaking (this includes Dragon Professional Individual.)**

   You are taken to Nuance's Tech Support page (shown in Figure 21-2), which has a Customer Login button.

3. **Click the Customer Login button.**

   You will be asked to create an account.

4. **Click the Create a New Account button.**

   At the prompts, fill in your information.

5. **Click Submit.**

   A screen appears that says you have created your account successfully and that you should check your email to validate the account.

6. **Go to your email and click the link.**

   You are congratulated for setting up your account and there is a button for you to use if you haven't already registered Dragon Professional Individual.

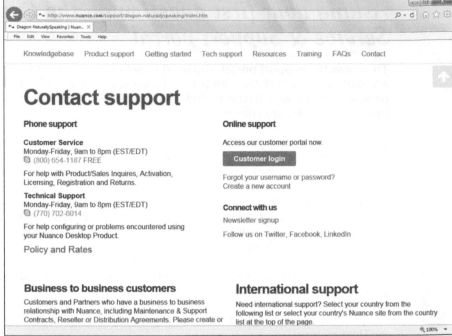

Figure 21-2:
Go to the
Customer
Login button
on the Tech
Support
page to
create your
free
account.

7. **Repeat Steps 2 and 3. Then log in to your account where prompted.**

   You are taken to the My Stuff area, where you see information about the products you registered.

8. **Click the Ask a Question link, and then click the Ask a Question link at the next screen.**

   Fill in your question where prompted. You must have a valid serial number if you are asking about your specific situation.

9. **Click Continue until you have answered all the questions.**

   You will arrive at a page that gives you a reference number for your question.

10. **Return to the My Stuff area and click the Notifications button to see the answer to your question.**

    You will also receive an email (at the email address you put on your account) with the answer to your question. If you need to continue the conversation, there is a link to the My Stuff area for you to post a reply.

They didn't do it

The people who answer the phones in technical support departments are the infantry of the software business. They may not be standing in muddy trenches, but they probably are sitting in windowless cubicles with nothing but a phone, a computer, and some reference manuals. They spend their days talking to people who are at best frustrated and at worst totally irate.

Chances are, the person you talk to when you call tech support had nothing to do with designing the product or with creating the mistake (if any) that you are suffering from now. He or she may well be as annoyed with the design of this particular feature of the product as you are, though it would be unprofessional of him or her to say so.

I know it may be difficult, but try to be pleasant and patient. Figuring out why software does what it does takes time, and the tech support folks are trying to solve in a few minutes something that has probably had you pounding your head against the wall for hours. If they could solve it faster, they would.

Talking to tech support on the phone

If Dragon Professional Individual does something you really don't understand and have a tough time explaining, or if it does something seemingly simple but gives you no information to work with (like failing to install or refusing to respond), you need to talk to a person on the phone.

I don't list pricing for tech support, in case it has changed since this book published. To determine what you will pay and the parameters under which you may call, go to www.nuance.com/support/dragon-naturallyspeaking/index.htm#contact_support.

The first thing to understand about Nuance's costs for tech support calls is that they are structured to cost more if you don't first use the question-based system through your free account. (See the preceding section.) Here are your options for speaking directly to a support person:

- **90-day product support warranty:** Unlimited calls are free during the first 90 days after you register your product or set up your account.

- **Post 90-day warranty:** You pay a fee for this call, and the fee is higher if you don't use the online question-based system first.

- **One version older than current or latest version released more than 2 years ago:** Here again, you pay a fee for this call, and the fee is higher if you don't use the online question-based system first.

- **Versions bundled with hardware or Original Equipment Manufacturer (OEM) release:** You pay a fee for this call, and again, the fee is higher if you don't use the question-based system first. (Are you detecting a theme here?)

> ✔ **Two versions prior to the latest version or one version prior to 2-year-old latest version:** No support available.
>
> ✔ **Trials and evaluations:** No support available.

Preparing before you call

A conversation with Technical Support proceeds much more efficiently if you gather the significant information before you call. (Being well-organized has the added benefit of establishing that you are not a complete idiot and therefore that you may be facing a real problem.)

You should also know what version of Dragon Professional Individual you have, both the release number (14, say) the edition and the serial number. This information displays from the DragonBar by choosing Help ⇨ About Dragon.

Nuance has taken great pains to handle most system configurations seamlessly. Still, a percentage of the real problems people have with Dragon Professional Individual (as opposed to the apparent problems caused by using the product incorrectly) occur from mismatches between the user's hardware and the hardware Dragon had in mind when it created Dragon Professional Individual. For this reason, the technical support person will likely want to know the following information:

> ✔ **Computer name and model:** They're looking for an answer like Sony VAIO VGN-Z or HP Pavilion 792N. It's probably on the front of your computer somewhere.
>
> ✔ **Processor type and RAM:** If you aren't sure about what you have, right-click Computer from your Start menu and left-click Properties to display the System Properties dialog box. The processor type and RAM should be on the General tab. If you are using Windows 7, choose Start Menu ⇨ Control Panel ⇨ All Control Panel Items ⇨ System.
>
> ✔ **Operating system:** Windows 10, for example. Restart your computer and you can't miss it.
>
> ✔ **Free hard drive space:** Find your hard drive (C, usually) in either Computer or Windows Explorer. Right-click it and select Properties. On the General tab of the Properties dialog box, you'll find Free Space and some number of megabytes. On Windows 7, double-click the Computer icon and you'll see Free Space displayed for your C drive.
>
> ✔ **Microphone name and model:** The obvious place to look is on the microphone.

Finding your product serial number

The first thing that Nuance wants to establish when you call the technical support department is that you are a bona fide customer. This is why they ask for your product serial number. It isn't a fool proof method, but it does eliminate some of the abuse. You find it on the DVD sleeve or for downloads, it's in the email you received.

During the call

Take notes. In particular, write down any changes that the technical support person tells you to make. If these changes don't solve the problem (or at least make it better), you may want to undo them later. This likely will not be the case. Most often, tech support folks will swiftly and professionally handle the issue.

A difficult problem can take more than one phone call to straighten out, and you may end up dealing with more than one person. This process goes much more smoothly if you can tell the current person you are talking to exactly what the previous person had you do.

Take very good notes if you end up doing something to the Windows Registry. (You'll know because you start using a program called RegEdit.)

Searching the Nuance Knowledgebase

If you like to look things up yourself rather than ask for help, the Dragon website provides ample reference sources you can look through. If the particular problem you're facing isn't absolutely unique to your system (and most problems aren't), chances are somebody has already asked Dragon's tech support people about it.

If someone has, you can look it up. When the technical support department staffers run into a new problem, they write down their solutions in their knowledgebase so that their own people can look it up rather than solve the same problem over and over again. Those answers are available to you on the website.

Scanning the knowledgebase

Whenever the technical support people at Dragon figure out how to solve a problem with Dragon, they write an answer for the knowledgebase. Follow these steps to scan the latest answers:

1. **From the front page of the Dragon website, click Support.**

2. **Click the Knowledgebase link under the Dragon NaturallySpeaking box.**

   Scroll down to the center of the page and you'll see a Search Nuance Knowledgebase prompt box, as shown in Figure 21-3.

3. **Type in the question for which you want an answer.**

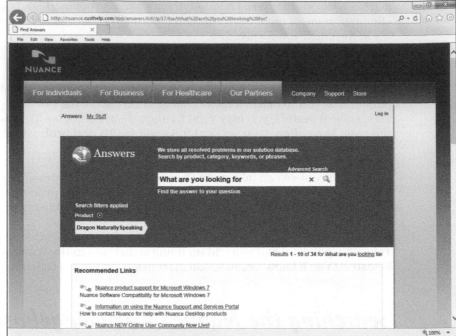

Figure 21-3:
Using the
Nuance
Knowledge-
base.

You'll find a list of answers arranged by date, with the most recent on top. It reads like a long troubleshooting guide, with the title of the note being the statement of a problem, such as "Registration reminder continues to appear after successfully registering the product." You can also do a search for a topic by saying, **"Search Nuance support for <topic>."**

Searching for technical information

Sometimes looking through the answers in order can be like searching for a needle in a haystack. Unless you know that the answer you want has been posted to the website in the last few days, you can look at a lot of message titles without finding what you're looking for. Fortunately, Dragon provides an Advanced Search button to help you dig deeper.

Accessing the Hardware Compatibility Guide

If you're buying a new system or looking to upgrade part of the system you have, you can use the site's Hardware Compatibility Guide to check whether Nuance has tested your system's performance with Dragon Professional Individual.

To access the Hardware Compatibility Guide select Support from the menu and click Get Support under the Dragon NaturallySpeaking box. The Hardware Compatibility link is on the left side. You can also go there directly by using `http://support.nuance.com/compatibility`.

When you arrive at the Hardware Compatibility page, click the kind of hardware you want to check out: microphones, notebook computers, desktop computers, recorders, sound cards, or miscellaneous to see a list of devices that Dragon has evaluated in its compatibility labs. (See Chapter 11 for more information.)

Finding downloads to update your software

On the same Support page (see Step 2 in "Scanning the knowledgebase"), off the home page is a link to downloads that are available for your software. Click the Search Software Downloads link.

Activating your software

On the same Support page (see Step 2 in "Scanning the knowledgebase"), off the home page you will see the Product Activation link. Click this if you have questions about the activation process.

Dipping into Product Resources

Nuance provides additional resources to help you learn how to use Dragon Professional Individual. The company makes it a point to provide a variety of formats because people have different learning styles. You will find the following information at `http://www.nuance.com/for-business/by-product/dragon/product-resources/user-documentation/index.htm` See the links for User Guides; Workbook; Cheat Sheets; Instructional Videos and Administrator Guide. Here's what you can find in each section:

- ✔ **User Guides:** Downloadable user guides help familiarize you with various aspects of the software.

- ✔ **Workbook:** Here you find the Dragon User Workbook to help guide you through program and its features.

- ✔ **Cheat Sheets:** This section contains datasheets for all the Dragon products as well as a list of white papers on a variety of subjects relating to the use of Dragon Professional Individual.

- ✔ **Instructional videos:** See brief videos that focus on specific features of the software, like Correcting Text or Creating Custom Commands.

The following system requirements apply to the Dragon Professional Individual edition of Dragon.

The system requirements for Dragon Professional Individual are as follows:

- ✔ **CPU:** Minimum: Intel dual core or equivalent AMD processor. Faster processors yield faster performance.

- ✔ **Free hard disk space:** 8GB.

- ✔ **Supported Operating Systems:** Windows 7, 8.1, 10 (32-bit and 64-bit); Windows Server 2008 R2; Windows Server 2012.

- ✔ **RAM:** Minimum: 2GB for 32-bit Windows 7, 8.1, 10; 4GB for 64-bit Windows 7, 8, and 8.1 and Windows Server 2008 R2; Windows Server 2012.

- ✔ **Browser:** Internet Explorer 9 or higher or the current version of Google Chrome or Mozilla Firefox for Online Help.

- ✔ **Sound card:** A sound card supporting 16-bit recording.

- ✔ **A Nuance-approved microphone:** See `support.nuance.com/compatibility` for more information.

A DVD-ROM drive may be required for installation, and an Internet connection is required for product activation.

Enhancing Community

In addition to making expert opinions and information available to you, the Internet also gives you ample opportunities to trade information with other users. Through these media, you can find out what problems other users are having; ask questions of your own; answer other users' questions; share experiences; commiserate; speculate about the motivations, intelligence, and personal hygiene of the people who wrote whatever part of Dragon Professional Individual you're currently having trouble with; and (most important of all) tell everyone about what a wonderful, readable, insightful book you have found.

Information you get on the Internet — especially from other users — comes without warranty. The vast majority of the users who post messages and comments are well-meaning people who just want to help, and a few of them are downright brilliant. But you should only trust them to the extent that they are making sense. You have no way to verify that they know what they're talking about, so caveat emptor.

Dragon Discussion Forum

The Dragon NaturallySpeaking Discussion Forum is public and active (it includes information about Dragon Professional Individual). It covers such topics as How to, Troubleshooting, and Specific hardware use. To participate, you can find the site, shown in Figure 21-4, at `http://nuance-community.custhelp.com/hives/be1ac29547/summary`.

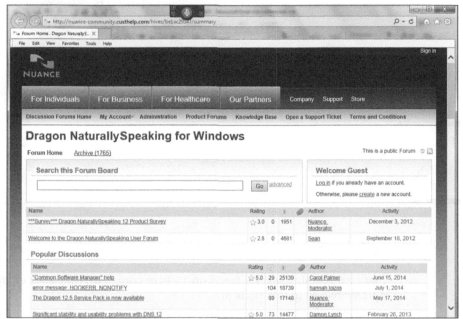

Figure 21-4:
The Dragon discussion forum.

Facebook

Like most major consumer software, Dragon has an official Facebook page. Some companies treat their Facebook pages as an afterthought. Nuance is not one of them. Nuance's Facebook page contains lots of quality content worth looking at.

You'll find comments from Dragon users along with answers from Nuance staff. You'll also see Customer of the Week highlights and pictures uploaded by Nuance at various tradeshows and other events.

Respond to a post and jump into the discussions going on. This Facebook page, shown in Figure 21-5, resides at `http://facebook.com/dragonnaturallyspeaking`.

Figure 21-5:
Dragon
Facebook
page.

Twitter

Nuance maintains several feeds on Twitter.com. Two that are pertinent to the topics covered in this book are

- ✔ **@Dragon Tweets:** Nuance has an active Twitter feed that focuses on answering questions, responding to user comments, and tweeting information. This is a great way to quickly get attention for a question that can be answered in 140 characters or less. I'm a big Twitter fan so I use this if I have a question. Nuance also mixes in content from its YouTube channel and training tips. This Twitter feed, shown in Figure 21-6, is at `https://twitter.com/dragontweets`.

- ✔ **@Nuance Mobile:** This feed, of course, concentrates on all things mobile. If you use a mobile device like an iPhone, iPad, iPod touch, BlackBerry, or Android, you'll find interesting information here about using them with Dragon. You can find this Twitter feed, shown in Figure 21-7, at `http://twitter.com/#!/NuanceMobile`. For information on using mobile devices with Dragon Professional Individual, see Chapter 14.

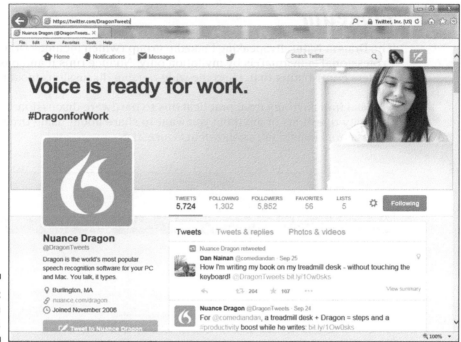

Figure 21-6:
Nuance on
Twitter.

Figure 21-7:
Nuance
Mobile on
Twitter.

LinkedIn

The Dragon NaturallySpeaking LinkedIn group (which includes Dragon Professional Individual) is by invitation only. Nuance runs it and has several staffers contributing to it. I find the wide-ranging discussions most useful.

You can find anything from practical tips to hardware discussions to productivity questions or anything you want to share about using Dragon Professional Individual, as shown in Figure 21-8.

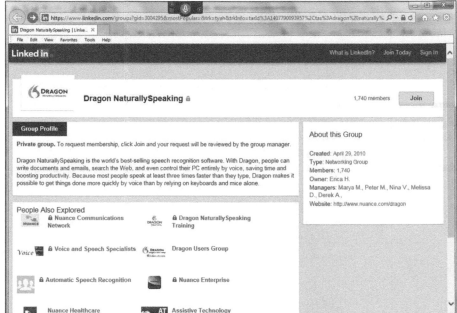

Figure 21-8: The Dragon group on LinkedIn.

Nuance on YouTube

If you browse over to Nuance's Dragon channel on YouTube, there's lots to see. Nuance's purpose for the channel is to tell you everything you'd like to know about its products and help you find the best ways to put them to use. There's a video on version 13, as shown in Figure 21-9, at `http://youtube.com/NuanceDragon`. In addition, you'll see lots of other videos uploaded by fans of the software.

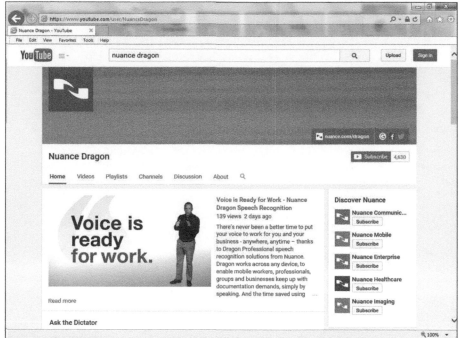

Figure 21-9:
Dragon
videos on
YouTube.

Part V
The Part of Tens

For some tips on using the microphone with Dragon Professional Individual, go to www.dummies.com/goprofessionalindividual.

In this part . . .

✔ When you're working with voice recognition programs, you're bound to run into snags along the way. See how to handle it when you dictate and nothing happens.

✔ You need to save your sanity and time when dictating. Find out how to avoid forgetting to turn off the microphone when you aren't dictating.

✔ Are you making voice commands that aren't being followed? I explain how to make sure the computer follows your instructions.

✔ Your Dragon assistant seems to be inserting extra little words. Find out how to correct that and get her back on track.

Chapter 22

Ten Common Problems

. . . .

In This Chapter

▶ Dictating but nothing happens

▶ Dealing with incorrect results

▶ Speaking commands that get typed as text

▶ Failing to control text with Full Text Control

▶ Discovering that Dragon Professional Individual inserts extra little words

▶ Dealing with slow dictation

▶ Uncovering Menu commands that don't work

▶ Tracking down Natural Language Commands that don't work

▶ Ascertaining that **"Undo That"** doesn't undo

▶ Realizing that **"Start"** doesn't start

. . . .

Did you ever own something that worked perfectly as soon as you took it out of the box, and never gave you a lick of trouble during its long, productive life? Neither have I. Problems are just part of the experience of owning something. And software problems . . . they are just part of the experience. Period.

So, without further ado, here are ten common problems that Dragon Professional Individual users face.

Dictating but Nothing Happens

The words leave your mouth, but they don't appear on the screen. Obviously, they must have taken a wrong turn somewhere. Suppose you follow the path the words should have taken, and see where they may have gotten diverted.

But before you take that trip, are you sure that *nothing* is happening? Say a few words into the microphone and see what happens. Does it say,

"Please say that again"? Okay, back to following the words after they leave your mouth:

- ✔ **First stop: the microphone.** Is it connected to the computer in the right microphone jack? (The red one is usually the correct one.) Try using the microphone for something else, like the Windows Sound Recorder. If you can record a sound through the microphone, then it isn't the cause.

- ✔ **Second stop: the sound card.** A poor sound card makes for poor recognition, but even poor recognition is a far cry from nothing. The sound card would have to be broken rather than just be poor quality in order to cause Dragon Professional Individual to stop dead in its tracks. Seems unlikely.

- ✔ **Third stop: Windows.** Double-click the speaker icon on the taskbar and look at the Microphone Balance. Is the Mute check box selected? Deselect it, if so.

    Another possibility is that Windows (for its own unfathomable reasons) has changed your device settings — redefined your microphone to be a printer or something equally helpful. (I think I'm exaggerating, but it's hard to be sure.) Running a microphone check will either fix the problem or give you a more specific complaint to take to Dragon Technical Support. (See Chapter 21.)

- ✔ **Fourth stop: microphone icon.** Is Dragon Professional Individual asleep? Check the microphone icon on the Windows taskbar or on the Dragon Professional Individual toolbar. If it's blue, it's asleep.

    If you are dictating directly into the Dragon Professional Individual document window, the preceding are all the obvious sources to check. But if you're dictating into a different application, there are other places to look for problems.

- ✔ **Fifth stop: the application.** Maybe you don't realize which window is active, and text is actually piling up somewhere that you aren't looking. Click in the window you want to dictate into to make sure that it's active. If you use the keyboard to type something, does it appear where you expect it? If not, the problem has nothing to do with Dragon Professional Individual.

- ✔ **Sixth stop: the DragonBar.** Look at the DragonBar and see whether the circle indicator is green in color. If it isn't green, that means you've lost support for the application you're in or you never had it.

Also, if you're using a nonstandard Microsoft application, it might be a good idea to use the Dictation Box. If this happens inside Microsoft Outlook or Microsoft Word, make sure you close them down along with Dragon Professional Individual and then restart them. This usually fixes it. Also, make sure that `WinWord.exe` or `Outlook.exe` is not running in the Processes tab of the Task Manager.

Still stumped? That's about as much help as I can give you from this distance in time and space. You need some one-on-one help either from Dragon Technical Support or from other Dragon Professional Individual users.

Dealing with Incorrect Results

If Dragon Professional Individual just doesn't get it right when you dictate, you're having what's called recognition errors or accuracy problems. Now, don't you feel better, having an official diagnosis of your problem?

No? Then turn to the chapters in Part IV of this book. So many different things can affect accuracy that I devote the entire part to them. If that sounds too wearisome, try the following first-aid:

✔ Make sure you actually speak each word fully and speak entire phrases. Don't pause between words, and don't skip them, clip them at the end, or slur them to other words.

✔ Make sure your microphone is positioned to the side of your mouth, about one-half inch away.

✔ Run the microphone check again: Choose Audio ⇨ Check Microphone.

✔ Choose Tools ⇨ Options, and in the Options dialog box that appears, click the Miscellaneous tab. Drag the Speed vs. Accuracy slider more to the right. Click the OK button.

If your problem is that Dragon Professional Individual repeatedly gets certain words wrong, make sure you use the Correction dialog box so that Dragon Professional Individual learns about its errors. (Say, **"Correct That"** after Dragon Professional Individual errs.) If you just select the erroneous text and dictate over it, Dragon Professional Individual will never learn.

Speaking Commands That Get Typed as Text

Few things are more frustrating than to select the most important line in your document and say, **"Italicize That"** only to watch the whole line disappear and be replaced with the words *italicize that*. (A quick **"Undo That"** or two usually gets back what you lost.)

This kind of problem can happen for a number of reasons. Here are some things to check or try:

- ✓ **Is the command supposed to work in this application?** I am not sure how many times I've threatened to reprogram my computer with a sledgehammer, only to discover that I had been dictating (well, yelling, actually) a Full Text Control command at an application that wasn't enabled for it or a Natural Language command when Natural Language Commands weren't available.

- ✓ **Get your pauses right.** On multi-word commands like **"Italicize That"** or **"Format That Arial Bold 16 Point,"** pause briefly before and after the command, but not at all in the middle.

- ✓ **Is Dragon Professional Individual hearing you correctly?** Watch the status box, or pay attention to what Dragon Professional Individual types instead of doing what you want. If it hears **"Italy Sized Hat,"** then it isn't going to italicize anything. If this keeps happening, you should do Word training on the particular commands that Dragon Professional Individual misinterprets. See Chapter 17.

- ✓ **Hold down the Control key.** Holding down the Control key while you dictate is a way to say, "Hey, assistant, this is a command I'm saying!" If this doesn't work, it's time to try to accomplish your purpose another way. For example, you might try saying, **"Press Control I"** instead of **"Italicize That."**

Failing to Control Text with Full Text Control

The most common reason Full Text Control doesn't work is that the application you're dictating into isn't a Full Text Control application. To easily determine if it is, look at the DragonBar on the right side where you see the circle. If the circle is green, you are in a Full Text Control application. If the circle is light gray, you aren't.

Discovering That Dragon Professional Individual Inserts Extra Little Words

Some days, you find your documents littered with little words like *in* or *to* or *and.* You are sure you didn't say them. Your Dragon Professional Individual assistant just seems to have an overactive imagination today.

These extra little words come from two places. The most likely explanation is that your microphone is positioned badly. If the mic sits in front of your mouth rather than to the side, your words are being punctuated by little bursts of air. Those puffs hit the microphone and make a short, sharp noise that Dragon Professional Individual interprets as a short word. It's also possible that the breath coming out of your nostrils is blowing across the microphone. In either case, move the mic farther to the side of your mouth.

The second possibility is that you are trying too hard to enunciate consonants. For example, maybe you had trouble a few lines ago getting Dragon Professional Individual to recognize your **"Format"** command. It heard *formal, form, for Matt,* or some other phrase that wasn't **"Format."** Then the next time you needed to format something, you tried too hard to make Dragon Professional Individual hear the *t* at the end. And Dragon Professional Individual did hear it — a little too well — and so it typed *format to.* The only solution here is to relax; go back to speaking the way you naturally speak. (That's why they call it Dragon Professional Individual, you know.)

Dealing with Slow Dictation

You dictate something to Dragon Professional Individual, and then you wait. How long is it going to take to figure out what you said? Did it even hear you? Should you repeat? Finally, the words show up.

You can deal with slow response time in the following ways:

- ✔ **Ignore it.** I'm serious. Don't wait around for the words to show up on the screen. Keep dictating. Dragon Professional Individual remembers as much as a half hour of dictation, so don't worry if you get a few lines ahead of it.

- ✔ **Change the settings.** From the Dragon Professional Individual window, say, **"Click Tools, Options."** When the Options dialog box appears, say, **"Click Miscellaneous"** then **"Press Tab"** several times until you select the Speed vs. Accuracy slider. Move the slider toward Fastest Response with the **"Move Left <*number*>"** command. When you have the slider where you want it, say, **"Click OK."** (You can also do all those steps with your mouse, if you prefer: Choose Tools ➪ Options, click the Miscellaneous tab, drag the slider left, and click OK.)

- ✔ **Liberate some RAM (memory).** Close any programs you don't need, and turn off background features of those you do need, like automatic spell checking.

✓ **Exit all your applications and restart the computer.** If you've been on the computer for several hours and have opened and closed a number of applications, Windows's bookkeeping may have gotten tangled. Restarting may give the computer access to resources it had forgotten about.

✓ **Install more RAM.** This isn't going to do you much good in the next 5 minutes, but in the long run, it's the best solution.

✓ **Turn off Natural Language Commands.** If you don't need the Natural Language Commands, just regular old dictation and the dictation commands that work in the Dragon Professional Individual window, turn off Natural Language Commands. Choose Tools ➪ Options in the Dragon Professional Individual window. In the Options dialog box that appears, click the Command tab, then click the More Commands button at the bottom. Once there, click to clear the check mark labeled Enable Natural Language Commands. Click OK.

Uncovering Menu Commands That Don't Work

When you say, **"Click"** and nothing happens, the likely problem is that your Use Menus That Are Compatible with Screen Readers check box is not selected. To check it:

1. **From the Dragon Professional Individual window, select Tools ➪ Options.**

   There's no point in telling you how to access this by voice, because that's exactly what isn't working!

2. **When the Options dialog box appears, click the Miscellaneous tab.**

3. **Find the Voice Enable Menus, Buttons, and Other Controls Excluding check box and make sure it is selected.**

Tracking Down Natural Language Commands That Don't Work

If the Natural Language Commands I describe in Chapter 8 don't work, the two most likely possibilities are

✔ **You aren't dictating into a compatible application.** Natural Language Commands don't work in every application you use. Make sure it's enabled for Natural Language Commands.

✔ **Someone has turned off Natural Language Commands.** To turn them back on:

 1. *Choose Dragon Professional Individual ⇨ Tools ⇨ Options.*

 2. *In the Options dialog box that appears, click the Command tab and then click the More Commands button at the bottom.*

 3. *Once there, make sure the check box labeled Enable Natural Language Commands has a check mark. If not, select that check box and click OK.*

 4. *On the window still open, click OK again.*

When all else fails, Dragon's integration for the application may not be working. Close the application completely and close Dragon Professional Individual completely. Reopening both should reconnect your assistant and the application.

Ascertaining That Undo Doesn't Undo

Often, particularly in Word, **"Undo That"** doesn't fully undo (an underdone undo?). It partially undoes. For example, suppose you highlight some text and speak the command **"Format That Arial 14,"** but instead of Dragon Professional Individual changing the format, it types *Format that aerial for teens* over your selected text. Not what you had in mind. So you say, **"Undo That"** and Dragon Professional Individual removes the offending text, but your intended original text is still missing!

In that event, you need to repeat the **"Undo That"** command. Many Dragon Professional Individual actions are actually made up of several Word actions, and **"Undo That"** only undoes one Word action at a time.

Realizing That Start Doesn't Start

You say, **"Start Internet Explorer"** or "**Start Microsoft Word**" or "**Start Quicken**" and nothing happens. What's the deal?

The **"Start"** command will start any application that is installed on your machine and has either

- ✔ A shortcut icon on the desktop
- ✔ An entry on the Programs menu

The catch, however, is that you have to say the name exactly as it appears on the shortcut or menu entry. So if the entry on the Programs menu is Microsoft Word 2010, then you need to say, **"Start Microsoft Word Twenty Ten."**

If the name on the icon or menu entry is too much of a mouthful to be worth pronouncing, or if you can never remember exactly what it says, rename it. Rename a desktop icon by right-clicking it and choosing Rename. You can do the same thing to the Programs menu entries, but you have to find them first. They live in the folder `C:\Windows\Start Menu`.

Another possibility is that you have too many programs on the Start list or on your desktop so the one you want to use can't open. Dragon Professional Individual tracks up to 500 menu and desktop items. If you are beyond that number, you will have a problem opening a program. Cleaning up the list can solve that problem.

Chapter 23

Ten Time- and Sanity-Saving Tips

. . . .

In This Chapter

▶ Using hotkeys in dialog boxes

▶ Positioning the microphone the same way every time

▶ Changing your mouse habits

▶ Drinking with a straw

▶ Turning off your word processor's automatic spell checking

▶ Working on small pieces of large documents

▶ Using dictation shortcuts

▶ Turning the microphone off when you walk away

▶ Selecting or correcting longer phrases

▶ Using the physical mouse and keyboard

. . . .

Sometimes the difference between doing well and just getting by is a well-placed piece of advice from a wiser and more experienced mentor. Go West, young man. Don't take any wooden nickels. Look before you leap — that kind of thing.

I looked all over for a wiser and more experienced mentor, but I came up short. That's the problem with cutting-edge software: "More experienced" means somebody who installed his copy last Thursday. Anyway, here are ten things I wish somebody had told me last Thursday.

Using Hotkeys in Dialog Boxes

I'm a big fan of hotkeys in general, but they really shine in dialog boxes. The varied features of dialog boxes, the radio buttons, check boxes, and so on, respond unevenly to voice commands. In some dialog boxes, you can say, **"Click Never Ask Me This Question Again"** and have a check mark show up in the Never Ask Me This Question Again check box. In other dialog boxes, it doesn't work. But saying, **"Press Alt S"** works every time.

Positioning the Microphone the Same Way Every Time

Misplaced microphones are the number one cause of error. Dragon Professional Individual learns best when you sound the same way every time you say a word. And even if you actually *say* the word the same way every time, it *sounds* different if your microphone isn't in quite the same location.

Develop your own precise way of knowing that the microphone is in exactly the right place. Maybe you can just fit a finger between the microphone and the corner of your mouth. If all that is too much trouble, get in the habit of running the microphone check from the Audio menu whenever you put your microphone on: Choose Audio ➪ Check Microphone from the Dragon Professional Individual menu bar.

Changing Your Mouse Habits

What habits am I talking about? I'm talking about all those things that you might be in the habit of doing with your computer's mouse: clicking toolbar buttons, using scroll bars, dragging and dropping, clicking links on web pages, and relocating the cursor.

Dragon Professional Individual has mouse commands, which I describe in Chapter 15. So you *could* keep all your same mouse habits and just use mouse voice commands instead of grabbing the physical object next to your keyboard. But that's not a great idea. The mouse commands (like **"MouseGrid"**) are usable in a pinch, but they get tedious if you try to do everything with them.

Instead, learn to do the same actions with other commands. Use the web commands with Internet Explorer, Google Chrome, or Firefox. Say, **"Press Page Down"** or **"Press Page Up"** instead of clicking the scroll bar. Use menu commands instead of toolbar buttons. Cut and paste with hotkeys instead of dragging and dropping. Use the **"Move"** and **"Go"** commands to put the cursor where you want. You can also try the **"Scroll Down"** commands to navigate. They work in applications like Microsoft Outlook.

Drinking with a Straw

Dictating is thirsty work. You can maintain a clear, steady tone of voice and avoid doing damage to your throat if you keep something to drink nearby and sip it occasionally. But there is no way to raise a cup to your lips without moving the microphone.

The solution is to drink through a straw! I admit, sipping hot coffee or cold beer through a straw is a weird experience, but most drinks are just fine.

Turning Off Automatic Spell Checking in Word Processors

Dragon Professional Individual is incapable of making a spelling error (unless you introduce a misspelled word into its vocabulary through the vocabulary-building process). So spell-checking is a waste of your computer's resources (which Dragon Professional Individual may already be stretching). If Dragon Professional Individual seems a bit sluggish when you're using a word processor, turn off that word processor's spell checker.

In Word, from the File menu choose Options ⇨ Proofing. Make sure the Check Spelling As You Type check box isn't selected.

While you're there, you can save some RAM by making sure the Check Grammar As You Type check box is deselected as well. In WordPerfect, choose Tools ⇨ Proofread ⇨ Off.

Working on Small Pieces of Large Documents

This tip is another RAM-saver. Large documents take up a lot of your computer's memory, memory that could be better applied to improving the performance of Dragon Professional Individual. Don't make your computer keep your whole novel in memory if you only need to work on one scene. Put the scene in a separate file and work on that file instead.

Using Dictation Shortcuts

You can save a lot of time by teaching Dragon Professional Individual some shortcuts. Teach your Dragon Professional Individual assistant to type "the Honorable Judge James J. Wackelgoober" when you say, **"The Boss,"** or to reproduce your full street address when you say, **"My Address."** See Chapter 17 for details.

You can also use shortcuts to gain some privacy for yourself. If, for example, you have a pet name for your spouse that you would rather not have overheard in the next cubicle when you dictate email, substitute some dull-sounding shortcut.

Turning the Microphone Off When You Stop Dictating

Dragon Professional Individual and the microphone that comes with it are usually good enough that they don't pay attention to random noises. The microphone doesn't, however, know that you have just picked up the phone or are talking to the person who just came into your office. I've had some interesting and lengthy gibberish result from such interruptions. It's good to get in the habit of pressing the + key on the keyboard (or clicking the microphone icon off) when you are interrupted or otherwise done dictating.

Selecting or Correcting Longer Phrases

When you dictate **"a hippopotamus"** and Dragon Professional Individual types "the hippopotamus," don't just say, **"Correct The."** Dragon Professional Individual may mishear it again, and there's bound to be a "the" in your document somewhere else that it will try to correct instead.

Speak the command, **"Correct The Hippopotamus."** Chances are good that only one occurrence of "the hippopotamus" is currently displayed and that Dragon Professional Individual will pick it out for you right away. Select an even longer phrase, if you can (**"Correct Tickle The Hippopotamus,"** for example).

Using the Physical Mouse and Keyboard

In theory, you can do just about anything with the Dragon Professional Individual voice commands. Voice commands like **"MouseGrid"** and **"Click"** give you a virtual mouse. The **"Press"** command gives you a virtual keyboard. So, you should be able to work without the physical mouse and keyboard — in theory. (Theory is a nice place, and I am thinking about relocating there. I hear it has an average temperature all year long.)

Sometimes, however, doing something by voice is simply a pain. Give it up. If you know in your heart that you can do it in three clicks of a mouse's tail, do it. You'll have better days, and you can figure out how to handle the situation with voice commands then. Meanwhile, you stay productive.

Chapter 24

Ten Mistakes to Avoid

. . . .

In This Chapter

▶ Running a lot of other programs simultaneously with Dragon Professional Individual

▶ Telling Dragon Professional Individual to shut down the computer

▶ Correcting what you ought to edit

▶ Editing what you ought to correct

▶ Cutting corners on any training

▶ Forgetting to rerun Audio Setup when the environment changes

▶ Signing on with somebody else's username

▶ Speaking into the backside of the microphone

▶ Creating dictation shortcuts or macro commands that sound like single common words

▶ Failing to proofread

. . . .

*E*verybody makes mistakes, and some people make really big and entertaining mistakes. I made a ton of mistakes with Dragon Professional Individual, and probably you'll make some, too, from time to time. Here's all I ask: Don't make these ten obvious mistakes that I guessed ahead of time. Be original. Be creative. Go out there and make brand-new mistakes that no one else has ever thought of before.

Running a Lot of Other Programs and Dragon Professional Individual Simultaneously

Dragon Professional Individual assistants are greedy beasts and, true to type, they grab lots of memory. They grab even more when Natural Languages applications run. Your word processor has its own memory greed, too. The same thing happens when you browse the web: It takes up a certain amount of memory, and Internet Explorer wants its own hoard of RAM. If there's not enough RAM for everybody, everything slows down.

So shut down programs that you aren't using. Plan your activities so that you don't have to run Dragon Professional Individual and Word and Internet Explorer all at the same time. Don't leave a big spreadsheet or a giant graphics program running in the background if you don't need it.

Telling Dragon Professional Individual to Shut Down the Computer

Certainly you can imagine an operating system that gracefully handles a shutdown request from one of its applications. *Get real, people.* This is Windows. It isn't always smooth sailing. You don't want to have to find some techno-gypsy to hold a cyber-séance to contact the files you were working on. Don't ask Dragon Professional Individual to shut down your computer.

Correcting What You Ought to Edit

Use the Correction process described in Chapter 5 only when your Dragon Professional Individual assistant has made a mistake that you don't want it to make again. If you just said the wrong thing, edit it. Although the program will take the final edit and learn from that, you don't need to blame your assistant for your mistakes.

Suppose, for example, that you're writing an email to tell a friend about the bonus that your colleague just got. But your Freudian subconscious gets the better of you, and you say *bogus* instead of *bonus*. If you then say, **"Correct bogus,"** you are in effect blaming Dragon Professional Individual for your error.

Dragon Professional Individual is a diligent little assistant, and will strive mightily to not make the same "error" again. And so it may start typing *bonus* when you really do mean to dictate *bogus*. It may even change its settings to reflect the possibility that sometimes your *n's* sound like *g's*. And then it starts turning *go* into *no*, and making other similarly mysterious mistakes.

Editing What You Ought to Correct

Dragon Professional Individual's performance will never improve if you don't tell it when it has made a mistake. Sometimes it seems easier just to say, **"Scratch That"** and repeat the phrase again, but in the long run, it costs you time because you'll see that same mistake in the future. See Chapter 5 for detailed instructions about correcting Dragon Professional Individual's mistakes.

Cutting Corners on Training

You can, if you're so inclined, skip any training and never fix mistakes. If you do this, Dragon Professional Individual will never be more than a toy. If you give training a little bit of time on a continual basis, you will reap great rewards. See Chapter 17 and make a commitment to regular training.

There is only one corner I recommend cutting: If you're using Dragon Professional Individual on a new machine and you already have user files on another machine, move the files over rather than retraining. See Chapter 19.

Forgetting to Run Microphone Check Again When the Environment Changes

So you get a great new microphone that you expect to improve Dragon Professional Individual's accuracy, and instead it gets worse. What happened?

Maybe you forgot to tell Dragon Professional Individual that anything had changed. Maybe your Dragon Professional Individual assistant is sitting there saying, "That isn't my master's voice! Where are the pops and clicks? Where is the background roar?"

The way to tell Dragon Professional Individual that something has changed is to run a microphone check. (See Chapter 2 for details.) You should also run it again if your voice volume changes (maybe you're tired) or if you move your computer to a new location. Anything that would make you sound different is an occasion to run the microphone check again.

Using Somebody Else's Username

You might think, "We sound alike. Why should I bother to train my own user? It won't make any difference." Trust me; it will make a difference. The performance will be poor, and if Dragon Professional Individual starts adjusting to your voice, it will start performing badly for the user whose identity you are borrowing.

Speaking into the Backside of the Microphone

Many microphones are noise-canceling directional microphones. That means that it has a front and a back. It tries to pay attention to what comes in the front, and tries to cancel out what comes in the back. The front has a little mark indicating that it's the front. Make sure you don't twist the microphone so that you're speaking into the backside.

Creating Shortcuts or Macros That Sound Like Single Common Words

One of the dumbest things a person could do with Dragon Professional Individual would be to create a macro command called **"The"** that deletes the entire current document. No one would be able to dictate for more than a sentence or two without accidentally invoking **"The"** and deleting her document. (I know you'd never do that. It's that "other" reader I'm talking to.)

But, dictation shortcuts can get you into trouble, too. What if you defined "two" to be a dictation shortcut for the numeral 1? Great confusion would follow.

Instead, make sure that any command or shorthand that you define consists of at least two words. **"Trash the Document"** would still be a dangerous macro to have lying around, but the danger would derive from rash decisions rather than accidental usage.

Forgetting to Proofread

Dragon Professional Individual doesn't make spelling mistakes, so spell-checking is useless. But that doesn't mean that your documents are perfect. They just have *correctly spelled* mistakes in them.

In some ways, that is worse. When you mistype a word, you usually wind up with nonsense. Your readers can deduce that a mistake has been made, and they can probably even figure out what you meant to say. But when your document has correct words that only sound like what you meant to say, your readers may think you are trying to be clever. When Mr. Jiro sees his name written "Mr. Zero," he may think you mean something by it. Don't forget to proofread your documents carefully so that you can avoid these types of mistakes.

Chapter 25

Ten Stupid Dragon Tricks

*N*uance created Dragon Professional Individual to handle dictation in contemporary English (or French or Italian or German or Spanish, if you have one of those versions). The idea was to make it easier for you to write letters or memos or detective novels or reports or newspaper articles. The vocabulary and word-frequency statistics are set up for this kind of contemporary writing.

But when people first sit down in front of a microphone to test Dragon Professional Individual, what do they almost inevitably start dictating? Something from memory, which usually means something they had to memorize in school. Something written in an earlier time, in other words — Shakespeare or the Declaration of Independence.

Dragon Professional Individual wasn't designed to understand this kind of stuff, and it makes lots of mistakes. Some of them are downright hilarious. This causes people to laugh at their poor, abused Dragon Professional Individual assistant, and to start feeding it stuff it couldn't possibly digest: nonsense rhymes, text in unknown languages, you name it.

This is cruelty, plain and simple. The folks at Nuance have encouraged me to condemn such behavior in no uncertain terms, and so I will: It is bad. Bad! Bad! Bad! Bad! Bad!

So, purely out of humanitarian concern, and so that you won't be tempted to do something like this yourself to your own poor, helpless computer program, I am (with great sorrow) publishing the results of my own Dragon transgressions. Remember: I am a professional. Don't try these at home.

In the unlikely event that you're the kind of person who would ignore my stern moral condemnation, you need to take two simple precautions to make sure that you don't screw up the Dragon Professional Individual training. (You don't want Dragon Professional Individual to *expect* you to talk like Shakespeare, do you?) Here are the things you shouldn't do:

- **Don't correct any mistakes that Dragon Professional Individual makes while you're playing.** If it interprets **"forsooth"** as **"fort's tooth,"** leave it alone. Who knows? You might really want to say "fort's tooth" someday.

- **Don't save your speech files when you are done.** If you don't save your speech files, it's as if the whole session never happened. You're like the stage hypnotist who says, "When you wake up, you won't remember any of this."

If you really, seriously want Dragon Professional Individual to learn to recognize previous uses of English — say, if you're a Shakespearean scholar or you frequently quote the Bible — it can, given time and training. Creating a new user for this kind of talk is best. Use the Vocabulary Editor to introduce mass quantities of that kind of writing, and then just correct Dragon Professional Individual whenever it gets something wrong. Forsooth, in a fortnight or so, your Dragon Professional Individual assistant will be a veritable maven of the bardly tongue.

Dictating "Jabberwocky"

Dragon Professional Individual is forced to interpret whatever you say as words in its active vocabulary. If you aren't saying words at all, it just has to do the best it can. Turning **"Beware the Jabberwock, my son!"** into "Be where the jab are walk, my son!" has to be seen as a heroic effort on the software's part. Ditto for turning **"Callooh! Callay!"** into "Colder! <colon> a!"

Here's the original text of "Jabberwocky" written by Lewis Carroll in *Through the Looking-Glass and What Alice Found There* in 1872:

'Twas brillig, and the slithy toves
Did gyre and gimble in the wabe;
All mimsy were the borogoves,
And the mome raths outgrabe.

"Beware the Jabberwock, my son!
The jaws that bite, the claws that catch!
Beware the Jubjub bird, and shun
The frumious Bandersnatch!"

He took his vorpal sword in hand:
Long time the manxome foe he sought—
So rested he by the Tumtum tree,
And stood awhile in thought.

And as in uffish thought he stood,
The Jabberwock, with eyes of flame,
Came whiffling through the tulgey wood,
And burbled as it came!

One, two! One, two! and through and through
The vorpal blade went snicker-snack!
He left it dead, and with its head
He went galumphing back.

"And hast thou slain the Jabberwock?
Come to my arms, my beamish boy!
O frabjous day! Callooh! Callay!"
He chortled in his joy.

'Twas brillig, and the slithy toves
Did gyre and gimble in the wabe;
All mimsy were the borogoves,
And the mome raths outgrabe.

Here are some other odd word choices and even odder interpretations that result when you dictate "Jabberwocky" into Dragon Professional Individual:

What was read:

'Twas brillig, and the slithy toves

Did gyre and gimble in the wabe;

All mimsy were the borogoves,

And the mome raths outgrabe.

What was heard:

Twist drilling, and a slightly to those did Dyer and Kimball in the law: all names he were the Borg wrote us, and a moment as out crowd.

What was read:

Beware the Jabberwock, my son!

The jaws that bite, the claws that catch!

What was heard:

Be where the jam are walk, my son! The John is that bite, the clause that catch!

What was read:

Beware the Jubjub bird, and shun

The frumious Bandersnatch!

What was heard:

Be where the job show bird, and shunned from the a spend your snatched!

Dictating the Gettysburg Address

I dictated this immediately after General Training, when the system was most likely to misunderstand.

Picture Lincoln on the train to Gettysburg, dictating the following into his portable recorder:

"*Or* score and seven years ago *homeowners* brought forth on this continent *emu* nation, conceived in Liberty and dedicated to the proposition that *old* men are created equal. Now we are engaged in a *Greek* Civil War, testing *weather* that nation or any nation so conceived and so dedicated *Campbell into work.*

"We are met on a *Greek* battlefield of that war. We have come to dedicate a portion of *battlefield* as a final resting-place for those who hear gave their *law is* that that nation might live. It is altogether *hitting* and proper that we should do this. But in *the* larger *cents,* we cannot dedicate, we cannot *concentrate,* we cannot *Howe of* this ground. The brave men, living *in* dead who struggled here have *concentrated* it far above our *war* power to add or detract. *The world will Littleton to normal* remember what we say here, but *he* can never forget what they did here.

"*Each use* for us *to* living rather to be dedicated here to the unfinished work which they *won't* here have thus far *sewn openly* advanced. It is rather for us to be here dedicated to *decree* task remaining before us — that *control* these honored dead we take increased devotion to that *callers* for which they gave the last full measure of devotion — that we here *Hialeah* resolve that these dead shall not have died *evening,* that this nation *undergone* shall have a *rebirth* of freedom, and that government *over* the people, *buying* the people, for the people shall not *parish* from the earth."

Dictating Shakespeare

Dragon Professional Individual did rather badly when I dictated Romeo's speech under the balcony, starting with, "What light through yonder window breaks?" But most of the mistakes are due to simple archaisms: "yonder window" becomes "the under Window," and "vestal livery" turns into "us delivery."

> "What light through the under Window breaks? It is the East, and Juliet is the son. Arise, fair son, and kills the in the us Moon, who is already sick and pale with grief, that now her mate art far more fair that she; the not her mate, said she is envy of; her us delivery is but sick and green and non-but fools to where it; casting off."

But it did even worse with Juliet's reply. The biggest problem here is that in the alpha-bravo-charlie way of saying the alphabet, **"romeo"** is the letter R. Stranger still, **"Capulet"** is interpreted as "Cap period." Because there is no capital period, Dragon Professional Individual produces an ordinary period instead.

> "O. r, r! Wherefore art that r? Deny the high father and refused I name; or, if now will cannot, be but sworn my love, and I'll no longer be a."

The bard's poetry fared no better. Dictating, **"Full fathom five thy father lies"** resulted in "Full phantom 555 their lives."

Antony's speech over the body of Caesar is at least recognizable, possibly because, as he says: "I am no orator, . . . but . . . a plain blunt man." But who is this Barry Caesar character, anyway?

"Friends, Romans, countrymen, land need your here is; I come to Barry Caesar, not to praise him. The evil that man to lives after them; the good is often incurred with their bones; so let it be with Caesar. The noble purchase have told you Caesar was ambitious: if it were so, it was a previous fault, and previously have Caesar answered it."

Hamlet *is* an orator, but the Dragon Professional Individual rendition of his speech needs a good editor. And don't we all wish for "no blur in the mind?"

"To be, or not to be: that is the question. Whether to is no blur in the mind to suffer the swings and arrows of outrageous fortune, or to take arms against the Sea of troubles, and by opposing and them?"

Dictating Proverbs

How about some ancient wisdom, Dragon-style? This is sooo close.

"A lie travels round the world while truth is putting her boots on."

The Dragon heard:

"A light travels round the world while truth is putting her puts on."

Dictating Limericks

Well, actually this one isn't so bad. I tried to dictate:

"There once was a man from Peru, Who dreamed he was eating his shoe. He woke up in the night With a terrible fright To find it was perfectly true."

Dragon Professional Individual almost got it. If only I could have told it that the lines were supposed to rhyme.

"Their once was a man from Peru, Who treat he was eating his should. He woke up in the night With a terrible frightened To find it was perfectly true."

Dictating "Mairzy Doats"

This one more-or-less speaks for itself (and please don't get mad at me if this little ditty starts playing over and over in your mind after you read it!):

"Mayors he doubts, And does he doubts, And little land see tiny. Get lead 92, would you? Get lead 92, we can you?"

Turning Dragon Professional Individual into an Oracle

You turn Dragon Professional Individual into an oracle by abusing the Vocabulary Editor. The idea is to be able to ask Dragon Professional Individual a question, and have it provide the answer. For example, you want to ask, "What is the answer to life, the universe, and everything?" and have Dragon Professional Individual answer "42" (or whatever you think the answer is).

The trick is to enter the answer as the written form in the Vocabulary Editor, and enter the question as the spoken form. So, for this example, do this:

1. **Choose Tools ➪ Vocabulary Editor.**

   The Vocabulary Editor eventually makes the scene.

2. **In the Search For box, type** 42 **and then click Add.**

   The Add Word or Phrase dialog appears.

3. **In the Spoken Form (If Different) box, type** What is the answer to life, the universe, and everything?

4. **Click Add and then click Close.**

You're done! Try asking Dragon Professional Individual the question.

Singing

Singing doesn't sound like speech at all. The tones jump around, and the pace is all wrong, too — at least from Dragon Professional Individual's point of view. It wants to insert extra words or syllables to account for those extended vowels, especially at the end of lines. There's also no room in the song for you to insert punctuation, capitalization, or line breaks, so what you wind up with looks pretty weird.

Everyone who saw the movie *2001: A Space Odyssey* remembers the computer HAL singing *Bicycle Built for Two* to his human colleague, Dave. I trained Dragon Professional Individual until it could recognize the spoken lyrics of *Bicycle Built for Two,* and then sang the first verse. It came out looking like this:

> "A. easy day easy to video around CERT true hot and the half crazy all for the love of you move it won't be a stylish narrated shy can do for the carriage but you'll look sweet upon the seat of a bicycle build afford to"

Dictating in Foreign Languages

I dictated (and didn't sing) the French verse of The Beatles song Michelle. I got something you can actually sing if you know the tune (but this version will never make the Hit Parade!):

> "Michelle, mob they'll Solely Mall key home trade BN owned song, Trade BN owned song."

Using Playback to Say Silly or Embarrassing Things

Certain things just sound hilarious when they are said by an artificial voice. Anything passionate or whimsical takes on a Kafka-esque absurdity when proclaimed in Playback's prosody-free manner.

The SyFy Channel has taken advantage of this phenomenon with its artificial announcer. After reading off the evening's schedule, the SyFy announcer has said things like, "I am living *la vida loca.*"

Index

• *N* •

• *O* •

• *P* •

About the Author

Stephanie Diamond is a thought leader and management marketing professional with 20+ years of experience building profits in more than 75 different industries. She has worked with solopreneurs, small-business owners, and multibillion-dollar corporations.

She worked for eight years as a Marketing Director at AOL. When she joined, there were fewer than 1 million subscribers. When she left in 2002 there were 36 million. While at AOL, she developed a highly successful line of multimedia products that brought in an annual $40 million in incremental revenue.

In 2002, she founded Digital Media Works, Inc. (DigMediaWorks.com), an online marketing company that helped business owners discover the hidden profits in their business. She is passionate about guiding online companies to successfully generate more revenue and find their company's real value.

As a strategic thinker, Stephanie uses all the current visual thinking techniques and brain research to help companies get to the essence of their brand. In 2014, she founded the Content Marketing Toolbox (ContentMarketingToolbox. com) where she helps companies accelerate their growth by communicating their value using content to customers using all the latest techniques.

Stephanie received a BA in Psychology from Hofstra University and an M.S.W. and M.P.H. from the University of Hawaii. She lives in New York with her husband and Maltese named Colby.

Dedication

To Barry, who makes all things possible.

To my family, for their encouragement and love.

Author's Acknowledgments

It is my great privilege to write this book. I want to offer great thanks to Wiley Publishing, Inc. for letting me introduce Dragon Professional Individual to a waiting audience of smart readers.

The following people were especially important in creating this book, and I offer very sincere thanks:

- ✔ To the wonderfully creative group at Wiley, Acquisitions Editor Katie Mohr and Project Manager Susan Christophersen. They made this project a dream!

- ✔ To the very sharp folks at Nuance Communications, Eric Guinazzo, Gregory Pane, Grace DuVal, Tom Vain, and Mark Jackson.

- ✔ To Matt Wagner, my agent at Fresh Books, for his continued hard work on my behalf.

Finally, thanks to you for choosing this book to learn about Dragon Professional Individual. I wish you enormous joy on your exciting journey into voice recognition.

Publisher's Acknowledgments

Acquisitions Editor: Katie Mohr

Project Manager: Susan Christophersen

Technical Editor: Grace DuVal

Editorial Assistant: Matt Lowe

Sr. Editorial Assistant: Cherie Case

Production Editor: Kumar Chellappan

Cover Photo: ©Shutterstock/lenetstan

Apple & Mac

iPad For Dummies,
6th Edition
978-1-118-72306-7

iPhone For Dummies,
7th Edition
978-1-118-69083-3

Macs All-in-One
For Dummies, 4th Edition
978-1-118-82210-4

OS X Mavericks
For Dummies
978-1-118-69188-5

Blogging & Social Media

Facebook For Dummies,
5th Edition
978-1-118-63312-0

Social Media Engagement
For Dummies
978-1-118-53019-1

WordPress For Dummies,
6th Edition
978-1-118-79161-5

Business

Stock Investing
For Dummies, 4th Edition
978-1-118-37678-2

Investing For Dummies,
6th Edition
978-0-470-90545-6

Personal Finance
For Dummies, 7th Edition
978-1-118-11785-9

QuickBooks 2014
For Dummies
978-1-118-72005-9

Small Business Marketing
Kit For Dummies,
3rd Edition
978-1-118-31183-7

Careers

Job Interviews
For Dummies, 4th Edition
978-1-118-11290-8

Job Searching with Social
Media For Dummies,
2nd Edition
978-1-118-67856-5

Personal Branding
For Dummies
978-1-118-11792-7

Resumes For Dummies,
6th Edition
978-0-470-87361-8

Starting an Etsy Business
For Dummies, 2nd Edition
978-1-118-59024-9

Diet & Nutrition

Belly Fat Diet For Dummies
978-1-118-34585-6

Mediterranean Diet
For Dummies
978-1-118-71525-3

Nutrition For Dummies,
5th Edition
978-0-470-93231-5

Digital Photography

Digital SLR Photography
All-in-One For Dummies,
2nd Edition
978-1-118-59082-9

Digital SLR Video &
Filmmaking For Dummies
978-1-118-36598-4

Photoshop Elements 12
For Dummies
978-1-118-72714-0

Gardening

Herb Gardening
For Dummies, 2nd Edition
978-0-470-61778-6

Gardening with Free-Range
Chickens For Dummies
978-1-118-54754-0

Health

Boosting Your Immunity
For Dummies
978-1-118-40200-9

Diabetes For Dummies,
4th Edition
978-1-118-29447-5

Living Paleo For Dummies
978-1-118-29405-5

Big Data

Big Data For Dummies
978-1-118-50422-2

Data Visualization
For Dummies
978-1-118-50289-1

Hadoop For Dummies
978-1-118-60755-8

Language &
Foreign Language

500 Spanish Verbs
For Dummies
978-1-118-02382-2

English Grammar
For Dummies, 2nd Edition
978-0-470-54664-2

French All-in-One
For Dummies
978-1-118-22815-9

German Essentials
For Dummies
978-1-118-18422-6

Italian For Dummies,
2nd Edition
978-1-118-00465-4

 **Available in print and e-book formats.**

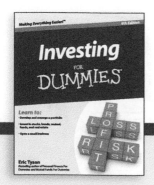

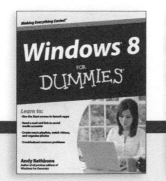

Available wherever books are sold. **For more information or to order direct visit www.dummies.com**

Math & Science

Algebra I For Dummies, 2nd Edition
978-0-470-55964-2

Anatomy and Physiology For Dummies, 2nd Edition
978-0-470-92326-9

Astronomy For Dummies, 3rd Edition
978-1-118-37697-3

Biology For Dummies, 2nd Edition
978-0-470-59875-7

Chemistry For Dummies, 2nd Edition
978-1-118-00730-3

1001 Algebra II Practice Problems For Dummies
978-1-118-44662-1

Microsoft Office

Excel 2013 For Dummies
978-1-118-51012-4

Office 2013 All-in-One For Dummies
978-1-118-51636-2

PowerPoint 2013 For Dummies
978-1-118-50253-2

Word 2013 For Dummies
978-1-118-49123-2

Music

Blues Harmonica For Dummies
978-1-118-25269-7

Guitar For Dummies, 3rd Edition
978-1-118-11554-1

iPod & iTunes For Dummies, 10th Edition
978-1-118-50864-0

Programming

Beginning Programming with C For Dummies
978-1-118-73763-7

Excel VBA Programming For Dummies, 3rd Edition
978-1-118-49037-2

Java For Dummies, 6th Edition
978-1-118-40780-6

Religion & Inspiration

The Bible For Dummies
978-0-7645-5296-0

Buddhism For Dummies, 2nd Edition
978-1-118-02379-2

Catholicism For Dummies, 2nd Edition
978-1-118-07778-8

Self-Help & Relationships

Beating Sugar Addiction For Dummies
978-1-118-54645-1

Meditation For Dummies, 3rd Edition
978-1-118-29144-3

Seniors

Laptops For Seniors For Dummies, 3rd Edition
978-1-118-71105-7

Computers For Seniors For Dummies, 3rd Edition
978-1-118-11553-4

iPad For Seniors For Dummies, 6th Edition
978-1-118-72826-0

Social Security For Dummies
978-1-118-20573-0

Smartphones & Tablets

Android Phones For Dummies, 2nd Edition
978-1-118-72030-1

Nexus Tablets For Dummies
978-1-118-77243-0

Samsung Galaxy S 4 For Dummies
978-1-118-64222-1

Samsung Galaxy Tabs For Dummies
978-1-118-77294-2

Test Prep

ACT For Dummies, 5th Edition
978-1-118-01259-8

ASVAB For Dummies, 3rd Edition
978-0-470-63760-9

GRE For Dummies, 7th Edition
978-0-470-88921-3

Officer Candidate Tests For Dummies
978-0-470-59876-4

Physician's Assistant Exam For Dummies
978-1-118-11556-5

Series 7 Exam For Dummies
978-0-470-09932-2

Windows 8

Windows 8.1 All-in-One For Dummies
978-1-118-82087-2

Windows 8.1 For Dummies
978-1-118-82121-3

Windows 8.1 For Dummies, Book + DVD Bundle
978-1-118-82107-7

Available in print and e-book formats.

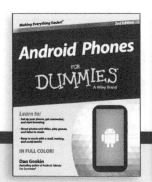

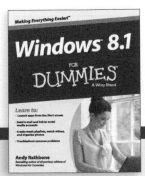

Available wherever books are sold. **For more information or to order direct visit www.dummies.com**

Take Dummies with you everywhere you go!

Whether you are excited about e-books, want more from the web, must have your mobile apps, or are swept up in social media, Dummies makes everything easier.

Leverage the Power

For Dummies is the global leader in the reference category and one of the most trusted and highly regarded brands in the world. No longer just focused on books, customers now have access to the For Dummies content they need in the format they want. Let us help you develop a solution that will fit your brand and help you connect with your customers.

Advertising & Sponsorships

Connect with an engaged audience on a powerful multimedia site, and position your message alongside expert how-to content.

Targeted ads • Video • Email marketing • Microsites • Sweepstakes sponsorship

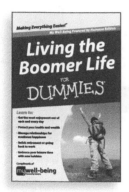

Dummies products make life easier!

- DIY
- Consumer Electronics
- Crafts

- Software
- Cookware
- Hobbies

- Videos
- Music
- Games
- and More!

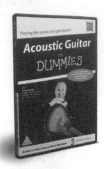

For more information, go to **Dummies.com** and search the store by category.

FOR **DUMMIES**
A Wiley Brand

Printed and bound by CPI Group (UK) Ltd, Croydon, CR0 4YY

25/04/2024

14489482-0002